PENGUIN BOOKS
BBC BOOKS

AGAINST THE STATE

Janet Coleman was born in New York in May 1945. She gradu-
ated from Yale University and received her Ph.D. in 1970. She
spent nearly two years in Paris as a post-doc Fulbright Fellow
at L'Ecole des Hautes Etudes, studying with Professor Paul
Vignaux, and then pursued research and teaching in the History
Faculty of Cambridge University. In 1977 she went to Exeter
University to lecture in the history of political thought and in
1987 she moved to the Department of Government in the
London School of Economics and Political Science, where she is
now Professor of Ancient and Medieval Political Thought. She
has lectured and studied abroad and her numerous publications
include *English Literature in History 1350–1400: Medieval Readers
and Writers* (1981) and *Ancient and Medieval Memories; Studies in
the Reconstruction of the Past* (1992). A four year research project
sponsored by the European Science Foundation culminated in
The Individual in Political Theory and Practice, which is forthcoming from the Clarendon Press. It draws together the work of
a team of fifteen European scholars, of which she was the
team leader, on the 'individual' in relation to the genesis of the
modern State.

Janet Coleman is a keen, if not always successful, allotment
vegetable grower; she describes herself as something of a
fantasy farmer who hopes, one day, to have a small holding
with free-range rare-breed pigs and a vineyard (preferably
before arthritis sets in). Her partner, formerly a professional
footballer, then builder, and now mature student of Social
Policy, likes the idea of the wine but is less convinced about the
pigs. Their Doberman, Georgia, is also dubious about the pigs.

D1585698

JANET COLEMAN

AGAINST THE STATE

STUDIES IN SEDITION AND REBELLION

INTRODUCED BY BRIAN REDHEAD

PENGUIN BOOKS
BBC BOOKS

To Gary and Georgia

PENGUIN BOOKS
BBC BOOKS

Published by the Penguin Group and BBC Worldwide Ltd
Penguin Books Ltd, 27 Wrights Lane, London W8 5TZ, England
Penguin Books USA Inc., 375 Hudson Street, New York, New York 10014, USA
Penguin Books Australia Ltd, Ringwood, Victoria, Australia
Penguin Books Canada Ltd, 10 Alcorn Avenue, Toronto, Ontario, Canada M4V 3B2
Penguin Books (NZ) Ltd, 182–190 Wairau Road, Auckland 10, New Zealand

Penguin Books Ltd, Registered Offices: Harmondsworth, Middlesex, England

First published by BBC Books, a division of BBC Worldwide Limited, 1990
Published in Penguin Books 1995
1 3 5 7 9 10 8 6 4 2

The author and publishers would like to thank the following for their kind permission to reproduce copyright material: 'Thatcher scoffs at Paris celebrations' by Paul Webster, The Guardian, 13 July 1989; 'Benn puts case for British Republic' by Alan Travis, The Guardian, 13 July 1989; The Complete Prose Works of Milton, ed. D. M. Wolfe, Yale University Press, 1953; The Sexual Contract by Carol Pateman, Polity Press, 1988; Karl Marx and Frederick Engels: Selected Works, Lawrence and Wishart, 1973; Economic and Philosophical Manuscripts of 1844, ed. D. J. Struik, Lawrence and Wishart; More's Utopia, ed. Paul Turner, Penguin Books, 1965; The History of the Church, ed. G. A. Williamson, Penguin Books, 1965; Freud, ed. James Strachey, The Hogarth Press

ⒷⒷⒸ ™ BBC used under licence

Printed in England by Clays Ltd, St Ives plc

CONTENTS

ACKNOWLEDGEMENTS

The research for this book was supplemented by material from interviews with numerous experts in different fields, who are named below. But in addition it was Brian Redhead's learning, critical abilities and charm which helped to make the interviews as exciting and challenging as they were and, therefore, such an interesting source of critical debate from which to work. The producer of the Radio 4 series, Christopher Stone, was more than a producer. In conducting some interviews himself, digging in archives, reading widely and taking on the unenviable task of reading and criticising the typescript, he helped to make the whole project a truly collaborative one. I am grateful to them both. The errors and infelicities that remain are truly mine own.

Janet Coleman

GOVERNMENT DEPARTMENT
THE LONDON SCHOOL OF ECONOMICS AND POLITICAL SCIENCE

The following gave generously of their time and expertise, and their views have done much to shape the content of both the radio series and this book. Their contributions are acknowledged with thanks.

CHAPTER TWO   SOCRATES

Julia Annas, Professor of Philosophy at the University of Arizona, at Tucson, USA

Thomas C. Brickhouse, Professor of Philosophy at Lynchburg College, Virginia, USA

John Camp, Assistant Director of the Agora excavations and
  Professor of Classical Studies at the American School of Classical
  Studies at Athens
Richard Kraut, Professor of Philosophy at the University of Chicago
  in Illinois, USA
Nicholas D. Smith, Associate Professor of Philosophy, Virginia
  Polytechnic and State University, Virginia, USA

CHAPTER THREE   MARTYRS

Stephen Benko, Professor of History at California State University
  at Fresno, California, USA
Dr Judith Herrin, Fellow of the Society of Antiquaries; most
  recently she was a Fellow at the Shelby Cullom Davis Center for
  Historical Studies, Princeton University, USA
Revd Dr Christopher Rowland, Dean of Jesus College, Cambridge
Amir Taheri, journalist, and formerly (1973–9) Editor-in-Chief of
  Kayhan, Iran's largest selling daily newspaper

CHAPTER FOUR   UTOPIANS

Professor Christopher Hill, formerly Master of Balliol College, Oxford
Professor Richard Marius, head of the Expository Writing Program at
  Harvard University, USA
Revd Dr Christopher Rowland, Dean of Jesus College, Cambridge

CHAPTER FIVE   OF CROWNED HEADS AND TYRANTS

Jonathan Ayal, Assistant Director, Royal United Services Institute for
  Defence Studies
Franklin F. Ford, Professor of Ancient and Modern History at
  Harvard University, USA
Professor Christopher Hill, formerly Master of Balliol College, Oxford

CHAPTER SIX   REVOLUTIONS

Stanley Ayling, retired schoolmaster and biographer
Richard Ashcraft, Professor of Political Science at the University of
  California, Los Angeles, USA, and Visiting Fellow at All Souls
  College, Oxford

Acknowledgements

Ted Honderich, Professor of the Philosophy of Mind and Logic at University College, University of London

Simon Schama, Professor of History and Senior Associate in the Center for European Studies at Harvard University, USA

CHAPTER SEVEN   MARX

Gerry Cohen, Professor of Social and Political Theory at the University of Oxford

CHAPTER EIGHT   FREUD

Dr Michael Ignatieff, writer and broadcaster

CHAPTER NINE   WOMEN

Dr Joni Lovenduski, Director of the European Research Centre at the University of Loughborough

Dr Sarah Perrigo, Lecturer in Politics in the Department of Peace Studies at the University of Bradford

Janet Todd, Professor of English at the University of East Anglia

CHAPTER TEN   TERRORISTS

Dr Robert Kupperman, Senior Adviser to the Center for Strategic and International Studies in Washington DC, USA

Richard Rubenstein, Professor of Conflict Resolution and Public Affairs at George Mason University, Virginia, USA

Amir Taheri, journalist, and formerly (1973–9) Editor-in-Chief of *Kayhan*, Iran's largest selling daily newspaper

Charles Townshend, Professor of History at the University of Keele

The Radio 4 series was presented by Brian Redhead. The consultant was Janet Coleman and the producer, Christopher Stone. The two Production Assistants who worked on both the series and the book were Dorothee Wigginton and Christopher Bacon.

INTRODUCTION

BY BRIAN REDHEAD

'Against the State' follows an earlier book and radio series, 'Plato to
NATO.' 'Plato to NATO' was an introduction to the history of
political thought; 'Against the State' is an introduction to the history
of sedition and rebellion. How do the two compare?

I f the history of political thought is the history of the
attempts over the centuries to answer the question: 'Why
should I obey the State? – the history of sedition and rebellion is the history of the attempts over the centuries to answer the
question: 'Why should I disobey the State, and how?' In truth, both
the questioning obedience and the questioning disobedience belong
to the same history because you cannot have the one without the
other. And the answers also have much in common.

The answers to 'Why should I obey the State?' have ranged from
the pragmatic: 'Because if I don't they will cut off my head'; to the
theological: 'Because it is God's will'; to the contractual: 'Because the
State and I have done a deal'; to the metaphysical: 'Because the State
is the actuality of the ethical idea'. The answers to 'Why should I
disobey the State?' are much the same: 'Because it presumes to cut
off the heads of those who dissent'; 'Because it is not God's will to
obey an unjust State'; 'Because the State and I have not done a deal';
'Because the State is anything but the actuality of the ethical idea'.

There have been many forms of State over the centuries, big and
small, democratic and oligarchic, governed by laws and governed
by whim, and all of them in their day have been opposed from
within. Their opponents have ranged from the single philosopher to
the terrorist gang, from a handful of holy men to an army of dissent.

1

Many of those who have chosen to disobey have been reviled in their lifetime and revered only in retrospect, though some have achieved immediate popular acclaim.

Sedition and rebellion are not simply things of the past, but they have a long history. This account of that history begins in fifth-century BC Athens with one man against the State, Socrates. Athens was a democracy and very much one in which you took part, if you were allowed to. Women took no part in it, nor did resident aliens, nor did slaves. Out of a population of a few hundred thousand only 40 000 had their say. But that say was more than the making of a cross on polling day; they turned up, and they spoke up. They would summon an assembly and as soon as a quorum of 6000 arrived the proceedings would begin. You got paid, not a lot but there was an attendance allowance, and you could even claim it if you showed up and the other 5999 did not. It was something of a lottery. But there were rude interruptions; first when the Pelopon-nesian War was not going well and 400 powerful men took charge – the Oligarchs. They said the Assembly should consist of only 5000 hand-picked individuals, but as far as we know that Assembly never met, and democracy was restored within the year. Then at the end of the War, Sparta imposed upon Athens the reign of the thirty Tyrants. They were set up simply to re-codify the laws, but they swiftly seized power. However, they too were deposed and demo-cracy was restored.

Socrates had plenty to say about all of this, arguing not for this system or that, but about what is right and what is wrong. It was not argument for argument's sake. It was not the theory but the practice that interested him. What people got up to and why. And for him, the many could be just as wrong as the few. Day after day he held forth. He knew what was wrong and he knew when he was right. He was inspired, commanded by the gods. Did he then hear a voice? Yes, he said, he did. And he referred to this voice or sign as something divine. But it always opposed him; it never directed him. When he was about to do something wrong or impractical or harmful or evil, it said: Don't. Which is another explanation of why he criticised the many as well as the few. If it was wrong it was wrong.

And he would not be silenced. If you would only shut up, they said, we will not prosecute you. But he would have none of it. My obligation to practise philosophy, he said, is more important than my obligation to the State. And even when they found him guilty he did not waver. The sentence was death, and if Plato is to be believed, Socrates was quite philosophical about it. His final words to the court and the 501 jurors were these: 'Now it is time that we were going, I to die and you to live, but which of us has the happier prospect is unknown to anyone but God.' He died precisely for what he believed in. Was he then a martyr?

Martyrdom is as old as mankind. Martyr means witness, from the Greek. It is the word used in the New Testament to describe John the Baptist. Strictly speaking, you don't have to die to be a martyr; it is enough simply to bear witness to something. But it helps if you are ready to die for what you believe in; people take you more seriously. In Judaism, martyrs are 'holy ones' who demonstrate loyalty to their faith by giving their lives 'for the sanctification of the divine name'. A Muslim martyr 'bears testimony to the truth of Islam and to the greatness of Allah'. He is 'ready to give his life to prove that Islam is authentic'. The early Christians were martyrs to martyrdom. They bore witness all over the Roman Empire, filling the dictionary of saints and inspiring a whole theology.

Martyrdom is not only defence; it is attack. It is not only defending the faith because it is persecuted by the State; it is attacking the State because the State is wrong in itself. Martyrs can be seen to be not only Against the State but Above the State. And there have been martyrs ever since Roman times, both outside the Church and among those within who hold competing views. There have always been those who believe that it is not good enough to accept the status quo, those who believe they must stand up for what they believe to be right and who are prepared to put their lives on the line. There are martyrs still. Not only Christian martyrs, but martyrs of, and for, many faiths and many causes, all over the world. They are standing up to what they see as oppression and injustice. They still bear witness, and they are still willing to pay the supreme price. Two weeks before he was killed, Archbishop Romero of San Salvador said: 'Martyrdom is a grace of God that I do not believe I deserve. But if God accepts the sacrifice of my life, let my blood be a seed of freedom and a sign that hope will soon be a reality. . . . A bishop will die, but God's church, which is the people, will never perish.' He did not, however, predict a paradise here on earth, in this world not the next. But over the centuries many Christians have. It is what millenarians believe the New Testament or more particularly the

Book of Revelation, promises, the Kingdom of God here when Christ comes again. And they put a date on it.

Thomas More's Utopia falls short of the Kingdom of God. It is perfect but not holy. More found fault in almost everything around him and not without reason. And he died for what he believed in. He too was a martyr, and yet I do not think he believed that we could have Utopia, only that we should have. In other words, we should hanker for perfection. He was executed for refusing to submit to the oath of royal supremacy and he died bravely. He laid his head on the block and said: 'Wait till I put my beard aside for that hath done no treason'.

A century later, in Oliver Cromwell's time, they really believed that there could be and would be something much better, nothing short of the Second Coming. It was not a question of if, but when. And indeed there were those who thought that once they had chopped off Charles I's head those who succeeded him were there not simply to exercise power but to embrace a new Kingdom of God. In his speech from the scaffold Charles had pointed out the error of their ways. 'A society,' he said, 'must give God his due, the King his due, the People their due. Truly I desire their liberty and freedom as much as anybody whatsoever. But I must tell you that their liberty and freedom consists in having Government . . . It is not in their having a share in the Government . . . A subject and a sovereign are clean different things.' Whereupon they chopped his head clean off. They said he was a tyrant. When England was declared a Commonwealth on 19 May 1649, the King's statue was thrown down and on the pedestal they engraved these words: *Exit tyrannus, regum ultimus*. The end of the tyrant, our last king.

Centuries earlier Aristotle had defined tyranny as a perversion of kingship. 'Tyranny,' he said, 'is a kind of monarchy which has in view the interest of the monarch only.' Two motives induce men to attack tyrannies – hatred and contempt, which is why tyrannies never last long, though they have been around a long time. The Bible is full of them. No doubt the regicides knew Aristotle as well as the Bible, and other authorities too. George Buchanan, a Scottish Calvinist, in a treatise called *The Right of the Kingdom* published in 1579, had argued not only that the people had the right to remove and kill a tyrant but so too had any one member of the public. Mariana, the Jesuit, who wrote a book called *The King and the Education of the King* argued that the people could call the King to

4

account. Normally, he said, it would be proper to have an assembly or at least a public meeting before the execution, but 'if you ask what can be done if the power of the public meeting is laid aside, anyone who is inclined to heed the prayers of the people may attempt to destroy a tyrant and can hardly be said to have acted wrongly'. Cromwell was fond of quoting both Buchanan and Mariana.

Charles was executed not because his regime was wilful and cruel – though it was – but because he expected unquestioning obedience. He could not accept that Parliament represented his people in the way Parliament thought it did. He was, as Christopher Hill says, an impossible man, though only God can say whether he deserved to die. The regicides paid the full price too, and they also died bravely. Like martyrs they died for what they believed in, convinced that they were not mere assassins but legitimate takers of life. But they had not achieved the great change they intended. The monarchy had been restored; the Revolution was still to come.

Revolution is an activity which can embrace everything and everyone mentioned so far – the philosopher, the martyr, the utopian, the tyrant, the regicide. It is something more than a political upheaval. It can overthrow not only a Government but a State. It is often accompanied by violence and terror, but it can be bloodless. Revolution, as Professor Ted Honderich reminded me, is usually best avoided but is sometimes unavoidable. There are always incoherences, suppressions and unsatisfied needs in the arrangement of a society and it is the task of the politicians to remedy them when they have exposed them. But sometimes the incoherences mount up unremedied until a definite crisis arises and they are only then surmounted by a revolution, or by a seeming revolution. What matters, however, are not the motives of the revolutionaries but the consequences of their actions. They can do more harm than good.

The Whigs who brought about the Glorious Revolution of 1688 could not be accused of that. The political struggle centred on the succession to the English throne. Charles II had reigned since the Restoration of the monarchy in 1660, but his heir, James, Duke of York, was a Catholic, and many English Protestants would have none of him. They tried to have him legally excluded but that came to nothing, and insurrection, albeit on a small scale, also failed. James succeeded to the throne in 1685 but lasted only three years. He took flight when William of Orange landed in England by invitation. England had imported a more suitable king. Parliament's will had been translated into law. This was a constitutional revolution in the strictest sense of the word. The constitution had been simplified; a slice of it, a layer of it, had been removed. And in a very English way it was explained that what had been altered was not the present, but the past.

The French Revolution was a very different matter. Burke saw through it and through Rousseau who argued that because Nature is a harmony (a very dubious proposition) all rational men want the same thing if only they realised it. But as people in real life are not always aware of their real will they must commission a wise legislator, a moral Sovereign, to interpret the General Will for them, to tell them what is in their own best interests. And so they got stuck with Robespierre and Mirabeau and the Jacobins and the Terror. There were of course genuine grievances too as well as grandiose ideas. They were not just egged on by a vision, Simon Schama told me, but spurred on by concrete discontent – like having nothing to eat. But that was not what finally provoked the Revolution nor what inspired its supporters.

The young Wordsworth wrote of

A people risen up,
Fresh as the morning star . . .

But then it got out of hand, and when Wordsworth arrived in the streets of Paris on 29 October 1792 to find the people standing there reading copies of Louvet's speech denouncing the crimes of Robespierre, he put all his foreboding into one line.

The earthquake is not satisfied at once . . .

Karl Marx was never satisfied with the French Revolution. Looking back on it from the next century he thought it had not gone far enough. The people had more liberty but not much more equality and fraternity. It may have been a political revolution but scarcely an economic or a social revolution. The whole purpose of Marx's thought was to abolish the State. His ideas were thought so radical that he was evicted in turn from Germany, France and Belgium, and finally took refuge in London in 1849. He died there at the age of 64, and his death certificate gave his occupation as author, the cause of his death laryngitis. But his voice was not silenced. For better or worse he has probably had more influence on twentieth-century politics than anyone else. This has been, among other things, the century of Communism, if not for much longer. Marx wrote many thousands of words explaining his theories, but he summed them up in a letter which he wrote on 5 March 1852.

What I did that was new was to prove:
1 That the existence of classes is only bound up with particular historical phases in the development of production;
2 That the class struggle necessarily leads to the dictatorship of the proletariat;
3 That this dictatorship itself only constitutes the transition to the abolition of all classes and to a classless society.

A classless society. Utopia, perhaps. But if the State is no more than a weapon in the class war, then when you achieve the classless society and have abolished the State as we know it, what do you have in its place – the ultimate democracy? And would Socrates have approved? The question is academic because it has not happened. Marx saw the evidence of the exploitation of the proletariat in nineteenth-century England, but he failed to see that capitalism could humanise itself, could build within itself a welfare state. He also failed to appreciate that capitalism could mend its business ways – by moderation and regulation, as Keynes recognised. Capitalism has certainly lasted much longer than Marx expected, whereas Communism will probably not survive the century. On the other hand it can be argued that the Communism we have seen is not the Communism Marx intended.

Freud was no less a revolutionary than Marx. He instigated a revolution in the way we think, and in particular in the way in which we think about ourselves. And in a sense he went further than Marx and talked not simply about the threat of the State but the threat of civilisation. People, he said, were threatened or felt threatened not only by the State, the government, the police, but by the whole apparatus of cultural convention, by the rules and customs and habits of a society of which the State's explicit prohibitions are only a part. That is real rebellion, a cry for the freedom of childhood, for male and female alike. But, he said, we must accept civilisation, the State, or we will destroy ourselves. Though Freud was very conscious of how oppressed within the family women could be. Over the centuries women have embraced many of the same rebellious causes as men. There have been women martyrs and women millenarians and, for that matter, women tyrants. But feminism is different. It is not simply about equal *rights*, but about equal *worth*, and that is a fundamental freedom. It also has a long history.

It began as a demand both for access to education and access to government. In 1698 Daniel Defoe wrote: 'I have often thought of it as one of the most barbarous customs in the world, considering us a civilised and a Christian country, that we deny advantages of learning to women.' The Established Church dismissed such heresy but women took advantage of the greater freedoms within the Non-Conformist Churches to argue against the idea that there are separate spheres of life for men and women. Even then they were told, by men, to get back to the boudoir – the boudoir, not the kitchen, for these objects of abuse were middle-class women. Working-class women knew their place even if they hated it. Mary Collier, a washerwoman, wrote a splendid poem in 1739 called *The Woman's Labour, an epistle to Mr Stephen Duck, in answer to his late poem called The Thresher's Labour*. In it she pointed out that woman's work is never done and she could see no end to it.

But others could, and over the next century and a half the arguments expanded from simple demands for equality to feminist utopias from which men are excluded. In the year in which she married John Stuart Mill, Harriet Taylor published *The Enfranchisement of Women*, a plea for women to be educated for the world and not for men. And Mill subsequently argued that the principle of the legal subordination of one sex to the other was wrong and ought to be replaced by a principle of perfect equality, admitting no power or privilege on the one side, nor disability on the other. That was the radical Liberal view. Others went further, like Charlotte Perkins Gilman, whose *Herland*, written in 1915, is a classic Utopia based upon feminist and socialist ideals. It was, however, a vision too far for most working-class women in the nineteenth century who found themselves exploited in the factory as well as in the home. They sought to join trade unions but were not always made welcome, so, egged on by middle-class women activists, they formed women's unions. And at least the TUC was committed to adult suffrage including votes for women. The victory for women's suffrage prompted more radical and socialist demands and in the process provoked some anti-feminism, and a re-run of the arguments of earlier centuries.

The Second World War, like the First, transformed the view of 'a woman's place', and after the War writers like Simone de Beauvoir and Germaine Greer called upon women to assert their autonomy in defining themselves. And the time was ripe for that assertion to become action. But not violent action, although Astrid Pröll, a founder of the Red Army Fraction in Germany and one of the Baader-Meinhof Group, did describe her colleagues to me as 'heavily armed social workers'. Terrorism is often said to have begun with the Reign of Terror which followed the French Revolution. It is not any old act of political violence. It is more organised than that. But it is not easy to define. The motives of terrorists vary – some are political, some religious, some achieve unholy terror. But like justice, terrorism must be seen to be done. Its organisation may be clandestine but its actions are public and deliberately so. They are there to frighten. And it is no comfort to know that many more people have been killed throughout history by government forces than by terrorist forces, though that may be one explanation for terrorism.

Is it then simply a technique, a calculated shock to paralyse the population? It is not easy to deter, because if a government responds to terrorism with acts of violence it is seen to be not so much taking on terrorism as taking up terrorism. It has to be vigilant and lawful. And why do people take up terrorism? One explanation is that when rising expectations are cruelly dashed – a 'shocking reversal' as one writer put it – then political violence frequently arises. But is it necessary and if terrorists overdo it with an indiscriminate use of violence do they forfeit what support they had? Some terrorists have sought to justify their actions by cataloguing the evils to which they are opposed. They look for a better society and can sound like Utopians or Millenarians, inspired by a vision of a better world to come, a Kingdom of God on earth, or whatever. They can quote everyone from Socrates to Marcuse as their intellectual sponsors, though Marcuse declines the compliment, and many people think they would be better consulting Freud. Some who take it up, give it up. But others take their place. Perhaps we must learn to live with it, hoping that more and more will take up something else.

These then are the subjects of *Against the State*, both the book and the radio series. All of the contributors to the programmes communicated not only their knowledge but also their enthusiasm. To talk with them was an education in itself. Only a fraction of what they had to say found its way into the final programmes. Far more is included in Janet Coleman's book. If the purpose of the radio programmes is to awaken interest, the purpose of the book is to point the way, wherever possible, to the words of those who wrote down their thoughts, and who expressed their reasons for being Against the State.

I ended my introduction to *Plato to NATO* by saying that to study the history of political thought is to engage in the great arguments of history, arguments that still rage. I can now say with confidence that the same is true of the history of sedition and rebellion. To seek to understand the arguments is to seek great satisfaction for there is nothing to match the satisfaction of understanding.

Socrates said that, so it must be true. As for terrorism, there are better ways of being Against the State.

CHAPTER ONE

SEDITION IN HISTORY

'So long as the State exists there is no freedom; when freedom exists there will be no State.'

T his may sound like the outraged sentiments of today's businessman who finds his taxation too high, the amount he has to pay for his employees' medical contributions exorbitant, the limits placed on him by trade restrictions and lending rates intolerable. He simply wishes that the State would get off his back and let him make a profit. But this statement was uttered by Lenin! How can two such opposing lifeviews end up agreeing that the State is an evil? And what could each mean by the State?

The nature of the State varies and has varied over time and geographical space. It has also varied in the degree to which it has intervened in people's social and economic lives. There have been different kinds of State throughout history and each type has been a different mixture of institutions and relations. The modern State as we conceive it today is thought to hark back to its beginnings in the sixteenth century. But prior to the sixteenth century in Europe and in the ancient world, states did exist.

What is usually meant by 'the State' in the context of known Western history involves more than a discussion of the apparatus of government at any particular period in history. We want to do more than simply describe the impersonal legal and constitutional order at a particular time, with its capacities to administer, to control territory, to centralise finance and regulate customary behaviour. When we discuss the State at a particular period in history we reflect on *where* this State is located in a society and *how* this State regulates the lives and conditions of its subjects or citizens. When we speak about different states throughout history we see that they maintained a range of differing views on the relationship between the individual and the community; on the relationship of power and dependency; on the relationship between the good life and the merely sufficient life; and on how a society's ethics is related to its economic arrangements. And we find that there has always been opposition to a given State's views on these matters. Throughout its history the nature of the State has always been contested. And this means that sedition has been one enduring mode of expressing opposition to certain interpretations of how a State *exercises* its power. There has also been an enduring tradition that rejects a specific State's own understanding of its *source* of power. Where does legitimate authority come from?

In this book, written to accompany the Radio 4 series, *Against the State*, I have not tried to answer the question: Why have there been states? And only in part have I dealt with the question: How have states come into existence and been maintained? Rather, I have focused on the problem of sedition's enduring tradition: How have individuals and groups throughout Western history sought to limit if not destroy the State's powers? In many ways the history of political thought is a history of justifications of different states. But there is a parallel tradition which tells the story of sedition and rebellion against the State.

Very few, if any, of the individuals and groups we examined with the help of many experts were against all authority. But more of them were against the State as it was constituted and justified in their own lifetime. Most were seeking an alternative notion of 'right order' among men, so that sovereign authority would be legitimate rather than arbitrarily and uncritically imposed. At the heart of many of these seditious analyses of right and legitimate order lay their theory of human nature. As a consequence, they discovered enormous tensions between their understanding of human nature and its purposes, and the claims of organised power with its explicit or covert objectives.

The further we reach back into history, the more certain seditious actions appear to us as heroic and courageous. Individuals and groups who acted against their states often seem to have been motivated in support of our own views of liberty, equality, individual rights, freedom of expression and creative action. But as we get closer to the present we grow nervous of those who advocate something more than a gentle or humorous critical perspective on the way things are. Is this pure hypocrisy? Are we possibly saying that before our own times, life in all earlier states was so much more intolerable that seditious acts were justified? By contrast, do we perhaps believe that our society, our State today, is actively pursuing and successfully achieving all those goals that rebellious and seditious individuals in the past sought? This may mean that we do not believe there can be anyone or any groups who are truly aggrieved today in modern states and that what minor grievances exist may be easily and satisfactorily redressed. There is, however, another way of looking at this. One might say that the modern State has been so successful in limiting our access to *plausible* alternatives to the way we do live, that we have lost all imaginative capacity to entertain serious alternatives to our own way of life. This would be an immensely serious indictment, amounting to the claim that the modern State has persuaded us to a degree that was never before so successful into believing that how we live is how we and everyone else ought to live. But with some historical reflection, we would find that the vast majority of citizens of past states also accepted that how they lived was how they (and everyone else) ought to live.

Who, then, were those men and women against their states, from the period of ancient Greece to our own times, who not only argued but acted in the light of an alternative vision of what social life could be? By telling their stories, it is hoped that we can uncover some of the reasons why we honour them by attributing to them a nobility of spirit that we deny to present-day actors who threaten today's states.

CHAPTER TWO

SOCRATES

S ocrates was born in *c.* 469 BC in the ancient Greek city-state of Athens. He is perhaps the most famous of ancient philosophers, and his fame is connected with his death by hemlock. This first chapter describes his life and attempts to explain why Socrates took up a position against his State.

High up on the Acropolis in Athens, one can look down on the ruins of the city Socrates knew. It was a city-state, the most powerful and wealthy of all the Greek city-states in the fifth century BC and also the most democratic until democracy was replaced briefly, in 404, by a vicious oligarchy of thirty Tyrants. Socrates just avoided falling foul of the Tyrants, one of whose commands he defied, as we shall see, and it is likely they would have put him to death had their government survived. But then Socrates did fall foul of the restored democracy which, in 399 BC, sentenced him to death for refusing to stop philosophising.

Socrates wrote nothing, but questioned everything. He was not concerned with administrative details or institutional proprieties but 'with deliberation on common purposes within the space of intellectual freedom'. He was not a particular friend of either democracy or oligarchy. In fact, he was a man apparently indifferent to any and all political institutions and structures, and this because he thought that the harder questions to ask and answer came before political questions: the harder questions concerned those underlying ethical attitudes men had to reflect on in order to answer the biggest question of all: how should a man live his life?

In Athens, as in other city-states of ancient Greece, there was a central space called the agora, which was the focal point of community life, the seat of administration, of the judiciary, the place for marketing and business, the scene of dramatic competitions and intellectual discourse. The buildings and monuments around the agora recorded the achievements of Athenian citizens. Memorials of great public deeds were set up there: the Battle of Marathon was depicted there to remind men of Athens how ordinary citizens had defeated the massive military machine of the Persian empire. It was said that other cities set up statues of their athletes whereas Athens honoured the statues of good generals and tyrannicides. Athenians would not be ruled by tyrants but would rule themselves. The agora was the spiritual centre of Athens, second only to the Acropolis on the hill, with its religious temples honouring the State's gods. The agora was the place where old laws that were tried and tested by time were invoked, and where new laws were proposed and first brought to public attention. Trials and private arbitrations were conducted in its buildings. It was said, 'You will find everything sold together in the same place in Athens: figs, witnesses to summonses, bunches of grapes, turnips, pears, apples, givers of evidence, roses, chick peas, lawsuits, irises, lambs, water clocks, laws and indictments.'

In the midst of this commercial activity, litigation and elections, the life of ancient Athens went on, including philosophical discussion. The public life in the agora was made sacred as a temple precinct and was marked off by boundary stones with basins of holy water at the entrance. It was here that Socrates walked and talked, questioning his fellow-Athenians about how a good man should live his life. The essence of his discussions was recorded for posterity by Plato and others in the form of dialogues.

What kind of democracy was ancient Athens? From the mid-fifth century and under Pericles, it was a radical participatory, face-to-face democracy. This means that of the several thousand residents, about 40 000 male citizens voluntarily participated in governing the city; women, children, the large resident alien population and slaves were excluded. But for the 40 000 men who were citizens, self-governance was a way of life and a duty. More often than not offices of state, juries and the like were chosen by lot. Citizens took turns in ruling and being ruled.

We do not actually know where Socrates, one such citizen, lived but it could easily have been a modest dwelling, very sparsely furnished, within walking distance of the agora. The men of Athens did not spend much time indoors: they were out in the wine shops or in the agora. We know that when he came to the agora, Socrates visited one Simon the shoemaker whose workshop archaeologists believe they have uncovered. Here he met those students who were too young to be considered full citizens.

North of the Temple of Apollo is a colonnade, known as the Stoa of Zeus, near what is now the Athens–Piraeus railway. Zeus was honoured here as the city's god of deliverance and freedom. The colonnade was a popular promenade and meeting place. At the north-west corner of the agora is the Royal Stoa which served, at least occasionally, as a meeting-place for the civic council, particularly when it functioned as a court in cases of homicide, arson and religious impiety. One of the chief magistrates, the King Archon, the second-in-command of the Athenian government, had his offices here. He was responsible for religious matters. It is here in the Royal Stoa that we have the scene of the preliminary proceedings in the trial of Socrates. According to Plato's dialogue, *Euthyphro*, the following interchange took place:

> *Euthyphro*: What revolution has taken place in your affairs, Socrates, that you have left your usual haunts on the north-east side of town and are now spending your time here waiting about the Royal Stoa? I don't suppose that you have actually got a case before the King Archon as I have.
>
> *Socrates*: No, Euthyphro, the official name for it is not a private case but a public action.
>
> *Euthyphro*: Really? I suppose that someone has brought an action against you; I won't insult you by suggesting that you have done it to somebody else.
>
> *Socrates*: No I haven't, but someone whom I don't know very well, a young man, undistinguished, one Meletus, has brought an action – mind, it's not trivial – against me. He claims to know how the characters of the young get corrupted and who the people are that are responsible. I am, he says, that corrupter of our city's young.

The charges brought against Socrates were twofold and stated as follows: 'This indictment and affidavit is sworn by Meletus, son of Meletus of Pitthos, against Socrates, son of Sophroniscus from Alopece: Socrates does wrong in not recognising the gods which the city recognises and in introducing other new divinities. He also does wrong in corrupting the young men. The penalty demanded is death.'

Even after sixty years of excavations, we do not know in which building the actual trial was conducted, but we do know that the trial lasted only one day, that a jury of 501 men was required, that jurors were paid for jury duty, and that the speeches made by both prosecution and defence would have been timed by water clocks, whereafter the vote was taken by ballot. Socrates, a citizen of the city-state of Athens, was tried and condemned to death by a jury of his fellow-citizens in 399 BC. Surrounded by friends in prison, he took the hemlock in the measured medicine bottle proffered by the State, and died. According to the description in the *Phaedo* by Plato, Socrates took the poison, his body went numb gradually, starting at his feet, the hemlock working its way through his legs until it eventually reached his heart and he died.

> *Socrates*: 'I suppose I am allowed, or rather bound, to pray the gods that my removal from this world to the other may be prosperous. This is my prayer, then; and I hope that it may be granted.' With these words, quite calmly and with no sign of distaste, he drained the cup in one breath . . .
>
> Socrates walked about, and presently, saying that his legs were heavy, lay down on his back – that was what the man recommended. The man (he was the same one who had administered the poison) kept his hand upon Socrates, and after a little while examined his feet and legs; then pinched his foot hard and said that when it reached his heart, Socrates would be gone.
>
> The coldness was spreading about as far as his waist when Socrates . . . said (they were his last words):
>
> 'Crito, we ought to offer a cock to Asclepius. See to it, and don't forget.'
>
> 'No, it shall be done,' said Crito. 'Are you sure that there is nothing else?'
>
> Socrates made no reply to this question . . . and when the man uncovered him, his eyes were fixed.
>
> . . . Such was the end of our comrade, who was, we may fairly say, of all those whom we knew in our time, the bravest and also the wisest and most upright man (*Phaedo*, 117A–118).

Today, as in his own times, it is thought by some, but by no means all, that the charges against him were extremely vague and that the religious element was at best disingenuous. As he stated himself, he was put to death by his democratic society because of his philosophical activity which, throughout his lifetime, had made him extremely unpopular. The Athenian democrats found it intolerable to be questioned and even more so that they were asked to defend their beliefs. As Julia Annas, Professor of Philosophy at the University of Arizona, Tucson, points out, Socrates' fate in an Athens priding itself on its greater tolerance than that of other city-states raises unresolved questions about the threat which intellectuals pose to any State. And this has led to the most diverse interpretations of his life and its significance.

Socrates wrote nothing. We rely for our knowledge of Socrates on the writings of Aristophanes, Plato and Xenophon, and their evidence conflicts. Plato presents Socrates as a witty and great metaphysical thinker, concerned with open debate in the agora, with anyone willing to discuss and be questioned by him. Xenophon presents him as a rather dull but worthy moralist. Aristophanes presents him as a buffoon but also as a dangerous, pernicious figure. It is Plato's view which most scholars have taken seriously over the centuries.

In our own century Sir Karl Popper has depicted Socrates as an individualist liberal who, in Plato's presentation, becomes the founder of a closed society, a society that does not permit a diversity of interpretations of the truth. Others have seen him as an authoritarian reactionary. According to either extreme view, he was undoubtedly indifferent if not hostile to politics as practised by his contemporaries in Athens. Some in his own time believed he had influenced many aristocrats who had interpreted him to suit their own anti-democratic prejudices. Such men then led a coup against the democratic State, and saw the replacement of the democracy with the oligarchy of the thirty Tyrants.

Like so many intellectuals, Socrates got people to think and then was held responsible for their thoughts. In fact, we know very little of his own personal attitudes beyond his lack of confidence in the average citizen to examine his own moral principles and, as a consequence, sacrifice wealth and status to a higher moral truth. Socrates' personal life cannot be recovered from the layers of later writings about him. But we certainly know he existed because there is enough continuity in the reports by various contemporaries to indicate that this immensely charismatic personality, who denied he was a teacher, none the less turned men around in their lives.

Most scholars down the ages have believed that we must examine

Plato's early dialogues to discover why Socrates should be found not only intellectually challenging but also possibly a scourge to the democratic or any other kind of political mind. The dialogues are thought to give a fairly accurate description of Socrates on which Plato would later build his own ethical and political views. It seems that after Socrates' death Plato became increasingly engaged in a kind of philosophical pamphleteering to justify Socrates' position and his own. Plato, born 427, knew Socrates when Socrates was already an older man. He was not in prison on Socrates' last day although in the *Crito* and *Phaedo* he wrote about the events and discussions which took place there. And although Plato was present at Socrates' trial, he was not really concerned to present the actual account of Socrates' speeches; rather, in the *Apology*, he gives us what he believed Socrates ought to have said. Just as Plato was able to pass on anecdotes and impressions of Socrates, partly through his own experiences of the man, so too did many later writers who had no first-hand experience of his teaching. The upshot is that different schools of philosophy have all claimed Socrates as their founder, schools at such variance with one another as the Cynics – who dropped out of Greek society altogether – to the Hedonists, Stoics and Sceptics. Socrates' own associates moved in many different directions, and even Christians were to be divided in presenting him either as the type of pagan philosopher whom they rejected or as a precursor to Christ. The figure of Socrates was so powerful as an uncompromising idealist, that he could become all things to all men.

At his trial Socrates told the citizens of Athens that they would be seen to have created a martyr. People would say Athens had killed 'the only wise man amongst them'. He did not consider himself wise, but others would. Others would recreate a hero whom they believed had acted against the State. Socrates, however, did not think that he had acted against the State. On the contrary, he thought he was God's gift to the State of Athens and that he was more devoted to that State than any other political citizen.

So what did he teach and why did so open a democracy need to silence him? Socrates is remembered for having been one man against his democratic State. He begins the Western tradition of political discourse on a decidedly anti-democratic, indeed anti-political note. But was he then the great apologist for all later closed societies and religious theocracies, or was he a radically free, supremely moral individual who lived the kind of ethical and philosophical life that every open society and State must not only tolerate but revere? Should he have been killed? Did he engage in sedition? If by sedition we mean a surreptitious, covert disobedience to the State by which one attempts to undermine government through secret acts, then Socrates was not seditious. Everything he did was out in the open. He spent his life arguing with anyone willing to talk with him, that wisdom in politics is a skill and it therefore presupposes a serious intellectual grasp of what one is doing or what one believes. He was totally committed to ideas, whatever their practical consequences. He exercised his freedom to speak his mind, but there was no law in Athens that guaranteed this as a right. His trial and his conviction were the result of people thinking he had taken liberties with Athenian free expression. He had misused it; he had gone too far.

We tend to think of Athens of that period as the model of democracy, but it was not a model of *modern* democracy. For instance, everyone was expected to engage in the practice of the State cults, and religious freedom was not recognised. Impiety was a crime although the law against it was vague. The virtues of this democracy were many, however. Every male over 18 who was a citizen (and therefore neither slave nor resident alien) could participate in direct discussion of the political issues of the day. Many of the offices were arranged by lottery. It was a democratic right to join in the discussion and not merely to vote on representatives. Can we say that Socrates disapproved of this?

In Plato's early dialogues Socrates notes that where the truth lies is not determined by vote, and he disparaged the ability of most men to recognise the truth about moral and political matters. What was wrong with the democracy of his own society, was that important decisions were made by majority vote. Socrates thought that most people lacked both the time and the temperament to develop any serious intellectual grasp of the issues at stake. And since political leaders depended on majority support, their power derived not from their wisdom but from their popular appeal, their image. Socrates was concerned throughout his life to show such prominent public figures that their views were unconsidered and had no intellectual backing. In this sense he was critical of democracies. But more to the point, Socrates' opposition to democracy or any constitution must be kept in perspective. He did not favour one form of government as opposed to another. He was critical of 'the many' because most men had given little thought to moral questions. And if you do not know what is just, how can you have well-defended views about this or that political question? This is more than merely saying you have to be well informed if well informed means having the empirical information to discuss a certain issue. You also need to have reflected on the more general and fundamental questions concerning what a good life is. If you have not so reflected, Socrates thought you were poorly qualified to discuss the political ways and means. Who then should decide whether people are qualified or not? Socrates made no such decision, although Plato later provided a detailed training programme to equip political leaders to make the correct moral choices.

Socrates, however, was not a political figure in the sense of having a definite programme for raising the level of discussion in a democracy. He simply button-holed people in the agora and questioned them on a one-to-one basis about their views on certain moral concepts. These people would say they had views on such concepts as justice, and Socrates would show them that in the end they could not defend their views. They would then go off annoyed at having been embarrassed in public. Socrates' method of questioning made people reflect on their strongly held beliefs, but often they did not appreciate the experience.

Although Athenians demanded proper intellectual qualifications from their doctors and architects and naval commanders, when it came to politicians, they thought that any man could do the job without training and skills. Socrates, however, believed that politics, perhaps more than any other 'profession', required a kind of moral 'training' which could only come about when someone had spent many years considering what justice and virtue consist in. By 'training' he did not mean the study of science, mathematics, grammar or rhetoric, but rather the intellectual enquiry into the distinction between what is good and what is bad. In Plato's dialogue, the *Apology*, Socrates makes the astounding statement that for man, the unexamined life is not worth living. This means that most human lives as we lead them are not worth living. If a person has not figured out the difference between justice and injustice, between good and evil, then his life is trivial. Therefore he encouraged some of the most talented young men of Athens to steer clear of politics because they would unwittingly harm themselves and others if they did not first spend many previous years examining themselves. If a man did not first examine his own ethical principles, he was in no position to advise others. And with such an examination his fellow-Athenians could only come to the same conclusion Socrates himself had reached: an awareness of his and their own ignorance.

But Athens required of its male citizens a continuous engagement in the political life through practical experience, typified by relations in the agora. For Socrates, such practical experience was nothing more than muddling through, providing ballast for one's own un-thought-out prejudices and habits. This kind of experience, Socrates said, positively 'unfits' a man for true engagement in politics. Politics is not about the proper procedure for chairing a meeting, nor is it about compromise between prejudices. It must be underpinned by a serious, indeed life-long, attempt at a thorough philosophical examination of your moral beliefs in order to discover true and unchanging ethical principles to guide your behaviour. The only way to come to an understanding of these principles is by hard thinking and philosophising and not through compromising truth in an attempt to be liked and accepted in the company of other men. According to Socrates, in some fundamental sense, politics as we know it, and as his fellow-Athenians knew it, does not matter at all!

In that case why bother with democracy or with politics? Become a complete human being first and ignore who runs the State – is this Socrates' message? Was his allegiance to Athens only a consequence of the comparatively greater freedom Athens provided for its citizens to ask the kinds of questions Socrates asked? Did he not see himself tied to Athens as *his* State which effectively made him who he was by its very laws and customs? While he argued that the first priority a man has is to discover the correct views on moral issues, we shall see that he argued this as an Athenian citizen and not as a man who believed that it did not matter in which State a man lives.

As Socrates described them, the customary values of democratic Athens placed great emphasis on wealth, status and physical plea-sure. He thought it was more important for people to acquire virtues, and to do so they had to engage in intellectual discussion in order to decide on the right conception of virtue. He was not particularly upset by the unequal distribution of wealth in his society or by any other socio-economic issue. He was most upset by the values his contemporaries had. And he was disturbed that his fellow-citizens did not take seriously their lack of an adequate moral theory. Athe-nian democracy could not be an efficient or just method of governing people because, in that democracy, political power was not in the possession of those who had acquired, through philosophy, a true understanding of the moral issues at stake in any decision. Since this knowledge mattered so much to him, Socrates did not over-value Athens' freedom of discussion and action by unreflective men. In this kind of society, men tend to concern themselves with the external trappings of wealth and show. Moral education and discipline should be what really matters. Political skills require the expert trained in ethical perception who is prepared to disregard the opinion of the many. And this ethical understanding does not come about through a reform of existing institutions. Rather, it requires a revolution in the fundamental beliefs of the many, a radical critique of people's morals. This would then create a revolutionary change in people's lives because only then would they take seriously the idea that prior to all political deliberation come the moral questions, the examination of good and bad.

As Professor Richard Kraut of the University of Chicago points out, most people today, as then, would respond by saying: 'I don't need to think about these moral issues; what I need is to live as I see fit.' Socrates knew this only too well. This is why he excludes the possibility that the many will ever develop moral expertise. It is the possession of the rare few who examine their lives continuously; for most men this is too much like hard work. Hence Socrates was against the values of *society*, and not simply of government. He was against the lack of interest that most people showed in fundamental moral questions. This made him an unpopular figure and because he insisted on his views so rigorously he was regarded, as Professor Kraut observes, as an 'arrogant bully'. People found him insufferable. In asking people to answer questions they thought they could easily answer, and in getting them to realise they had not adequately thought out their positions, he punctured their pretensions. People so irritated were ready to accept that he was both impious and a corrupter of the city's youth.

Chief among Socrates' conclusions is that injustice must never be done. But he also argued that the laws of a State need not limit a citizen's opportunities for dissent and even disobedience. Rather, political life is about a balance between the needs of citizens and the needs of the State. Without a certain loyalty to the State in which one is born and educated, the State cannot survive, and we ourselves do not flourish. But there is a moral standard by which a State is to be judged and when it fails to meet that standard a citizen must disobey. In the *Apology* Socrates said that he would not stop practising philosophy because he had a higher obligation to practise philosophy, a higher obligation than that which he owed the State. His message was that sometimes it may be necessary to do something even if one is ordered not to do it by the authorities. The State cannot control your thinking about what is the ethically right thing to do. The orders or commands of a State's government are not the last word in deciding what to do. The State can order you to do certain things that none the less you must not do. There are moral imperatives that must be fulfilled first. But you cannot simply ignore or disrespect all that a State has done for you, and indeed the State's benefits are similar to the benefits a child receives from its family. Socrates believed one owed it to one's government to explain why one disobeys when, on those occasions, one thinks disobedience is justified. But he thought it impossible to give the State a final authority to decide on moral issues. There was always the possibility of the State being wrong. The State's order as to what was to be done could not be the final arbiter. Legal requirements in any State had to be transcended by a higher moral imperative. Socrates can be seen to have been loyal to Athens as in principle a law-governed city but he was not loyal to particular interpretations of what was lawful when the many had decided it. He could not obey a court decision that required him to stop philosophising. This would have been tantamount to living the unexamined life, to living a trivial life, which he said was not worth living. But he would obey the court decision that he die if he did not give up philosophising.

In the *Apology* he said that, especially in a democracy, no man would remain unharmed if he genuinely opposed the State and prevented unjust and illegal things from being done in the city. Most men, he argued, would always be either corrupt or at least ignorant of what truly harms them and their fellows. The Athenian multitude, like most men anywhere and at any time, was an unknowing, unreflecting multitude. And the truly reflective, just man, who knows that injustice must never be done, will in the end come to grief in this kind of State.

Socrates valued the extraordinary freedoms his native city gave its citizens but he would not confer moral legitimacy on any statute simply because it had been adopted by a majority. Should we then see him as an upholder of autonomous choice against majority pressure? Socrates told of having a divine voice that came to him and had come to him since childhood. This voice opposed him when he was about to do something wrong. We must not be parochial about this divine sign, even if we think that such private religious phenomena can be explained psychologically and socially. The Greeks accepted religious phenomena and voices at face value. But they were suspicious of anyone claiming to hear this voice on his own, unregulated by the State religion. In this way Socrates seemed a radical innovator. His voice told him not to go into politics, and instead to question people about their moral beliefs. And in some of the early dialogues he challenged the traditional religious beliefs that the gods acted immorally. He insisted that gods never acted immorally.

In the end, Socrates placed allegiance to this private divine voice which spurred him on to philosophise above an allegiance to his State. Effectively, his divine voice required that he question the most basic values of his society. This questioning placed great emphasis on man's intellectual ability and on the power of knowledge. The divine voice did not tell Socrates what to do, but what *not* to do. It stopped him from doing wrong and urged him on to pursue philosophy. He believed that once you investigate and establish what is right, you will proceed to do it. In this sense he was a rationalist. For him intellectual understanding had the power to move humans above all other forces. But he was not the kind of rationalist who questions all institutions. Rather, he took Greek customs and religion at face value, accepted both, but transformed them personally. Yes, we admire justice and piety, but what do we mean by these terms?

Is society damaged by this kind of questioning of its basic values? This is a question that Plato went on to treat in his *Republic*. Can young people be too vulnerable to hear the truth or to question accepted values, opposition to which they cannot yet handle? Only if we adopt views that are prevalent in modern liberal democracies can we say with assurance that Socrates was not really a dangerous figure and that we need more rather than less of him. Judged against the opinions of the time, however, it was fair for people to raise questions of whether their society could tolerate this kind of challenge to their values. Socrates certainly saw the role of the philosophical citizen as one which helps others to discover the proper conception of virtue. No one could really teach virtue, but a sensitive, enquiring mind could elicit satisfactory definitions from each individual without providing answers. Socrates provided no answers to his questions. He believed, rather, that philosophically sensitive questioners should give criticism and guidance rather than answers. But in Athens there were numerous professional philosophers, called Sophists, paid by ambitious and wealthy citizens, who were supposed to impart political virtues to men who merely sought political power and success in terms of wealth. In reality, such professional philosophers taught rhetorical persuasion rather than the skills to examine one's own moral principles, and Socrates believed that the students of such philosophers emerged from their studies morally blind. This moral blindness seemed predominant among men of political power. A man who knows that injustice must never be done will therefore have to disobey his State's command if such commands are made by a morally blind legislator. A State that ordered an end to one's moral investigation would have to be disobeyed.

If we then go on to ask if Socrates was engaged in civil disobedience the answer must be a qualified yes. Professor Kraut argues that the kind of disobedience he practised was 'civil' in that it was respectful of the State. But he did not use tactics for raising a grievance against the State's laws in order to bring to the attention of the authorities and the general public that a law was unjust. He provided no strategy for changing the law. Rather, he simply emphasised that sometimes it may be necessary to do something even if one is ordered not to do it by the authorities, or not to do something one was ordered to do. At his trial, in response to the hypothetical suggestion that he should just leave Athens alone in peace and quiet, Socrates said that this simply could not be done by anyone committed to moral truth. But he realised that most democrats could not be persuaded of this. Love it or leave it is precisely the kind of political response to the philosophical mind which Socrates could not accept.

'If', he said, 'I were to say to you democrats, that philosophical enquiry just happens to be the greatest good for men; that this greatest good consists in constructing arguments every day about virtue and the other things about which you hear me conversing as I examine myself and others, and if I say that an unexamined life is not worth living for man, you will be even less persuaded.' Indeed, he believed that he should never have been brought to court at all, that if certain citizens had had a grievance against him, they should have taken him aside to instruct him in his errors. Unwilling to leave Athens, because in other States he would have received the same if not worse treatment as an irritating alien; and religiously dedicated to philosophical enquiry as a way of life, Socrates clear-headedly realised he would have to disobey any order prohibiting him from examining himself and others. For he said 'death does not mean a thing to me'. And government, no matter how powerful, could not frighten him into doing what he considered unjust. It was not a matter of determining whether a particular decree of whatever government was legal or not, but whether it was just or not.

But if one must never knowingly commit an unjust act, could Socrates be a citizen of any State? Is he and his type always to be a martyr to a higher truth than is allowed by whatever constitutional structure or positive enactment? Can democracies, any more than other States with more limited franchise, cope with this kind of moral absolutism?

At his trial he gave an honest defence. He denied the charges against him, saying that he taught no doctrines and simply asked questions. He also said he did believe in the gods of the State. Was he as forthcoming as he perhaps should have been on this last issue? Was his divine voice a deviation from customary religious practices? He did not address the question of whether he had radically different views of the gods from the commonly accepted religious ones of his time. He did insist that he was a law-abiding citizen and did his duty. But he had also acted on his principles.

Just after the close of the Peloponnesian War, a war between Athens and Sparta which Athens lost, and five years before Socrates' trial, the Spartan general Lysander pressurised Athens into adopting a new oligarchic regime of thirty Tyrants, ostensibly to re-codify Athenian law. Some of the thirty were associates of Socrates and relatives of Plato. Socrates says in the *Apology*:

When the oligarchy came into being the 30 sent for me and four others to come to the rotunda and they ordered us to bring from Salamis Leon the Salaminian so that he would be killed. Such orders they gave to many others since they wanted to spread the blame for his death as widely as possible. However, I then proved not by talk but by action that – to put it in an uncultivated way – death doesn't mean a thing to me. Rather to do nothing unjust or unholy, that is my whole concern. That government, powerful as it was, didn't frighten me into doing anything unjust. When we came out of the rotunda, the other four went to Salamis and brought in Leon, but I walked away and went home. And perhaps I would have been killed because of this, if the government had not been overthrown soon afterwards.

Now Professors Brickhouse and Smith – the authors of *Socrates on Trial* – believe that the government's command was not a legal one. But there is little doubt that Socrates accepted that a government established by force *could* give *legal* orders and that furthermore a revolutionary government could give orders that circumvented the legal machinery of a prior constitution, thereby creating a *new* legal system which demanded obedience. But Socrates' appeal was to something higher than political arrangements and legality as defined by systems of government. Because he was committed to avoiding all wrongdoing, the breaking of bad laws is and must sometimes be justified. Socrates believed that under any government a man must either try to persuade the State to do what is right, or if he is unsuccessful then he must take the consequences. If one does not succeed in persuading the State, and Socrates clearly believed he would not be capable of persuading the multitude at his trial of his philosophical calling, then he must obey the State's decision that he die, rather than renounce his position. To the end he abided by the laws of Athens. He did not escape from prison when his friends provided the means. At the same time he was willing to die; some say he chose to die for his beliefs. He saw himself as a hero and as an extremely courageous man. But he did not pursue his own death in order to fix his own moral opinions more fully, says Professor Annas. He had not *intended* to get himself killed and his trial makes it clear that he hoped for acquittal, so that philosophy might win. But philosophy was his mission and if he was to be prevented from philosophising, then his unexamined life would not be worth living. He warned Athens that in killing him, *others* would see him as having been martyred.

In the final analysis, Socrates did not disobey the State. He was given a choice of penalties: either stop philosophising or face death. If he had chosen to stop philosophising he would have obeyed the State but disobeyed God. But in choosing to die he disobeyed no one. The only actual sufferer was himself or, as he believed, Athens, which was getting rid of her only true benefactor. Socrates accepted the death penalty as the only possible solution to obeying everyone to whom obedience was owed, although he maintained his innocence and insisted that the State had passed a faulty judgment. But he had made an agreement with the State to abide by its laws. In accepting the death penalty, Socrates believed he had found the solution to being both a good man and a good citizen. He continued to do what he thought just and satisfied the State by accepting its laws, which punished him for his action.

If Socrates' message is that people must be morally vigilant in all States so that injustice is never done, will such a man get into trouble under any regime except one in which philosophers are in power? Even if you are treated unjustly you must never do injustice in return, Socrates said. Treating people wrongly, doing wrong things to them, is acting unjustly. Since most people would not agree to this and instead would argue that it is appropriate to harm one's enemies, Socrates simply confirmed his view that political life in these imperfect States would always be tragic settings for revenge and continuing injustices. He believed in the necessity of States and their benefits to men. But he thought that the values of his society were corrupt. He did not make this into a universal principle regarding all societies: indeed, if a society were to practise what he preached, encouraging its citizens to enquire about moral issues deeply, then Socrates would not advocate resistance to such a State. Was he then Athen's philosopher-king – the only man suited to rule?

Certainly he had no more political power than any other citizen. He did think that the State should give its citizens moral education and that his Athens was not doing its job. He was political in the sense that he thought that *he* was doing the State's job. He argued that Athens needed him as her gadfly, stinging the sluggish beast into active moral reflection. He was her most devoted citizen. And he wanted and needed others to join him. But he was aware that only a handful of people could and would take moral discussion seriously. His questions in the agora were addressed to anyone willing to talk with him but he was well aware that only a few men would seriously engage in this hard work of self-examination. There was, then, an élitist component of his thought which was to be taken much further by Plato for whom only a selected few could and should rule the best State.

But if someone argues that only a very few are capable of achieving a profound moral understanding that makes them morally fit to govern, is he not prescribing a kind of totalitarianism? We must remember that Socrates did not actually propose a State ruled by the few. The natural consequence of his questioning, however, did lead to the strong demands that Plato was later to make: once the proper moral theory had been worked out, understandable only by the few, then it was necessary and right that they alone should rule. And they would do so not in their own interest but in the interests and well-being of all. But can we be assured that Plato's enlightened few would never be corrupted?

Professor Kraut has observed how it has become the common view in our century that, however unenlightened we are, a political system where everyone has some political power is *less* likely to be corrupted than that in which a few possess concentrated power. But Professor Kraut insists that Socrates' questioning dealt with something *prior* to this problem of power in the hands of few or many. He was determined to refocus men's concerns so that they might ask what was wrong with their habitual social life. The focus of human moral life should, he believed, be on the meaning of moral well-being and happiness. He believed that his fellow-citizens merely accepted the prevailing standards of what a good life, in its unexamined form, was. They accepted cultural norms and habits and tried to achieve wealth and status. Socrates' whole aim was to try to get people to solve the question 'How should a man live?' as an *intellectual* problem. And public figures who have no concern for the intellectual quest which determines what is right and wrong *prior* to policy statements are, for Socrates, an ignorant and potentially harmful lot.

But should moral education be the State's concern? Here we see the dividing point in contemporary political theory. The widely held liberal view is that since there is no certain way of determining the best life among the competing claims, the State should stand back and remain neutral regarding this question. The State should only intervene as an umpire – regulating the competing modes of living. It should not itself take on the task of educator. But not everyone accepts this view. There is something inadequate if not paradoxical in the insistence that the State should play no part, have no role and exercise no guidance in getting its citizens to question at a deeper level what kind of life is worth living. Indeed many people think that

Socrates had the right view: that politics must have a moral focus and that it must be based on the right kind of life to have. Many people think that Socrates' criticism of the lack of moral initiative in his ancient Athens can and should be applied to the modern liberal State; that both have failed in their main task. Did Socrates expect too much of the State? Do we today consider it appropriate for the State to mould our moral perspective? Undoubtedly Socrates believed that the State could do this, but should it? Socrates criticised the inadequate use of what he took to be an undoubted State power: to educate its citizens in moral reflection on the sort of life that was worth living.

At his trial, as reported in Plato's *Apology*, Socrates said

Gentlemen, I am your very grateful and devoted servant, but I owe a greater obedience to God than to you and so long as I draw breath and have my faculties, I shall never stop practising philosophy and exhorting you and elucidating the truth from everyone I meet. I shall say, my good friend, you are an Athenian and belong to a city which is the greatest and most famous in the world for its wisdom and strength. Are you not ashamed that you give your attention to acquiring as much money as possible and similarly with reputation and honour and give no attention or thought to truth and under-standing and the perfection of your soul? This I assure you is what my God commands. And it is my belief that no greater good has ever befallen you in this city than my service to my God, for I spend all my time going about trying to persuade you, young and old, to make your first and chief concern not for your bodies nor for your posses-sions but for the highest welfare of your souls, proclaiming as I do: wealth does not bring goodness but goodness brings wealth and every other blessing both to the individual and the state . . . [and] if you put me to death you will not easily find anyone to take my place. God has literally appointed me to this city as though it were a large thoroughbred horse which is inclined to be lazy and needs the stimulation of some stinging gadfly. God has attached me to this city to perform this office. Hence it is not an enjoyment but a mission.

. . . And I tell you, my executioners, that as soon as I am dead, vengeance shall fall upon you with a punishment far more painful than your killing of me. You have brought about my death in the belief that through it you will be delivered from submitting your conduct to criticism. But I say the result will be just the opposite. You will have more critics whom up till now I have restrained without your knowing it. And being younger, they will be harsher to you and will cause you more annoyance. If you expect to stop denunciation of your wrong way of life by putting people to death, there is something amiss with your reasoning.

We may well take seriously the charge against Socrates that he was guilty of impiety, introducing his own private god into Athens. But it is clear that he himself recognised that the danger Athens really took him for was as a critic of her conduct. Athens brought about his death in the hopes of silencing such criticism. But he lived on in the testimonies of others as a lone, heroic voice against a State that neglected to encourage in its citizens the living of an examined life which was the only life worth living at all.

CHAPTER THREE

MARTYRS

D uring the reign of the Roman Emperor Marcus Aurelius, in the summer of AD 177, there took place in Lyons in what was Roman Gaul one of the most terrible dramas in the Church's early history – the persecution and martyrdom of forty-eight Christians. So far as we can tell, this second-century Christian community was probably made up of Greek-speaking Christian traders and merchants who had settled in Gaul on the Rhône. The story of their persecution was retold in the fourth century by the Bishop Eusebius of Caesarea in his *Ecclesiastical History* (Book 5, Chapters 1–3). His information came from an anonymous letter giving an account of the martyrdoms which was sent by survivors to the Eastern churches in Asia and Phrygia. This letter remained one of the most inspiring documents for later Christians because in a distant city in Gaul these early martyrs had demonstrated a tremendous faith that had threatened the Roman authorities.

The Christian martyrs of Lyons pose a set of much larger questions for us. Were early Christians opposed to the Roman or any other State, and does Christianity, in some fundamental sense, cast a shadow over all politics? Is martyrdom a political statement expressing some radical opposition to a particular State or all States? And to what extent may we detect a continuous tradition of martyrdom in the context of political life from the early days of the Roman Empire to our own times?

In seeking some answers to these questions we must begin by asking: what is a martyr? The Revd Dr Christopher Rowland, who is Dean of Jesus College, Cambridge, replies that in Greek it simply means 'one who bears witness'. In religious terms it means bearing witness to God and his purposes over and against those who do not accept God's ways. Strictly speaking, martyrs need not die for their faith. But their faith requires that, in modern terms, 'they put their heads above the parapet and risk getting them blown off'. In the case of the early Christian martyrs living under Roman rule, many not only took this risk but actively sought death.

After the crucifixion of Jesus of Nazareth, Christianity as a religious sect had small beginnings. It came up from below to influence the lower orders of Graeco-Roman society. In the early days, Christians were people who left no mark on classical literature and the culture of their time. What they did leave were cemeteries, burial inscriptions, some buildings and letters describing intermittent persecution. But it must be said at the outset that initially the Roman State into which it was born did not have a policy of widely persecuting Christianity's adherents. But there were persecutions and these were more often than not local, even unofficial events. The drama in Lyons was one such event. It serves as an example of how we learn about these early martyrs from contemporary Christians who watched in distress and wrote for the record in order to teach others of the glory of these deaths which set an example. Such persecutions constituted enormous events for Christians. For the Roman State, they were relatively insignificant. But the Roman Empire would eventually decline and fall, while Christianity would persist throughout the ages. And the difference in values between Rome and Christianity lies at the heart of our story.

Indeed, the values emphasised in Christian history writing were different from those expressed in Roman history. When Eusebius came to include in his Church history the account of the sufferings and deaths of the Lyons martyrs, he said:

I know that other historians have confined themselves to the recording of victories in war and triumphs over enemies, of the exploits of commanders and the heroism of their men, stained with the blood of thousands they have slaughtered for the sake of children and country and possessions. But I want to tell you about peaceful wars, fought for the very peace of the soul and men who in such wars have *fought manfully for truth rather than for country; who have fought for true religion rather than for their dear ones*. My account of God's commonwealth will therefore be inscribed on imperishable monuments because it is the unshakeable determination of the champions of true religion, their courage and endurance, their triumphs over demons and victories over invisible opponents, and the crown which all this won for them at the last, which will enable my account to be famous for all time.

For Bishop Eusebius, Christian history was a story of voluntary martyrdom, a story of baptism by blood which ensured the creation of a universal 'State' in heaven that emerged from the unspeakable physical torments of certain Christians, suffered at the hands of their neighbours and of the Roman State. In their eventual hour of triumph, which only came about during the fourth century when the Roman State officially tolerated Christianity among other religions and then named Christianity as the State religion, Christian writers like Eusebius looked back to the persecutions of Christian martyrs of the early centuries as that heroic age of the Church.

The letter about the martyrs of Lyons had spread extremely rapidly in the Greek-speaking East and then had been included in a *Collection of Martyrdoms* for consolation and encouragement to those who would be determined in their efforts to oppose any attempts to wean Christians from their faith. Eusebius says that at that period in some parts of the world the persecution of the Church flared up again more fiercely, and as a result of mob onslaughts in one city after another countless Christian martyrs came to their glory. This was the story of the successful Christian revolution against the Roman Empire, and it has often been told.

The anonymous letter quoted by Eusebius not only tells us what happened on that day in 177, but it gives us an insight into early Christian values. 'The severity of our trials here, the unbridled fury of the heathen against God's people, the untold sufferings of the blessed martyrs, we are incapable of describing in detail.' But then the terrible details are given. With numerous citations from Scripture, especially the New Testament, the heathen, the Roman citizens of Lyons, are described as swooping down on Christians with all their might, giving Christians a foretaste of Satan's coming which undoubtedly is imminent.

Dr Judith Herrin, author of *The Formation of Christendom*, observes how it is clear that in times of tension between racial or ethnic communities, food shortages or increasing taxation which could generate social discord, the Christians came on the rough end of their pagan neighbours' feelings. This is precisely what seems to have occurred in Lyons. And it is possible that Christians were suspected of plotting some treason and of being fundamentally anti-Roman. If this was the case in Lyons, we shall see that it would be repeated elsewhere and at other times. The Christians in Lyons felt themselves entirely innocent but they suddenly found themselves debarred from houses, baths and the forum, and in fact from being seen anywhere. The letter says they heroically endured whatever the surging crowd heaped on them – abuse, blows, dragging along the ground, plundering, stoning and imprisonment. Then they were marched into the forum and interrogated by the tribunal and the city authorities before the whole population. When they confessed Christ they were locked up in gaol to await the governor's arrival.

One young Christian, full of love towards God and neighbour, was incensed by the charges against Christians, and boiling with indignation, he applied to speak in their defence to prove there was nothing godless or irreligious in their society, but his application was dismissed. He was asked, 'Are you a Christian?' And he confessed, 'I am,' and was admitted to the ranks of the martyrs . . . Some of us confessed readily while others hesitated because they were in no fit condition to face the strain of a struggle to death. We were worried about whether they would confess along with us others: we were not afraid of the punishments inflicted but looking forward to the outcome and dreading lest anyone might fall away.

The arrests went on day after day and those who were worthy filled up the number of the martyrs; from our city were collected all the active members who had done most to build up our Church life. Heathen servants of some of the Christians, ensnared by Satan and fearing torture themselves, falsely accused us of secret banquets at which we ate children or where we committed Oedipean incest and of things we ought never to speak or think about or even believe that such things ever happened among human beings. When these rumours spread, the people raged like wild beasts against us.

While it was clear that among these Christians were distinguished and wealthy doctors and merchants, the martyrs remembered in this account are the humble like Blandina.

Blandina was one through whom Christ proved that things which men regard as mean, unlovely and contemptible are by God judged worthy of great glory. Because of her love for Christ shown in her spiritual power and not vaunted in her appearance, she was able to calm our fears. When we were afraid of the physical torture and when her earthly mistress, who was herself facing the ordeal of martyrdom, was in agony lest she should be unable even to make a bold confession of Christ because of bodily weakness, Blandina was filled with such power that those who took it in turns to subject her to every kind of torture from morning to night were exhausted by their efforts and confessed themselves beaten. They could think of nothing else to do to her. They were amazed that she was still breathing for her whole body was mangled and her wounds gaped. But the blessed woman wrestled magnificently, grew in strength as she proclaimed her faith and found refreshment, rest and insensibility to her suffering in uttering the words: 'I am a Christian. We do nothing to be ashamed of.'

Blandina was hung on a post and exposed as food for wild beasts in the amphitheatre. She looked as if she were hanging in the form of a cross and through her ardent prayers she stimulated great enthusiasm in those others undergoing their ordeal. In their agony they saw with their outward eyes in Blandina, their sister, the One who was crucified for them. She was a small, weak and despised woman who had put on Christ, the great invincible champion, and in bout after bout she had defeated her adversary and through conflict had won the crown of immortality . . . she was indifferent now to all that happened to her because of her hope, and sure to hold on to all that her faith meant and of her communing with Christ. Then she was sacrificed, the heathen themselves admitting that never yet had they known a woman to suffer so much or so long.

Sanctus was another example of near superhuman courage in the face of the entire range of human cruelty. And the letter tells us something of importance concerning Christian attitudes to nationality and the State: 'With such determination did he stand up to their onslaughts that he would not tell them his own name, race, and birthplace or whether he was slave or free. To every question he replied, in Latin, "I am a Christian." This he proclaimed over and over again, instead of name, birth place, nationality and everything else and not another word did the heathen hear from him.' Sanctus' indifference to the State is a key to early Christian values. These contrasted sharply with the values of their Roman neighbours.

We must remember that Roman culture was in many ways highly

civilised but it also displayed an ugliness and violence that today shocks and repels. Amphitheatres throughout the empire had constant spectacles of blood-letting. Sometimes slaves who were trained to fight each other with nets and weapons entertained spectators while another day it was Christians fighting with wild animals. Violence hovered close to the surface of daily life. And in this context, violent martyrdom enabled Christians to embrace death in all its forms, 'winning them the mighty crown of immortality'. Christians who feared confessing were jibed at by the Romans as cowards, and they 'lost the honourable glorious life-giving name'. And their belief in the resurrection after death was seen as a foreign cult which treated torture with such contempt. That certain Christians went willingly and cheerfully to their death enraged Romans who said: 'Let us see if they will rise again and if their god can help them and save them from our hands.'

Christianity was effectively destroyed in Lyons during the summer of 177. We do not hear of Christianity as an established faith there until the fourth century. The persecution of forty-eight Christians, either in the amphitheatre or through suffocation in filthy prisons, eliminated what little basis of a Church there was for a very long time.

How many Christian martyrs were there during the first few centuries? It is still debated among scholars whether there were few or many. But the forty-eight at Lyons were, for later Christians, a beacon. During the later fourth and fifth centuries hundreds of accounts, known as the *Acts of the Martyrs*, were composed and their deaths were celebrated in churches. But can we uncover the kernel of truth in these stereotyped stories of ghastly human suffering at the hands of communities and the State? And what did Christian martyrs believe not only about themselves and their faith but also about the society in which they lived that led them to choose death rather than renounce their religion?

It is clear that *death alone for the faith* made a Christian a martyr, for without suffering death he was not perfected. It also appears that no one could claim the title of martyr merely as a confessor unless his confession of Christ was sealed by death. The theology of martyrdom in the early Church shows that there was a great concern among some early Christians to seek death in order to attain to the closest possible imitation of Christ's passion and death. At Lyons we see that suffering and tribulation belong to the very nature of the primitive Church. The Christian, like the Jew, was expected to confess and if need be to suffer for the Name. And the Christian was also called upon not merely to suffer, but to undertake the life of positive witness, because with Jesus, it was believed, the final era of world history had dawned. The Day of the Lord is at hand and, as Luke says, 'Christians are to live like men awaiting their master' (Luke 12). The Second Coming was around the corner. History was going to end and they had to be prepared. The reputedly eternal Roman Empire was not eternal.

But were they against the State in the sense of undermining its authority or did they simply want to ignore it? Many have argued that there is no evidence that Christians regarded their quarrel specifically with the authorities let alone with the Roman Empire. They saw their acts in terms of salvation from all society and not in narrowly political terms. The devil was their enemy and Christ their advocate. Satan was the lord of death and against him the Christian athlete pitted his might with the crown of immortality as the prize. Here they took up the vital legacy of Judaism. And indeed, the problem which Christians posed to the Roman Empire was fundamentally the same as that posed by Judaism, namely the reconciliation of the claims of a universal theology with those of a temporally and geographically more limited empire. Jewish martyrdom is in origin the basis of the Christian understanding of martyrdom. The martyrs of the Maccabean revolt, 167 years before the rise of Christianity, provided the models.

In the West, the problem of those who saw themselves ultimately as citizens of an unworldly State would continue to dominate history for a further 1500 years. Lyons set the stage. There the claims of State and the pressure of popular opinion confronted in the starkest of terms the claims of Christian confession and witness. Christianity was, therefore, a new social movement, but it was also seen to be more than this. Their own abhorrence felt for other religions, pagan and Jewish, throughout the empire, their love for one another and their sometimes heroic endurances made them appear to their non-Christian contemporaries as atheists. Strangely enough, *atheism* was the real and damning charge against them at the end of the first century. What this meant for Romans like the Emperor Domitian was that Christians were uninterested in the survival of the empire, uninterested in earthly social and political life, disinterested in law and certainly unconvinced of, if not hostile to, the pagan belief in the immortality of the State. They were perceived to have a noxious psychology of the two cities well before St Augustine in the fifth century would make the language of a city of God and a city of man common currency. They were perceived to have a belief in an exclusive, gathered Church with its martyrs and saints, with its hope of a millennial triumph over all earthly kingdoms. And they persisted in this peculiar interest in resurrection after life in the body to the detriment of history and the well-being of the State. Trading in a nationality for membership in a Christian grouping, theirs was a secret society intent on imitating Christ's martyrdom. And so, official Roman policy towards the Church, when not simply seeing Christians as an irritation, gradually became hardened into the command 'recant or die'.

But where does one look for the explanation of what was an excessive legal procedure that was the direct opposite to the normally accepted standards of Roman jurisprudence? Such standards provided equal recourse to the law and equal treatment by that law to all Roman citizens. Why were Christians singled out as was no other group in society? Was it finally understood that Christians were a threat to the Roman State?

Unlike Jews they had no story to tell of an existing nation with a tradition of obedience or disobedience to God during a long period of organised political life. As the martyrs of Lyons demonstrated, they considered themselves to be a *new* nation, a third race, created not by the recognition of laws but through voluntary baptism wherever one was in the world. And yet they often affirmed their concern for the empire and the emperor. But in defiance of Rome their new individually chosen nation was to be eternal and destined to dissolve all other temporally and geographically defined nations. The Gospels and Acts presented new beginnings, a new history. The story begins with Christ's martyrdom and continues with the martyrdom of his confessors. They called it a new nation, forged from the blood of human suffering for the Name. Christianity is a faith based on the death of its first leader and his miraculous resurrection after three days. Dr Judith Herrin believes that here is a type of sacrifice everyone can understand, a trial and a death to serve as a model for all followers of Christ.

In the course of their suffering Christians showed a disdain for 'the wild and barbarous pagans' among whom they lived. They offended their pagan neighbours and even frightened them, because their collective belief suggested they were intent on damaging the interests of the State. Hence local popular hatred is a prime mover in this tragic story. In a century like the twentieth we know what pogroms are. Their pagan neighbours had to show that the Christian claim to immortality was vain. Their neighbours feared the Christian violation of the State gods and the religious rites which held Roman society together over centuries. At first the Roman authorities seemed either indifferent to or extremely ignorant of just what Christians did believe in these early days, but what was clear was that they were secretive, apparently arrogant in their superior allegiance to something above Roman traditions and that they numbered men and women who saw themselves as a class apart even from the average Christians: martyrs ready for combat and rushing to their death. Whatever else the Roman authorities felt about Christianity when they felt anything at all, was that they feared its fanaticism.

The Christian view of history was indeed bizarre for Romans. How can people dote on continuing affliction and see persecution as something not to be regretted or avoided but accepted even with rejoicing? Why did these early Christians feel they had to suffer after Christ had already presented himself for the supreme sacrifice, having been nailed to the cross on behalf of all? Acts shows the disciples rejoicing at the onset of Herod Agrippa's persecution in AD 44 and earlier it shows them happy in having been found worthy of suffering for the Name (Acts 5). Stephen's speech sums it up: 'Jesus', he says, 'marked the culmination of all prophetic suffering in the age-long encounter between righteousness and hardness of heart.' As an imitator of Christ, Stephen prays for his enemies' forgiveness (Acts 7) and is granted a vision of Christ's glory in his final moment. Stephen is both prophet and martyr, an example that would set the seal on the martyr's life for the next centuries.

But Paul, too, passionately believed that suffering, beatings and death were the symbol of his own right to be called an apostle (II Cor. 4, 6 and 11). He was concerned to be identified with Jesus and his suffering. Only through affliction which, after Christ's death, had to be carried on again and again, did one attain God's kingdom.

But if it was the case that Jesus' suffering was meant to be efficacious for all mankind why, then, did Christians have to continue to suffer at all? Paul's answer, the answer of the Pharisaic Jewish tradition in which he grew up, insisted on there being a predetermined period of natural disaster, of war and confusion and persecution before the arrival of the End. Jesus had only shortened, not abolished, the period of tribulation. Christian suffering completed what still remained of the afflictions in the world before the imminent Second Coming. To Paul, as to most of his Hellenistic-Jewish contemporaries, the souls of martyrs were destined to eternal bliss and through their suffering they were guaranteed a share in Christ's sufferings and hence in his future glory. The Revd Dr Christopher Rowland reminds us of that remarkable letter in the New Testament from Paul to the Colossians where he speaks of filling up in his body that which is lacking in the suffering and tribulations of Christ. Although we do not speak of St Paul the martyr, early Christian evidence suggests that he did die for his faith in one of the persecutions under the Emperor Nero. In this early period, the Christians hoped the world would end and the empire cease to rule. They knew what *their* world looked like but as they could not speed its coming, they had to wait and suffer in the meantime. And when the State persecuted them it justified their view that the State was wicked and evil.

How can we understand this in the twentieth century? Isn't all of this terribly extreme? How can any society, no matter what its tolerance of religious and social beliefs of others, tolerate this kind of psychology? By the end of the first century, martyrdom had come to mean among Christians dying after confessing the faith. For some, it meant actively seeking death. But there was no need for the Christians to take up arms against the State, against Rome. This would be done for them in due time: the enemy would be destroyed and the destruction would be eternal. Meanwhile the Christian was to be both imitator and witness for his Lord and accept the hatred of the world, a world to which he himself was indifferent.

Can Christianity, then, be seen as a revolutionary movement at its inception? Is it true to say that implicit in Christianity is a defiance of the State? Today, as in the past, some think this must be the case. Dr Christopher Rowland believes that Christians are consciously engaged in some kind of political struggle – in the early centuries with the paganism of the Roman Empire – but also, in a wider sense, with the State, all States. He believes that Christianity casts a shadow over the kingdoms of this world.

If the literature cited, along with St John's Book of Revelation, stood alone for this early period, we could not hesitate in answering yes to the question: are Christians engaged in some kind of struggle with the State, all States? Indeed we might ask of these early Christian martyrs: did Revelation egg them on to martyrdom? Revelation 17–18 condemned the earthly city of Rome in horrific terms as it also condemned every aspect of the material world 'that waxed rich by the power of her wantonness'. John the Divine sees in his vision of a woman, a great whore 'that sitteth upon many waters with Babylon inscribed on her forehead, and she is drunk with the blood of the saints and martyrs of Jesus'. Here is a direct reference to all the client rulers, the merchants, the shipowners, the military commanders of the Mediterranean. But the Book of Revelation had mixed fortunes in the life of the early Church. Christopher Rowland emphasises that many Christians viewed it with great suspicion because of its subversive character. And the attitude of other New Testament writers towards the Roman Empire presents a different picture, varying from enthusiasm to violent hostility.

Jesus' own teachings and actions at different moments in his earthly life present contradictions. Yes, the cleansing of the temple was a violent affront to the ruling, pro-Roman Sadducees. And in the final phase of the struggle some of the disciples were carrying arms, and Luke (22) says they were prepared to use them. And yet Jesus said that the man who lives by the sword perishes by it. And the tribute money story in the end shows Jesus advising payment to the State for if the heart is true to God the purse may belong to Caesar without offending him. Some have argued that there is little doubt that in the last resort Jesus accepted *de facto* civil government as a good in itself, as did the moderate Jews of his day. He was prepared to criticise abuses in contemporary society including the severity of the law courts. But never does he advocate radical changes to the existing system. Is this because the existing system had only a short course to run? Surely he suggests that if one is forced to labour, one does so cheerfully. Temple tax is to be paid. Matthew is not criticised for being a tax collector nor are Roman centurions criticised for their calling. Rather the Christian is counselled to adopt a policy of non-resistance; to submit to the wrongs suffered in the present world. Caesar has a certain authority over men but not total authority.

Others hold a different view. To Christopher Rowland, it is not clear that Jesus is saying that Christians must render to Caesar what is his due. If Luke's Gospel is anything to go by, there were some people there who thought Jesus was indicating that Caesar should get nothing. One of the charges with which Pilate confronted Jesus was his unwillingness to pay taxes to Caesar.

But even if we interpret Jesus as meaning that Christians had a dual allegiance, to render unto Caesar that which was his, and to God that which was God's, this was a teaching that rankled with Roman authorities, for to them, religion and State were one. Christians had a double allegiance and an obligation of unequal value. In the case of a conflict of duties the Christian was to follow in the words of Peter 'the duty that one owes to God rather than to men'. But then what do we make of what Paul says to the Corinthians: 'let every soul be subject to higher powers, for there is no power but from God and those that are ordained of God. He that resists the power resists the ordinance of God... for he that is called in the Lord being a bondsman is the freeman of the Lord' (Romans 13).

Did the early Christians have any idea of the role of the State as satisfactory? It varied. Some certainly believed that the State remained on a lower plane for Christians (Acts 5:29) and civil requirements and responsibilities had to be shaped to the more important requirements of the coming age. But when it came to the test of practical situations, most Christians appear to have lived the double life. Even Paul was proud of his Roman citizenship.

But Dr Rowland believes that the martyrs made themselves into 'a holy huddle' and set a revolutionary theory in practice. In the beginning they were hardly a force for Rome to reckon with. But by the third century things had changed. These men and women did not regard the call to arms of Revelation, the call to vengeance against the Beast or emperor, as a literal call to organised battle. Their real weapon was faith and not force. In the short interim before the imminent Second Coming, the Christian was called upon to suffer rather than to inflict suffering since his citizenship was in heaven and not within geographical boundaries. But should he actively seek this suffering? Dr Judith Herrin believes that some of them definitely tried to engineer to be in the right place at the right time so as to bear witness and achieve the crown of glory.

Many Christians kept repeating that their kingdom was not of this world. But some Roman authorities were aware that many Christians of the first generations after Christ's crucifixion saw Rome as the embodiment of idolatry, the power of empire as the power of anti-Christ, and their literature warned of the overthrow of such government, presaging the millennium (see Chapter 3) that was anticipated by the martyrs' death. By the mid-third century when Christianity had developed its organisation under bishops, so that a hierarchy run by brilliant men was deeply entrenched in specific communities, like Cyprian in Carthage, Rome took notice.

Were these Christians provocateurs? Occasionally, Judith Herrin says, they must have been seen as this. How much toleration could any State be expected to extend to the kind of radicalism that believed that a Messiah had come and a new age was round the corner? Early Christians threatened social stability. Rome had maintained a long enduring peace throughout her far-flung territories during which period she raised to greater prominence than ever before the cult of the emperor as a god. The traditional pagan rites and ceremonies to the State's gods, the veneration of Caesar's image, all this was idolatry for the Christian as for the Jew. The second commandment had forbidden the worship of graven images. 'Come now', said uncomprehending Roman officials, 'just a bit of incense burned to propitiate the gods; celebrate and venerate the emperor with the rest of us. Simply go through it all *pro forma*, just go through the motions and you'll be all right.' But as with the case of Polycarp, a very old man dragged before a bored Roman official, so too others refused to engage in idolatry. To Romans, then, they were the enemy within. Christianity, like Judaism, was not only incompatible with the social practices of pagan neighbours, but was also, at times, seen as a dangerous rival ideology, threatening the good order of society. The whole nexus of cultural attitudes and practices through which government organised human relations, morality, justice, was threatened. A Roman's religion and his contribution to the preservation of the State were intertwined. For the Roman, his religion was a national cult based on ancestral usage and custom. And so they asked: 'Who were these Christians with a "tradition" of no antiquity?'

As we have seen, the answer was that they were secretive, suspected of black magic and of conspiracy against the State, of an exclusive loyalty to their own kind alone against the more numerous outsider. They would not even attempt to meet customary requirements of loyalty to the community and its values. In areas where Christians were actively hostile to collective State rituals, social pressure led to their persecution. Indeed, the Roman religion of duty and authority had no place for fanatics who looked forward to their own salvation, actively provoked their own doom, and displayed little concern for the rest of humanity other than their own kind. This Roman incomprehension, lack of patience and intolerance is, of course, not simply an ancient phenomenon.

If this were not the story of the Christian Church would we be ready to accept the beliefs of such people in our own communities? Celsus, an educated man, put it this way:

> Not only are Christians members of a secret and illegal organisation; there is not a chosen people, as they believe. Rather every race and every species must play its part in the earthly community, observe the laws and serve harmony. What we have with Christians is a revolt against community. It is futile for the race of Jews and Christians to cluster like bats or ants coming out of a nest, or frogs holding council round a marsh, or worms assembling in some filthy corner, disagreeing with one another about which of them are the worse sinners. Christians are like worms who say: there is God first and we are next after him in rank since he has made us entirely like God and all things have been put under us, earth, water, air and stars, and all things exist for our benefit and have been appointed to serve us.

Celsus believed this was the basis of their uncooperativeness and arrogance towards their fellow-men. And he insisted that this kind of unfounded arrogance of Christians was what attracted women and slaves to it!

> In private houses also we see wool workers, cobblers, laundry workers and the most illiterate and bucolic yokels who would not dare to say anything at all in front of their elders and more intelligent masters. But whenever they get hold of children in private and some stupid women with them, they let out some astounding statements as for example, that the children must pay no attention to their fathers or their school teachers but rather obey the Christians; father and school teachers talk nonsense and are unable to do anything good but are taken up with empty chatter. The Christians alone, they say, know the right way to live and if the children would believe them they would become happy . . . The more reckless even urge the children to rebel, and if they like, they should leave father and their schoolmasters and go along with the women and little children

who are their play-fellows to the wool dresser's shop or to the cobbler's . . . that they may learn perfection. And by this they persuade the children.

If this is the way Christians were perceived then it is not surprising the Romans thought seditious elements were seen to be at work in society. The social order was being undermined, or so it was feared, by Christians within families themselves. Minucius Felix provides a further, classic, senatorial class statement of grievances against Christians in the late second century:

> Fellows who gather together illiterates from the dregs of the populace and credulous women with the instability natural to their sex, and so organise a rabble and profane conspirators, leagued together by meetings at night and ritual fasts and unnatural repasts, not for any sacred service but for rites, a secret tribe that shuns the light, silent in the open but talkative in hid corners, they despise our temples as if they were tombs. They spit upon the gods, they jeer at our rites, they despise title and robes of honour.

The rigourist martyr-inspired code of behaviour found a permanent place in the Latin West, that is, in North Africa and in Rome. It inherited many aspects of a Christianity with its roots in Asia Minor where the Book of Revelation came from. As Dr Rowland points out, this sort of Christianity saw things in dualist, black-and-white terms. And our very knowledge of Christianity in North Africa begins with a story of martyrdom, that of Perpetua in Carthage. Here there was a continuous protest against the world from the outset. Defiance of the world and a belief in the power of martyrdom made them members of a chosen race ever ready for death. They have been called 'a full *militia christi* whose storm troopers (*agonistici*) they formed in the fight against Satan. Their deaths were the "seed" of the Church'. Especially in the writings of Tertullian (*c.* AD 200) we see an increasingly virulent strand of Christian opposition to the State, an opposition to everything that Rome stood for.

Tertullian was a superb political journalist who probably trained as a lawyer. He is said to have been a man in lifelong revolt, against the rigour of his father's house, against the Romanisation of North Africa – Tunisia and Algeria – against all the outward forms of Roman civilisation. He favoured men and women prepared to die rather than accept the conventional form of loyalty to State authorities. In his writings we see that nothing is found noble in the pursuit of ancient philosophy and we see the renunciation of the Olympian deities, and also the laws and institutions of the cities of the day. 'We bid farewell to the arrogance of Romans and to the idle talk of the Athenians.' Instead, he said, Christians believe that 'there ought to be one common polity for all and not different codes for different states'.

Tertullian started life as an orthodox Christian but ended it as a Montanist who believed fervently in prophecy and that the kingdom of God would actually come down on earth. But even his early work (*De Spectaculis*) summed up the whole protest movement of Latin and especially African Christianity with which Roman authorities had to deal. Writing early, between 197 and 200, he said: 'It is therefore against these things that our business as Christians lies: against institutions of our elders, against the authority of traditions, against the laws of the masters of this world, the arguments of lawyers, against the past, against custom and necessity, against the examples of prodigies and miracles that have fortified this bastard pagan divinity.' He declared war against all that Roman administration stood for, against the rule of secular law and the binding authority of custom. There was, for him, no possibility of ever having a Christian emperor. Caesars *are* necessary to the world but 'nothing is more foreign to us than the State. One State we know, of which we are citizens – it is the universe. What greater pleasure is there than a contempt for pleasure and the activities of this world?'

By the end of his life Tertullian was a sectarian, outside the mainstream Church, against the authority of tradition: either you are on the side of the kingdom of God or you are on the side of the kingdom of the devil. This direct opposition to the State would continue as a stream of Christian thinking for centuries. Tertullian summed up one of the extreme manifestations of the Western Latin Christian hostility to the State and his voice strikes our ears oddly, uttering in an ancient tongue all the hostility of later anarchists, perfectionists and radical individualists without reverence for tradition. His rejection of Rome's literary and philosophical heritage was part and parcel of his rejection of civic obligations. 'What', he asks, 'is there in common between Athens and Jerusalem? What between Plato's Academy and the Church? Nothing. After Christ we desire no subtle theories, no acute inquiries after the Gospel. Christians must renounce wealth and riches for possessions are sinful. Wealth belongs to the world of things and this world belongs to Satan.' But he does not thereafter advise Christians to take up arms against the State. Martyrdom is the means to victory. It is the final act of vengeance against and defiance of the world.

As he grew older, and more sectarian, he became more strident: 'The fact that Christ rejected an earthly kingdom should be enough to convince you that *all* secular power and dignities are not merely alien from but hostile to God.' And so there can be *no* reconciliation between the oath of allegiance taken to God and that taken to man, between the standard of Christ and that of the devil. The soul *cannot* serve two masters, God and Caesar. Hence, 'I owe no obligation to forum, assembly place or senate'. Society and its obligations came a poor second to the uninhibited search for and service to religious truth. If the opposition to the established order led to death, no matter. 'I refuse to call the emperor God; the capitol is a temple of devils. Government itself is part of the devil's pomp. And nothing could compel a Christian to say otherwise.'

It is obvious that a strand of early Christianity would not compromise with the State. But Tertullian's attitude would not quite triumph. The Greek-speaking Church, in the Eastern part of the Roman Empire, absorbed and refined the ethical and philosophical legacies of Greece and Rome, and ensured that the Church would survive *in* the world. But in the Latin-speaking West, the apocalyptic tradition continued to dominate the hopes of many Christians throughout the third and fourth centuries, martyrdom stirring the passions among Latin-speaking Christians so that the compromised dualism of Christians' allegiance to Church and State would never be satisfactorily resolved. Indeed the more some scholars like Dr Rowland read both Old and New Testaments, the more convinced they are of the interesting proposition that in its very nature Christianity *is* against the State. Even in John's Gospel where Jesus says 'My Kingdom is not of this world' Dr Rowland interprets that to mean *not* that Christ's kingdom is otherworldly. Jesus' statement means that the inspiration for the character of kingship and the kingdom of God is different from what one might expect from observing the kingdoms of this world. Christianity casts a shadow over the State.

Did martyrdom continue in Christian history after the period of the early Church? Dr Judith Herrin asks us to recall those evangelising missionaries – to Scandinavia, the Baltic and Eastern Europe during the early Middle Ages, to China, to the New World. But after the Emperor Constantine in the fourth century officially tolerated Christianity among other sects, one might have expected martyrdom to become redundant and even more so once Christianity was adopted as the State religion of Rome at the end of the fourth century. Dr Herrin notes that beyond the confines of the empire Christians were still persecuted. And even within Christian Rome and especially during the sixth century, the idea of martyrdom remained a focus, and a model for Christians. Monasticism as a form of collective asceticism in a community that was set apart from society had been established in the West during the fifth century, and to some, the act of entering a monastery was seen as a spiritual martyrdom, a witness to religious truth.

Martyrdom as witness, martyrdom as a suffering in a completely unprotected way where men and women are evidently without force of arms and only have their faith, their inner belief, remains a model that Dr Herrin believes has and will always appeal to a certain sort of mentality. What appears to be sufficient for martyrdom is a belief that one is on the side of the angels and that one's suffering will bring eternal life. Most religions have their saints and martyrs: Christianity is not a necessary nor sufficient condition. Dr Herrin notes that many individuals in the twentieth century have given their lives for humanitarian causes – in the protection of Jews during the Second World War though they themselves were not Jews, or in attempts to protect Gypsies when they were subject to persecution.

Dr Rowland believes there is no antidote to martyrdom. If one were found, presumably the kingdom of God would have come. So long as the kingdom of God has not yet arrived, then Christians who remain faithful to the teachings of Jesus will always be ambivalent about the State. And this, Dr Rowland believes, raises an important question about the Christian's quest for perfection. 'If you would be perfect, as God is perfect' is a phrase that remains a constant reminder. Nowadays, Christians who become part of the Establishment are reminded by a Christian tradition to ask: should it really be like this? Shouldn't one be looking for something more? The Church, even the Established Church, reminds its members of this.

More obviously, the Church in Latin America has had its members who have paid with their lives for being outspoken witnesses to the sufferings of the poor and their non-violent resistance to the government. Oscar Romero was killed in 1980 by supporters of what is now the governing party of El Salvador: here was a Bishop of the Roman Catholic Church who died for his faith and for his belief in Christ's message to the poor, impotent and abused. He joined the ranks of the victims of 'death squads' who have tried to eliminate a defiant and subversive Church that has been committed to non-violent resistance to the State. It is not surprising that they talk of the liberation of Salvadoreans 'in the blood of the martyrs'. And it is clear that they see a continuity in the tradition of Christian martyrdom from the early Church to the present.

Protestants and Catholics, Jews and Muslims have all had their martyrs, paying the ultimate penalty for what they believed. And they have been not only against the State but also against organised religion itself. Often what is so significant about the martyr's ordeal is that he is helpless and is fortified only by faith. And so the twentieth century has its martyrs, not only in the more visible Martin Luther Kings but in his nameless companions who were prepared to be harmed or even die when on pacifist marches against the segregation of buses and education in the American South. We have the Ghandis known by other or no names who pursued their ends by force of faith alone. And in this century of all centuries, some would say, we have had Jewish martyrs, who passively accepted Nazi gas chambers to the consternation of some modern Jews. Why did they not resist? Why was the revolt in the Warsaw Ghetto, for example, not more widespread?

It has been thought by those who have had the psychological stamina to confront the holocaust and its victims, that those Jews who were most religious saw themselves as martyrs, and so were better able to come to terms with the Nazi State's evil. It was religious Jews who most actively interpreted their experience of the concentration camps and their deaths as their voluntary witness to their faith.

But is it the State in its all-inclusiveness, attempting to take over the religious and secular aspects of human life, that is in true opposition to the psychology of martyrdom? Throughout history people have testified to being filled with the spirit of God, be it a 'daemon', as with Socrates, or 'possessed' of a 'dream' as with Martin Luther King. Is the indwelling vision, which ignores or transcends the political, one of the great motive forces in history which effectively thwarts any State and its demands for collective uniformity? And must the vision be so strong that life is, to put it crudely, cheap? To be filled with God is, as Professor Stephen Benko, the author of *Pagan Rome and the Early Christians*, explains, to be *en-theos*, enthusiastic. Is the State the natural opponent to all enthusism? History is filled with the theatricality and extrovertism of enthusiasts willing to put their heads above the parapet. Should we then consider martyrdom a demented psychology or one necessary to human flourishing? Is a live Christian, Jew or Muslim better than a dead Christian, Jew or Muslim?

Perhaps one of the most terrible questions to answer is whether today's urban guerrillas, willing to die for a cause, are also martyrs. Why is it so difficult for us to accept as anything other than repellent a contemporary singularity of vision which comes close to willing one's own death for a cause firmly held?

One answer would surely be that the early tradition of martyrdom sought harm to no one except, and sometimes incidentally, to the martyrs themselves. Jewish and Christian martyrdom was not engaged in a forceful revolution against the State in order to ensure an historical city of God within history. The creation of a city of God was God's work and not man's. But as we shall see, not all Christians would be willing to wait.

The early Christians believed that man's history was providentially determined by God. Men were not seen as taking ultimate control of events. But when men's attitudes changed with time, they came to believe that history was shaped by them. Martyrdom would then be transformed into a consciously engineered revolutionary fervour so that what society looked like would depend on what men made it look like. It could thereafter be argued that men's social and political creation conformed to God's will. In this light the Judaeo-Christian legacy of martyrdom has been added to by a distinctive Islamic tradition of martyrdom.

Amir Taheri is the author of *Holy Terror – the Inside Story of Islamic Terrorism*. His view is that a martyr in the Islamic tradition is a person who bears witness and testifies to the truth of Islam and to the greatness of Allah with his life. He must give up his life to be called a martyr. But what is strikingly different from the Judaeo-Christian tradition is that the Muslim martyr must fall with his sword in his hand, he must fight and kill. If Christ was not a warrior in this world to early Christians, Mohammed was. And so from the beginning of Islam, warrior martyrs were there. The uncle of the Prophet killed many people on the battlefield before his own tragic fate got the better of him. Both at home and abroad, in certain circumstances, enhancing the spread of Islam by killing its enemies and getting yourself killed in exchange, in the eyes of some Muslims, would make you a martyr.

But the idea that you can commit an act of murder and be happy to take the risk of being killed yourself, knowing that you will be a martyr, is to others who do not think this way, extremely frightening. And yet, incomprehensible as it may seem, perhaps we need to be reminded that this tradition of martyrdom fits into a parallel tradition of religious violence in both Judaism and Christianity. Surely it is *not* so discontinuous with the Old Testament tradition of the chosen Jewish nation fighting its enemies with God on the side of the Israelites. Nor is it discontinuous with the crusading armies of medieval Christendom, wielding their swords against Jews and Muslims in a Holy War to regain Jerusalem.

It would seem that martyrdom belongs to a wider spectrum of violence by enthusiasts for causes that have been against either a particular State or the State itself. What appears to be shrouded in paradox is the general attitude that is prevalent in Western, liberal societies. But whether or not we oppose violence and find contemporary martyrdom distasteful, and whether or not we appear to have been prepared to condone it and even honour it in the past, let the last word go to Archbishop Oscar Romero. Two weeks before he was killed, Archbishop Romero said, 'Martyrdom is a grace of God that I do not believe I deserve. But if God accepts the sacrifice of my life, let my blood be a seed of freedom and a sign that hope will soon be reality. . . . A bishop will die, but God's church, which is the people, will never perish.'

CHAPTER FOUR

UTOPIANS

I magine living in a State where everything is perfect: the laws, the morals, the politics, where there is no greed, no envy, no private possessions. In 1516, Thomas More gave it a name – Utopia; but the image of perfect men in a perfect State in this world and not the next has its origins many centuries before the sixteenth.

From its earliest days Christianity inspired its adherents to consider the possibilities of human perfectibility. Christ said: 'Be you therefore perfect, as also your heavenly Father is perfect' (Matthew 5:48). Whether or not human nature and social groupings *could* be perfected was discussed against a background of intermittent persecution by a Roman State whose values, forcibly imposed by institutions, were seen as both corrupt and corrupting. Early Christians expected Christ's imminent return to earth where he would rule over a perfect kingdom of his saints. This expectation took up the thread from Hebrew sources and was fostered by the description of the millennium, the thousand years of peace and harmony as set out in the vision of St John's Revelation 20: 1–15:

> And I saw an angel coming down from heaven having the key of the bottomless pit, and a great chain in his hand. And he laid hold of the dragon, the old serpent, which is the devil and Satan, and bound him for a thousand years. And he cast him into the bottomless pit, and shut him up, and set a seal upon him that he should no more seduce the nations till the thousand years be finished. And after that he must be loosed a little time. And I saw seats, and they sat upon them; and judgement was given unto them, and the souls of them that were beheaded for the testimony of Jesus and for the word of

God and who had not adored the beast nor his image, nor received his character on their foreheads or in their hands; and they lived and reigned with Christ a thousand years. The rest of the dead lived not, till the thousand years were finished. This is the first resurrection. In these the second death hath no power; but they shall be priests of God and of Christ; and shall reign with him a thousand years.

People interpreted this fundamental text in very many ways. Mille-narianism, from the Latin *mille*, meaning 1000, has come to refer, says the Revd Dr Christopher Rowland, author of *Radical Christianity*, to that way of looking at the future which expects the fulfilment of God's promises to be in this world, within history, as opposed to another one, beyond history. Throughout history, people with a millennial outlook have been active in trying to bring it about: by self-improvement, by ascetic practices, by the renunciation of the evils of their age, or even by force.

Millennial sects have persisted into our own times, too, ranging from Seventh-Day Adventists to Jehovah's Witnesses. Christopher Rowland reminds us that if former President Reagan's utterances are anything to go by, he believed there was going to be a moment called the Rapture, when the elect would be snatched away, just in time, before a limited nuclear war would take place. It is said that the Reagans have now retired to what was originally number 666 St Cloud Road, Bel Air, California, but which they had changed to number 668 to avoid an association with the Beast of the Apocalypse in the Book of Revelation. Christopher Rowland also notes that many conservative Christians in America continue to prepare for nuclear war in the belief that it will happen, and this is buttressed by a particular reading of the Book of Revelation.

Millenarianism does not lead to a particular set of political ideas. But throughout history, Christopher Rowland emphasises, there has been a frequent presumption that men can live now as saints in preparation for Christ's Second Coming. A second, perhaps more significant, presumption is that the ideals of a secular, political society cannot lead to this perfection in and of men's lives, that politics always provides distorted goals for human beings.

This seeking after perfection through a renunciation of material things, and even a renunciation of the State and its ways, occurred in the ancient world when a group of religious Jews went out into the wilderness of Judaea to set up an alternative society (from the second century BC until *c*. AD 70–80). Their writings, known as the Dead Sea Scrolls, were only discovered in 1948. They described a Rule of Life that they believed could not have been implemented in the Hellenistic cities where urban Jews lived, and, in their view, compromised their faith.

Christopher Rowland points out that this idea of a perfect society of perfect men existing here on earth as distinct from a kingdom of heaven, thereafter entered Christian thinking as millennialism. There have been various interpretations of what the millennium will be like when it happens. Perhaps most prominent has been the belief in the imminent Second Coming, preceded by calamities and the emergence of Antichrist on earth, who, after being chained for a thousand years, would be absent from Christ's earthly reign over his kingdom of saints. But then, after the thousand years of peace, there would be the loosing of Antichrist, he would seduce the nations, a final battle would ensue, God would devour both Satan and the wayward nations, and the Final Judgement would judge the living and dead 'according to their works'. Those written in the Book of Life would be saved and they would enter the beloved city; others would be damned eternally and 'cast into the pool of fire'.

To some extent this religious view was a rejection of life as it was enforced by political structures, institutions and rules of behaviour of the secular state. But to what extent did the millennial outlook see the State as unnaturally and coercively intruding on human lives?

By the end of the fourth and early fifth centuries, the early Christian millennial hopes of the city of saints were famously transformed by St Augustine, the Bishop of Hippo in North Africa. He too conceived of a city of God (and a city of Man) but in terms similar to Plato's ideal Republic, written *c*. 390 BC: in so far as the city of God exists on earth and in history, it exists *only as a mere shadow* of the eternal city, the kingdom of God in heaven. On earth there *are* members of that city of God but they are not collected into a social whole. They are diffused throughout society and the Church and they act as pilgrims in this world, not yet united in the perfect city or church. None the less, they share a love of God rather than a love of the world. For Augustine, there is no city and no church on earth and in history that is perfect. The Church is not the arena of perfection. The city of God comprises those predestined to join the communion of saints in heaven after history. All men are divided, not in terms of the perfection they have achieved here but in terms of the object of their love, be it God on the one hand, and the world and self on the other.

Augustine's abstract doctrine of the two cities was rather quickly converted into another which taught quite literally that the city of worldly man *is* to be identified with the secular city, and the city of those who love God *is* to be identified with a community of perfected saints owing no allegiance to the temporal order. They live as a perfect community in the midst of a secular State which preaches and acts in ways which are the contrary of the ideals of communal Christian perfection.

During the Middle Ages there were monks living in monasteries who proclaimed that their life alone was saintly and a foretaste of the city of God. Not only did monasteries see themselves as enclosed, perfected societies owing no allegiance or obedience to secular authorities, they also meticulously arranged their own spiritual and economic survival to constitute alternatives to the way men lived in the world. Odo, the tenth-century Abbot of Cluny in Burgundy, believed that his monastery was the perfect city of God prior to the assumption of his monastic community as a whole into heaven and eternity. And he was concerned to convince men and women outside the monastery to enter the monastic city, so that they would transform their allegiance to secular structures and superiors into an allegiance to the new perfect city, in order to be saved forever. He too believed that the end of history was near.

This 'social perfectibilism', as it might be called, would be taken up later in the Middle Ages by laymen and women who, instead of joining monastic communities, set up what they saw as their own perfect communities in which they believed they had found the key to a literal imitation of Christ's life and that of the early Church of the community of the Apostles. In so far as they saw their collective lives as *more* perfect than that of the contemporary Church and State, these groups (and there were many of them) came into direct conflict not only with the increasingly powerful and hierarchically organised Church but also with the increasingly centralised State.

The late-twelfth-century renegade Cistercian monk, Joachim of Fiore, identified the kingdom of God as about to be realised, in history and imminently. He said it would be inaugurated by human agents who lived like the angels. The Franciscan Order, founded early in the thirteenth century, harboured elements within it who came to interpret Joachim as having foretold their arrival on the scene. Their new order of mendicants did not live in enclosed monastic cloisters but went into the world teaching by example that the life of Christ could be imitated. They owned nothing, begged for daily provisions, regarded themselves as *minores* – beneath all authority and dignity, as were all the social marginals (the weak, the poor and the ill) in society. They were Europe's first social workers and Red Cross combined. The radicals among the Franciscans, who later came to be known as the Spirituals, posed a threat to the established and wealthy Church because they affirmed that their way of life was more perfect than that lived by any other group or individual within the ecclesiastical hierarchy. And some did indeed believe in the millennium, calculating its precise arrival. The Spiritual Franciscans were eliminated from the Franciscan Order in the early fourteenth century: many were burned at the stake and their writings destroyed by the Church which judged them heretics.

But we might well say that such apparently egoistical perfectibilism cannot easily be tolerated. Indeed, in its major, official sects, Christianity has always been opposed to the view that men can, in this life, live flawless lives. Christianity did promise perfection in a *future* life, sometimes to all men, sometimes to all men who diligently sought after it, sometimes only to an elect. But in this life, at least according to the central stream of Christian thinking, nothing more can be achieved than a kind of *progression towards* individual perfection, and this progress itself is dependent on the assistance of God's grace. There have been disagreements about the degree of terrestrial perfection to which even God's grace can carry men and women, but it has generally been admitted that not even God's grace made men perfect in this life, although this was and is effectively within God's power should He in future choose to bestow it on humanity.

But throughout Christian history, many Christians have been dissatisfied with this conclusion. Such men and women sought complete perfection, whether by renunciation of the world and the rules and ideals of the secular State and organised Church, or by direct union with God, or by an overwhelming conversion, or by placing themselves entirely in God's hands, or by an exercise of will. Some perfectibilists tried to live within small communities of like-minded believers, insisting that perfection would be achieved in a fellowship of the perfect. They were certain that they had simply put into practice the fundamental ideals of Christian orthodoxy which the current institutional Church refused to implement and which secular society merely ignored. The Church condemned them as heretics and the State saw them as seditious.

The Decrees of the Council of Vienne of 1312 list what one such perfectibilist group living in France, known as the Free Spirit, did believe, and it is rather shocking.

That man in his present life can acquire such a degree of perfection as to render him wholly sinless. This means that he has no need of the laws of society and government to keep him in check. And he has no need of a hierarchical Church with its priestly intercessors. That in this perfected condition a man can freely grant his body whatever he likes.

That those who are in this degree of perfection and in this spirit of liberty are not subject to human obedience, for as they assert, where the spirit of the Lord is indwelling, there is liberty. That man can attain the same perfection of beatitude in the present as he will obtain in the blessed life to come.

That man, as an intelligent nature, is naturally already blessed. That the perfect soul does not need to practice acts of virtue or heed ethical rules.

That the carnal act is no sin since nature inclines one to it.

That the members of the Free Spirit sect should not stand up when the body of Jesus Christ is elevated in the host nor show reverence to it, for it would be a mark of imperfection in such perfect men to descend from their perfect purity and contemplate the symbolic sacrament of the Eucharist or the passion of Christ's humanity.

These perfect men live like Christ, are made one with God so that they are totally and physically Godlike.

They cannot be commanded by anyone since they have total liberty as a result of their being possessed of the divine.

In sum, they believe that man can attain such a degree of perfection in his earthly life so as to be incapable of sin. In this perfection he can achieve no additional grace because such would give him perfection superior to Christ.

When such beliefs were put into practice, as they were in fifteenth-century Bohemia, a new social order, that of the Taborites, was created. Their members revolted violently against their feudal over-lords, confiscated their property and set up a perfect city of commu-nal ownership where there were no ethical rules of behaviour, no laws and no hierarchies of command. They were crushed by the Bohemian authorities. But their very attempt tells us something about a tradition of Christian perfectibilism that neither began nor ended with Taborites in Bohemia.

During both the Middle Ages and the early modern era, much political thinking was carried on within a religious framework and employed a religious vocabulary. The search for perfection that led to salvation frequently necessitated a consideration of those histori-cal conditions that could provide men and women with as perfect a space and time as possible while they were alive. The perfect Christian society was meant to be a collective enterprise, where members were voluntarily poor. They shared the communal pos-sessions of the whole and usually rejected private property. Members believed that the historical conditions and values of secular society would be transformed, that positive laws would no longer be required because Christian norms would be written in men's hearts. And throughout the medieval and early modern periods there were some who were prepared to be militant because they believed that both theoretically and practically society *could* make a progressive effort, spiritually and structurally, towards what they perceived as its proper end. Men would never be at home in the secular state. They required a perfect Christian society.

Such ideals were shared by orthodox and heterodox alike because they were seen as implicit in the Bible's presentation of the life of Christ and the Apostles. In so far as the Bible was the model for the Christian life in history, members of perfectionist groups did not, on the whole, confront social and economic reality and injustice in the State directly. Rather, they rejected economic reforms in favour of the ideal of voluntary poverty, austerity and humility, all in an attempt to keep alive the ideal of an economically primitive, self-sufficient community reflecting an agrarian and simple paradise that was ready for the transference to the heavenly Jerusalem. Social and economic problems were recast as problems that required not new institutions for their solution but rather the reform of the inner man within a Christian collectivity. This Christian collectivity rejected the order imposed by the institutions of states. The State as a set of institutions with a legal framework could not be reformed. It must be transformed by the reform of the inner man. Only then would the State be effectively destroyed.

If the State is the men who comprise it and fill its offices and institutions, then reformed men with Christian rather than secular goals simply do not construct the State. They construct a Christian utopia.

It is in the light of this long perfectibilist tradition that we look at one famous Lord Chancellor of England's 'little proposal' for a near-perfect community that was an alternative to Henry VIII's England: Thomas More's *Utopia*. Thomas More's life and times are immensely well documented except for his last days. His son-in-law, William Roper, wrote his biography twenty-two years after More died, which in some ways gilded the man's memory. More was a graduate of the Inns of Court, a member of the royal council of Henry VIII, Henry's Lord Chancellor, a devout Catholic layman, a family man, a humanist scholar and friend of Erasmus and, in the end, a martyr. He became *Saint* Thomas More only in 1935.

In 1516 he wrote what Professor Richard Marius, the author of one of the most recent biographies of More, calls 'an amusing little Renaissance humanist tract' in Latin, the first part of which is not amusing at all. Here, More describes in devastating fashion the ghastly situation of the poor in England, but then in Book 2, he provides a near-ideal alternative society. He called this new society Utopia, a word he coined to mean both 'good place' and 'no place'. Utopia is a Greek pun. In Latin, More called it *Nusquamia*, meaning no place, an ideal world. It was soon translated into English and then into other European languages.

The fundamental ideas of his utopian society, and the social ills they were meant to eradicate, would serve as the basis of most future critiques of the State, some of which would inspire seditious attempts to construct alternative and more perfect communities. More contrasted in some detail the unhappy conditions of European society, and specifically life in Tudor England, with conditions in an ideal country where human life was organised in the best possible way. His criticisms are trenchant and, in spite of little jokes here and there which would be enjoyed and understood perhaps only by an élite group of humanist intellectuals, it seems pretty clear that he meant what he said, both in his criticism of England and in his suggestions on how political and social life ought to be ameliorated. According to More, the wrong people with the wrong social training, education and values – which taught them to focus on self-interest and self-aggrandisement – were in power. More did not write the equivalent of a Green Paper or a policy study for discussion. He wrote a work of fiction, in Latin, about a sailor who discovered an ideal society on an island.

Richard Marius points out that More wrote *Utopia* for a humanist audience, in part as a *jeu d'esprit*. He knew the scholar humanists like Erasmus and Budé, and wanted to join them in a playful critique of European society, but the playfulness turned to something very serious with More. Part of that seriousness was a belief that the social and economic ills of society, if treated as *political* problems in the courts of Europe, would be shifted aside and ignored.

Several medieval perfectibilist groups believed that the Judaeo-Christian paradise on earth was dependent on God's transcendent will and therefore would be realised by God alone in history. None the less many believed, as we saw, that their own efforts to create an alternative perfect community was either an expression of that will or sanctioned by God. In *Utopia* More makes an even more positive statement that a near-paradise on earth is man-made, but based on those natural, reasonable principles which Christianity expresses and which even non-Christians can and do naturally come to recognise as true about the world and mankind. The humble citizens of Utopia

> sensibly believe in a single divine power, unknown, eternal, infinite, inexplicable and quite beyond the grasp of human minds, diffused throughout this universe of ours, not as a physical substance but as an active force. This power they call 'The Parent' . . . there is one Supreme Being who is responsible for the creation and management of the universe . . . his Supreme Being is identical with Nature, that tremendous power which is internationally acknowledged to be the sole cause of everything . . . [this is] the most reasonable religion.

And when Utopians were told about Christ, 'Christianity seemed so very like their own principal religion' that they accepted it, not least, for the important reason 'that Christ prescribed for his own disciples a communist way of life which is still practised today in all the most truly Christian communities'! (ii. 18).

Utopia was not to be the city of God because it was not Christian. But it is a State which is as Christian as can be without its inhabitants receiving divine revelation. Professor Richard Marius believes More had a problem all his life in reconciling reason with faith. He wanted to believe reason and faith were compatible but in the sixteenth century this was difficult to sustain. Richard Marius has characterised the sixteenth century as a time of profound scepticism during which there was a fear that the cold tide of unbelief was about knee high and rising. More wanted to fend off that tide of unbelief by making reason and faith compatible as he did in Utopia. For More, Utopia was a reasonable society which, upon hearing of Christianity, was prepared through reason to accept it.

More's Utopia is a Renaissance Christian development of earlier Christian proposals for a better life in community and in history before salvation. We know that More admired the monastery. For a while he lived in a Carthusian house and Richard Marius thinks he always regretted not having stayed in the monastery. We are told that he wore a hair shirt all his life, presumably under his Chancellor's robes. Richard Marius describes him as one of those late-medieval Christians – so much like his contemporary, Luther – who felt the impulsion of the flesh and the stain of sin along with the fear that was probably mixed together with much doubt. For such men the monastic life was attractive. As we shall see, Utopia has much in common with a monastery, except that it is a monastery with wives. In Utopia, as in all monasteries following the Benedictine Rule, the inhabitant or monk is given something to do all day long to prevent idleness. According to Richard Marius, More hated idleness perhaps more than he hated almost anything on earth.

Like the millenarian perfectibilist dreams of earlier Christianity, More's *Utopia*, in its attempt to improve the social and economic abuses of sixteenth-century England, initially spawned more literary fantasies than it did political movements. This is because as More himself explained through his main character, Raphael Hythloday, to treat socio-economic issues as *political* problems during the sixteenth century was to court political impotence.

Most kings are more interested in the science of war than in useful peacetime techniques. They are more anxious to acquire new kingdoms than to govern their existing ones properly. Besides, privy councillors are either too wise to need or too conceited to take advice from anyone else though of course they are always prepared to flatter the king's favourites by agreeing with the silliest things they say . . . Suppose in such company you suggest a policy that you've seen adopted elsewhere, or for which you can quote an historical precedent, what will happen? They'll behave as though their professional reputations were at stake and they'd look fools for the rest of their lives if they couldn't raise some objection to your proposal. Failing all else, their last resort will be: 'This was good enough for our ancestors, and who are we to question their wisdom?' Then they'll settle back in their chairs with an air of having said the last word on the subject – as if it would be a major disaster for anyone to be caught being wiser than his ancestors! And yet we're quite prepared to reverse our ancestors' most sensible decisions. It's only the less intelligent ones that we cling on to like grim death. I've come across this curious mixture of conceit, stupidity and stubbornness in several different places. On one occasion, I even met it in England! (i. 43).

What did More think was wrong with sixteenth-century England? The world traveller Raphael Hythloday is told of the current ills of society by the kindly but uncomprehending Archbishop of Canterbury, the most Reverend John Morton, who was also Cardinal and at the time Lord Chancellor of England. More uses fictional conversations between Hythloday and real people to make his critical point. The Archbishop tells him that thieves and robbers are being hanged all over England. 'Considering how few of them get away with it, why are we still plagued with so many robbers?' Raphael says he is not surprised: 'This method of dealing with thieves is both unjust and socially undesirable. As a punishment it's too severe and as a deterrent it's quite ineffective . . . Petty larceny isn't bad enough to deserve the death penalty and no penalty on earth will stop people from stealing if it's their only way of getting food.' The real problem is

> that there are lots of noblemen who live like drones on the labour of other people, their tenants, and keep bleeding them white by constantly raising their rents. For that's their only idea of practical economy – otherwise they'd be ruined by their extravagance. And they have vast numbers of idle retainers who have never been taught any method of earning their living . . . Now a sacked retainer is apt to get violently hungry if he doesn't resort to violence. For what's his alternative?

But there are other things that compel men in England to steal. Sheep have turned into man-eaters!

In those parts of the kingdom where the finest and so the most expensive wool is produced, the nobles and gentlemen, not to mention several saintly abbots, have grown dissatisfied with the income that their predecessors got out of their estates. They're no longer content to lead lazy, comfortable lives which do no good to society – they must actively do it harm by enclosing all the land they can for pasture and leaving none for cultivation. They're even tearing down houses and demolishing whole towns – these kind souls have started destroying all traces of human habitation and turning every scrap of farmland into a wilderness. Hundreds of farmers are evicted from the thousands of acres of enclosed land.

For More, land enclosure for sheep initiated a cycle of crime and punishment in a society that was morally degenerate despite its claim to embrace Christian ideals. People cast off the land were turned into outcasts in their own society and forced to turn to crime in order to live. More continues his story by making use of quasi-fictional conversations with representatives of some of the most influential professions in society to illustrate the problems he believed England faced. Chief among them was England's lack of realisation and acceptance that *social conditions, not individuals, were to blame for crime and social unrest*.

A prominent lawyer tries to deny More's premises with a familiar argument: 'There's adequate provision already. There are plenty of trades open to these people from the land. There's always work on the land' (despite the argument Raphael has just made that sheep farming only requires a few shepherds in contrast to all the farmers previously needed for crop cultivation and now discarded). The lawyer says, 'they could easily earn an honest living if they wanted to, but they deliberately choose to be criminals!'

More emphasises that individuals are not to blame but society is. 'Instead of inflicting these horrible punishments, it would be far more to the point to provide everyone with some means of livelihood so that nobody's under the frightful necessity of becoming first a thief and then a corpse.' He recognises only too well that if social reforms are seen as damaging to the interests of those empowered to implement change, then change will not occur. As Plato, whom More admired, had also noted, a happy state of society will never be achieved until philosophers are kings or kings take to studying philosophy. But since there is no room at Court for philosophy, and kings are too deeply infected with the wrong ideas from their childhood to take a philosopher's advice, More writes fiction. As Raphael says: 'What do you suppose would happen if I started telling a king to make sensible laws or trying to expel the deadly germs of bad ones from his mind? I'd be promptly thrown out or merely treated as a figure of fun.'

Here, More is considering the problem that the powerful members of society are required to effect changes but because these men are themselves a product of a degenerate society which has shaped their attitudes, they are virtually incapable of doing so. And if a king grew up in a good society he would be of little use since the society, through its own norms and controls, would maintain itself without him. This is what a republican commonwealth, as opposed to a monarchy, meant for More's contemporaries. It was what humanists were looking for. The imposing State bureaucracy would not be needed; one would simply have a true commonwealth maintained *by* the governed *for* the governed. The undermining of what could have been a true commonwealth by the two major self-interested social groups – the nobility and the landlords – was to be discussed in greater detail by numerous later radical groups.

If these are More's criticisms of his contemporary society, then what does his good society look like? More describes it as an island like Great Britain with cities that are neatly arranged. It has a tidal river like the Thames. The Latin original describes it as a republic rather than as a monarchy. But the English translation of 1551 gives the impression that Utopia could be a monarchy and that Utopos was its king. This was an interesting and significant mistranslation and a misreading of More's message.

Utopia was founded by a mythical conqueror, Utopos, who transformed 'a pack of ignorant savages into what it is now, perhaps, the most civilised nation in the world'. Utopos, who in the Latin version, remember, is never called king, achieved social change rapidly, indeed in a kind of revolution. He landed, got control of the country, cut a channel between Utopia and the mainland and created an island. Utopia was quickly separated from the rest of its immediate environment like a monastic community in the wilderness. Utopos, the mythical founder, is in a long line of mythical founders – from Sparta's Lycurgus who set up the constitution and then left the country; to Plato's philosopher-king; to the millennialist dream of Christ as king in his heavenly Jerusalem; to the Republican ideal of a prince who sets up what will be self-governing cities, each with its own elected governor or mayor. The communities set up in Utopia are geographically separate throughout the island but all have identical structures, regulations and life-styles.

It is a terrifically conformist society. Richard Marius emphasises that life is lived communally and possessions are held in common in this fatherly republican state. Money and the passion for money are abolished. Community takes precedence over and invades all aspects of life from work and taking meals in common, to recreational activities around which the day is organised. People are working and learning all the time. All are expected to work as work is not only necessary for the survival of the community but is also a healthy and fulfilling activity. Education is respected but few members of the community spend much time pursuing purely academic and philosophical activities. As in monasteries, travel between communities requires permission before the individual starts his journey. If he is absent from his own community for less than one day, he will be welcomed by another community, given food, and not required to work. But if he stays longer, he is expected to work and live in the community as if it were his own.

Utopos is the founder of the system but he does not rule. Rather, there is an internal ranking of citizens which acts as a general monitoring of society by its more senior male members. Utopia relies strongly on customary methods of social control and not on the regular imposition of rules and force by some external agency or organ of the State. It is maintained by the citizens who have internalised the reasonable rules of behaviour and values for governing their own lives and for maintaining this harmonious, busy and ordered society.

Thomas More socialised Utopian citizens in both a personal way and for the well-being of the collective whole. Citizens keep the society and themselves integrated into the harmonious whole by constant attention to internalised rules and norms which they learn from childhood. The society therefore does not suffer from unemployment, social and economic insecurity, lack of education or the effects of externally imposed and ill-thought-out policy. To modern liberals the cost of these benefits looks rather high.

Crime *does* still occur, although rarely. It is the product of the failure of certain individuals in an ideal environment and must be severely punished. But it is not widespread. If More believed in Original Sin, and as a Catholic he presumably did, then the evidence provided in Utopia is only sufficient for us to infer that his view of man is that he is sufficiently good to enable any badness in his 'fallen nature' to be corrected by good social norms.

One of the means by which temptation to crime is discouraged is that luxury items, especially gold, are brought into daily use. Gold serves as chains for slaves or as chamberpots and toys. Utopians, who now associate gold either with childish toys or manacles, are not inclined to warlike behaviour and do not seek wars abroad to obtain gold or wealth. They preserve gold only to pay off mercenaries who fight their wars for them. Warfare for them is a 'quite subhuman form of activity' and they only go to war in self-defence, to repel invaders from friendly territories or to liberate victims of dictatorship, which they do in a spirit of humanity because they feel sorry for them. Most important, Utopia is self-sufficient, and private life is effectively destroyed by having the bright light of public scrutiny shining everywhere.

More's discussion of aspects of Utopian life is frequently spiced with amusing examples. But the attention he pays to policies of full employment, social and economic security, social integration and education, suitable punishments for offenders and foreign relations, including his justifications of war and colonial activity, do not suggest that he was joking, however learnedly. It is not surprising that a certain tradition of European Socialists and Communists took More's agenda seriously, seeing Utopia as a programme for action. Karl Kautsky, the German Communist of only a few generations ago, wrote his own serious commentary on what he took to be More's blueprint for a more satisfactory future. How much More intended his little fiction to be a blueprint for action and how much merely a cerebral experiment to incite readers to reflection, can never be known. But if it was only to inspire reflection it was meant seriously.

Utopia is religiously tolerant because More believed men naturally come to certain spiritual conclusions about an overarching Supreme Being, and they do so the more readily *when* their social lives are harmoniously arranged. Like Erasmus, he seems to have believed that education can seriously change society. The Utopian life-style, with its many parallels with other perfectibilist Christian visions, was in accord with Christian principles; indeed, not unlike those lived by Christ and the Apostles. He notes that Christian England was Christian in name but not in deed. Raphael Hythloday says:

> For fear of sounding ridiculous, we'll have to hush up, even in a Christian community, practically everything that Christ taught – most of His teaching is far more at variance with modern conventions than anything I suggested, except in so far as His doctrines have been modified by ingenious preachers . . . But I can't see what good they've done. They've merely enabled people to sin with a clear conscience.

For More, the changes in society which *practising* Christianity entailed would provide a beginning to the solution of economic and social problems created by the State. As Raphael says,

> When I consider any social system that prevails in the modern world, I can't, so help me God, see it as anything but a conspiracy of the rich to advance their own interests under the pretext of ordering society. They think up all sorts of tricks and dodges, first for keeping their ill-gotten gains, and then for exploiting the poor by buying their labour as cheaply as possible. Once the rich have decided that these tricks and dodges shall be officially recognised by society, which includes the poor as well as the rich, they acquire the force of law. Thus an unscrupulous minority is led by its insatiable greed to monopolise what would have been enough to supply the needs of the whole population! . . .
>
> And yet how much happier even these people would be in Utopia. I'm sure that even the rich are well aware of all this, and realise how much better it would be to have everything one needed than lots of things one didn't need – to be evacuated altogether from the danger area, than to dig oneself in behind a barricade of enormous wealth. And I've no doubt that either self-interest or the authority of our Saviour Christ – who was far too wise not to know what was best for us and far too kind to recommend anything else – would have led the whole world to adopt the Utopian system long ago if it weren't for that beastly root of all evils, pride. For pride's criterion of prosperity is not what you've got yourself but what other people haven't got. Pride would refuse to set foot in paradise if she thought there'd be no underprivileged classes there to gloat over and order about . . . Pride, like a hellish serpent gliding through human hearts, or shall

we say, like a sucking fish that clings to the Ship of State, is always dragging us back and obstructing our progress towards a better way of life. But as this fault is too deeply ingrained in human nature to be easily eradicated, I'm glad that at least one country has managed to develop a system which I'd like to see universally adapted.

Pride, for More, is not easily eradicated but a reversal in social values and the construction of a commonwealth based on principles that reverse the political values of most European states can make a serious dent in pride's domain. 'Rethink a truly Christian society which practises what it preaches', seems to be More's message, whether or not what results from this rethinking looks precisely like his island Utopia. The politics of states with their underlying values steeped in pride and greed can never serve as the model for reflection. According to Raphael, 'The Utopian way of life provides not only the happiest basis for a civilised community but also one which, in all human probability, will last forever. They've eliminated the root causes of ambition, political conflict and everything like that.'

More ends his work with an ironic question: Aren't these laws and customs really ridiculous, especially, 'the grand absurdity on which their whole society was based, communism without money? Would this not mean the end of the aristocracy, and consequently of all dignity, splendour, majesty which are generally supposed to be the real glories of any State?' . . . Precisely.

He and Raphael will, perhaps, discuss this further some time in the future. This from the man who was to become the Lord Chancellor of England. But More, it seems, did not always practise what he preached. Recent research by people such as Richard Marius has shown that in real life More was a pretty ruthless landlord himself, enclosing land in just the way he criticises Tudor landlords in the first part of *Utopia*. Furthermore, as Richard Marius says, his attitude towards women would today be considered awful. And he was in favour of burning heretics. Even in Utopia the penalty for adultery is death on the second offence. And although he was champion of the poor in Utopia, Richard Marius sees not a shred of evidence that More ever had any special concern for the poor during his life. He was an enormously successful careerist. But although he rose to the King's Council and to the Lord Chancellorship (1529), he was willing to lose it all at the end.

More's political problems began when he refused to go along with the King and his intention to divorce his wife Catherine. Therefore, when Henry VIII got the submission of the clergy to withdraw from the Roman Catholic communion, he then called for More's resignation. More refused to swear to the oath attached to the Act of Succession that Henry was head of the Church of England. Thus More took the final step. Henry, that secular man, could not be the head of the Church of Christ. So More was tried. It is likely that by now Henry wanted More to die and therefore the only acceptable verdict from the jury had to be death. Like Socrates, More died magnificently. It is not clear that he lived as magnificently. But he said at the end that he had gone so far that he could not now go back and save himself, without shaming himself. His last works were devotional tracts filled with proposals on how best to conquer death. He was beheaded in 1535.

Both *Utopia* and his last act of courage, says Richard Marius, are seen as confessions of what reason and faith ought to be and what the State ought to be. Certainly More believed in the necessity of the State to keep order. He never sought to lead violent opposition to government. But it was the values behind government that he sought to change. Perhaps he thought that in some way the government of his time might be overthrown and that then his witness would count for something. At the end of his life he said in various ways that eventually the King would come to himself and that England would come back to the Catholic Church. Richard Marius observes, with sadness, that More would have the hardest time were he living today, in realising that England never did come back, that the Church would forever be sundered and that the unity he sought and the certainty that he found in that unity, would be forever gone.

Thomas More's death, the last years of his life, and his little humanist tract *Utopia*, all served, in different ways, to inspire future uncompromising perfectibilism in English history. Most notably, during the seventeenth century the continuing thread of Christian millenarianism revived the same questions and saw them answered by men and women who actually set up alternative societies. As Professor Christopher Hill, the author of many books on seventeenth-century England, tells us, in the turbulence following the death of King Charles I, Gerrard Winstanley, the leader of one such utopian community, the Diggers, believed the time had come to establish that specific epoch in human history, God's kingdom on earth. Winstanley and his companions were to be God's agents, and they took possession of common land on St George's Hill, Walton-on-Thames, in 1649 in a symbolic act of co-operative ownership. The Diggers tried to establish a communist system of economic equality, for they believed that the earth was a 'common treasury of livelihood to the whole of mankind'. They appealed to Cromwell that it was their collective responsibility to help in the establishment of God's commonwealth.

Based on his theological convictions that the world, the whole of the common land, belonged to ordinary people, Winstanley insisted that it was the Fall which had established private property. If the kingdom of God was now at hand, then the abolition of private property was its necessary precondition. After a year, Winstanley and the Diggers were suppressed by the local gentry and clergy.

Some seventeenth-century millenarian groups, like their medieval precursors, went even further, arguing that to live in the kingdom of God, as did the angels, meant the sharing of women and men in common as well as the abolition of marriage. Human perfectibility would go hand in hand with social perfectibility. The latter would not be a reform of the existing State but its replacement by a complete, alternative structure, based upon fundamentally different values. Winstanley's view of the Second Coming of Christ was that it would be 'reason rising in men and women'. But precisely when all this was going to happen had been a subject of great controversy among Protestants from the sixteenth century onwards. Throughout the Middle Ages it had been the job of chronologists and historians and mathematicians to work out the date of the millennium from hints in the Bible. Professor Hill goes on to observe that by the early seventeenth century a consensus had been reached among scholars that at least the decisive event that would inaugurate the millennium – the destruction of Antichrist, the Pope – would occur in the 1650s.

He adds that Milton, in 1641, spoke seriously of Christ as 'shortly expected king'. Parliamentarian propagandists made a great play of God's Englishmen fighting to bring about His Kingdom on earth. The victory of Parliament would bring it to pass. King Charles would be succeeded by King Jesus. There was a bit of millenarianism in everyone then, and even in Cromwell, as we shall see.

God's kingdom on earth, the Christian utopia as an idea, would continue to attract enough support throughout history to inspire attempts to overthrow the State. And Richard Marius has observed that states have frequently seen utopians as the dangers they are because they believe themselves to have all the answers and those answers are not the State's answers.

Perhaps the fundamental criticism of utopians is that they refuse to bend with the human fallibility that is everywhere and which gives men individually the chance to say 'I can do better than that' through gradual reform. Utopianism turns away from the State as it is and, as we shall see in later chapters, it has often violently turned away. But some would say that it is precisely the extremist perfectibilism of utopianism that has sped history along, for without such people and their uncompromising beliefs we would still be living oppressed by the values of the bad old days.

Then there are others who, Richard Marius reminds us, have taken a look at the Utopian paradise and, with Max Beerbohm, said: 'Oh, excuse me, I thought it was hell'. But can we live and improve ourselves and society without the utopian mirror that shows us what is wrong with our society and its values? Even if we cannot achieve a utopia, it is not certain that we can do without the insistent image that the world can be better than it can ever *be*. We need to 'hanker' for perfection.

And so utopianism, in theory and practice, asks us whether it is sufficient merely to criticise social and political abuses in a piecemeal fashion without having a whole picture of the goal to which humans must aim. That whole picture, which serves as an ideal goal, may have to be opposed to the State and its values.

We shall see that there is an extraordinary continuity in aspects of millenarianism and utopianism that can be traced into the nineteenth century when some men predicted the withering away of the State. An alternative vision of social life would replace the conditions which the State offered. We shall meet this alternative vision when we encounter Karl Marx's critique of the capitalist State and then we will have to ask if Marx's dream had anything in common with More's.

If we wonder who would enjoy More's Utopia, we might answer with Richard Marius that it would be a marvellous place for generals, and for engineers who want to build bridges that won't fall down. But it would be an absolutely terrible place for the poet, or for the person who wants a red house when everyone else's is not red.

More's Utopia is one man's idea of what society ought to look like, but if we believe that we are so diverse and that no amount of social engineering can ever make us anything but diverse, then this ideal vision for some would be the nightmare of others.

Historically, Richard Marius points out, Utopian visions have helped to undermine the State and there has been no shortage of utopians since Thomas More. Utopian theories have, perhaps, best served their purpose when they allow us to look at the problems of a State and encourage us to be more reasonable than the State in solving them. At the very least, utopias are mirrors. But they have sometimes been more than this, as we shall see in the next chapter on Cromwell's England.

CHAPTER FIVE

OF CROWNED HEADS
AND TYRANTS

At two in the afternoon of Tuesday, 30 January 1649, Charles I stepped out of the window of the Banqueting House in Whitehall on to the scaffold. The crowds who had come to witness his beheading were kept at a distance by the soldiers, too far down the street to hear his final words. But the King knew that if he did not speak it would appear that he submitted to the guilt as well as to the punishment. Reading from notes, he insisted that society must give God His due, the King his due, the people their due. But subjects and sovereigns were different things. Charles had always insisted that he ruled, as had his ancestors, by divine right. He was not raised to sovereignty by the people but by God. And the people, his subjects, had no right to rebel against him.

Was Charles I a tyrant? They said so at the time when England was declared a commonwealth on 19 May 1649. We turn now to tyrannicide, perhaps best defined as the legally justified political death of the one at the top who is judged to have misused his power. And the story that led to Charles's death begins at the end of the sixteenth century.

In 1579 George Buchanan, Calvinist, wrote what was to become an enormously influential treatise, *The Right of the Kingdom in Scotland*, in which he justified the people's right to repudiate a legitimate prince. The Catholic, Mary Queen of Scots had been deposed in 1567 and Buchanan argued for the people's right of resistance on the grounds that the people themselves institute a ruler by means of a straightforward contract, without intermediaries, between the prospective ruler and the whole body of the people as signatories. Since each individual must be pictured as agreeing to the formation of a commonwealth for his own security and benefit, then surely it follows that the right to remove and kill a tyrant must be lodged not only with the whole body of the people but even with every individual citizen. Even if someone 'from amongst the lowest and meanest of men' takes upon himself the task of 'revenge' against 'the pride and insolence of a tyrant' such action is 'judged to have been done quite rightly' with 'no question ever being made against the killer'.

In France, Catholic theologians also adopted a radical justification of political resistance, rebellion and tyrannicide. In *The King and the Education of the King*, the Jesuit Mariana wrote that since the people have established their commonwealth themselves there is no doubt that they can call a king to account. Normally a properly constituted assembly or at least a public meeting of the people is required to remove a tyrant. But 'if you ask what can be done if the power of the public meeting is laid aside – anyone who is inclined to heed the prayers of the people may attempt to destroy a tyrant and can hardly be said to have acted wrongly'.

As Europe entered the seventeenth century, above the din of voices arguing more traditionally for the divine right of monarchy and the impermissibility of resistance to it, the unthinkable was being uttered: that the ultimate right of tyrannicide could be exercised by any private person who may wish to come to the aid of the commonwealth.

By the middle of the century, Oliver Cromwell had found it quite sufficient to reassure himself about the lawfulness of executing Charles I by engaging in 'a long discourse about the nature of the regal power according to the principles of Mariana and Buchanan'. And indeed by the beginning of the seventeenth century the very concept of the State – its origins, its nature, its powers, its right to command obedience – had become the most important subject of debate in European political thought.

But the relative calm of political theory's logic followed on from what was required that men do in practice. So that when Charles Stuart walked from St James's Palace to the scaffold erected at Whitehall where he was to be executed, it was more the blood and anguish of the preceding decade than simply high-blown theory alone that caused this momentous event: regicide.

On the scaffold, Charles, forbidden from making any public appeal, spoke to his chaplain. His last words show why he died:

For the people truly I desire their liberty and freedom as much as anybody whatsoever; but I must tell you that their liberty and freedom consists in having government, those laws by which their lives and goods may be most their own. IT IS NOT THEIR HAVING A SHARE IN THE GOVERNMENT; THAT IS NOTHING APPERTAINING TO THEM; A SUBJECT AND SOVEREIGN ARE CLEAN DIFFERENT THINGS.

It is on this unrepentant and inflexible interpretation of government that Charles's downfall and the two civil wars of the 1640s hinged.

In 1641 Charles had been presented with a wide-ranging attack on the position of monarchy as a whole in the form of Parliamentary grievances known as the Grand Remonstrance. It is precisely because the picture of limited monarchy, monarchy limited by Parliament, presented in this document sounds so reasonable and anything but extraordinary to modern ears that we must pause to reconsider. Because, for the time, the demands made *were* extremely radical. The Grand Remonstrance was not so much a new and revolutionary political theory as a response to Charles's own temperament, the very person of the King who was perceived to have been ruling in an arbitrary way. He had ascended the throne in 1625 at the age of 24. His government had been a personal and secretive one. He was even opposed to those constitutional royalists who argued that the monarch's function was to protect the law, order and property of England against arbitrary claims. He was perceived as harbouring absolutist tendencies and, with some justification, his absolutism was linked with the support he received from Catholics and pro-papalists at home and (especially) abroad. His wife, Henrietta Maria, was a French Catholic, the daughter of France's King Louis XIII. Charles, like absolute monarchs on the Continent, refused to allow any distinction to be drawn between the office of king and his person; instead he saw policy as made in private where offices at the administrative and policy-making level were granted for life to favourites and viewed as freeholds. And he maintained extensive and extremely expensive patronage networks. He was incapable of seeing any need for distributing favours to those who were more important at a local level. And, taking over the views of his father James I on absolute and divine kingship, Charles expected unquestioning submission. Not only had he inherited his father's theory of monarchy by divine right but also his vast debts and commitments to an immense annual expenditure. In short he was seen to have been an impossible man. As Professor Christopher Hill describes the situation, Charles believed that it was his religious duty to double-cross everybody who disagreed with him, so he told the most fantastic lies, played people up and then betrayed them. He could not accept that Parliament were the representatives of his people as Parliament thought they were. Many of Charles's policies were regarded as assaults on the rights of his subjects, to which were added further grievances occasioned by Archbishop Laud's intransigent views on Church government.

And so Parliament went further and in June 1642 the two Houses issued 19 propositions to the effect that the King's power was limited by Parliament. Although the King's assent to parliamentary legislation was necessary, the propositions insisted that his assent should be automatically forthcoming once parliamentarians had decided on legislation.

Charles described the propositions as 'a mockery and a scorn' and rejected them. The demands of the two Houses, he said, must subvert government, and he described what government was: it was the King's preserve. Parliament was barred from sharing in government and from selecting those who governed. Judged by the standards of monarchical authority of the past, the 19 propositions were indeed radical and even personal. Some clauses insisted that the King's children were to be educated by and married to only those approved by Parliament. The King was to accept Church reforms as advised by Parliament. Laws against Catholics should be enforced and Catholic peers disqualified from sitting in the House of Lords. And the King's privy councillors should be appointed with Parliament's approval. Charles answered that he would not change the laws of England. And in August 1642 Charles raised his standard to signal the formal opening of the Civil War.

'The whole business of the matter,' it was said at the time 'was whether the king was above parliament or parliament, in ruling, was above the king'. Those who fought for Parliament above King believed they were fighting for parliamentary liberty so that Parliament would be the supreme trustee of English law. Behind this fight for parliamentary liberty lay another battle: that over the manner of religious worship. And religion and politics were inseparable in the seventeenth century. From the pulpits raged those sermons that incited men to sedition against Charles's State. Some argued for a limited monarchy; others for no monarchy at all. Englishmen seemed more united in what they would not have. But they could not unite on what they should have. Charles's intransigence produced heady times.

By 1646 Charles gave himself up to the Scots, having long left London of which he had lost control, and having roamed the north of England where he was checked by the combined armies of Scotland, Yorkshire and the Eastern Association. Parliament had signed the Solemn League and Covenant with the Scots in 1643 and in 1647 they handed him over to the English Parliament. But Parliament was divided by two parties, Presbyterians and Independents, effectively pro-monarchical conservatives and anti-monarchical radicals. Cornet Joyce was placed in charge of securing the prisoner from Parliament's control in order to place him under the aegis of the New Model Army. There were negotiations between the Generals and the King to establish a limited monarchy, but numerous members of the Army, as well as radically democratic groups like the Levellers, were extremely suspicious. They did not trust the King, were suspicious of monarchy in general, and demanded a more democratic constitution.

The King escaped the Army's custody, Presbyterians in Parliament attempted to secure a negotiated settlement with him, but now even the Generals felt that Charles could not be trusted. In hiding on the Isle of Wight, the King was approached by Parliament once again in 1648, but a petition signed by 40 000 persons living in or near London protested against any such settlement which would retain the monarchy and the House of Lords. The petition, supported by the Army, was presented to the House of Commons. The protesters claimed that it was only the House of Commons which was chosen to represent the people and hence it was the supreme authority in England.

The Levellers, in favour of widespread constitutional reform, insisted that punishment should be executed upon Charles I as the very cause of the shedding of blood. He was responsible for the Civil War, a war against his own people. And the Adjutant General Allen, at a prayer meeting at Windsor, declared that the Army had reached a clear and joint resolution: 'It is our duty, if ever the Lord brought us back again in peace, to call Charles Stuart, that man of blood, to an account for that blood he had shed and mischief he had done to his utmost against the Lord's cause and the people in these poor nations'.

In November 1648 the Council of Officers adopted the Remonstrance of the Army and presented it to Parliament: 'That the capital and grand author of our troubles, Charles Stuart, may be speedily brought to justice for the treason, blood and mischief he is guilty of'.

Oliver Cromwell, the Member of Parliament for Huntingdon and later Cambridge, a deeply religious man and a political agitator, a cavalry leader for the parliamentary cause, had extended his own troop into a regiment culminating in the formation of the New Model Army. Cromwell, in his dual role as Member of Parliament and Army leader, wrote to General Fairfax. He said he concurred with the feelings of his officers of regiments that impartial justice must be done upon offenders. 'I am persuaded they are things which God puts into our heads'.

On 6 December 1648 Colonel Pride went with soldiers to the House of Commons and with a list of those MPs proscribed by the Army, turned them away or locked up those who resisted. Pride 'purged' the Commons of all those in favour of a restoration of Charles. Fewer than sixty Members of Parliament remained as the Rump. The purge transferred power to what had previously been the Independent minority in Parliament and the way was now clear for the trial and execution of the King. A last effort was made to save Charles by making him surrender his right to veto parliamentary bills and by giving up lands of the Church. But he refused.

On 2 January 1649 the Commons sent up to the Lords an Ordinance creating a special court to try the King accompanied by a resolution that 'by the fundamental laws of this kingdom it is treason in the King of England for the time being to levy war against the Parliament and kingdom of England'. And on 6 January the House of Commons overthrew both the King and the House of Lords in three resolutions from the purged Rump Parliament.

That the people are, under God, the original of all just power;

That the Commons of England in Parliament assembled, being chosen by and representing the People, have the supreme power in this nation;

That whosoever is enacted or declared for law by the Commons in Parliament assembled, hath the force of law and all the people of this nation are concluded thereby, although the consent and concurrence of king or house of Peers be not held thereunto.

Although any right of the Lords to disagree with the Commons was denied, the House of Lords was not yet abolished. And the Lords returned their own Ordinance which said that any future king levying war against Parliament would be guilty of treason and tried accordingly. The Act of 6 January rehearsed the accusations against Charles Stuart for having conceived the wicked design of introducing arbitrary and tyrannical rule, having thereby levied war against Parliament and the kingdom as a whole to the effect of having miserably wasted the nation. It would be insufficient to imprison Charles since 'by sad experience . . . their remissness only served to encourage him and his companions in the continuance of their evil practices'.

A High Court of Justice was set up with 135 Commissioners who would act as judge and jury. The Chief Justice of Cheshire, John Bradshaw, was chosen President of the Court. The poet Milton wrote later how Bradshaw surpassed in glory 'all former tyrannicides in the precise degree in which it is more manly, just and majestic to judge a tyrant than to kill him misjudged'. Charles was not to be assassinated. He was to be brought to trial and legally condemned as tyrant. Bradshaw wore beneath his scarlet robes a suit of armour and a hat lined with steel to ward off attempts on his own assassination. Charges were officially drafted against the King. And Cromwell said he wished to be prepared to answer the King 'when he comes before us, for the first question that he will ask us will be by what authority and commission we do try him'. One of Cromwell's companions gave the answer: 'In the name of the Commons and Parliament assembled and all the good people of England'. To Algernon Sydney who had been chosen one of the judges and who objected that the King 'can be tried by no court and that no man can be tried by this court', Cromwell responded: 'I tell you, we will cut off his head with the crown upon it'.

The King was charged with being 'tyrant, traitor, murderer and a public and implacable enemy of the Commonwealth of England'. And on 30 January 1649 Charles was brought to the scaffold. When the executioner performed his task and raised the severed head aloft, reportedly a great sigh went up from the crowds who watched. A 17-year-old boy who was present said he would remember as long as he lived the sound that broke from the crowd: 'Such a groan as I never heard before and desire that I never hear again'.

Charles had been judged to have committed high treason against the nation. But it was argued further that the King's whole position was founded on a contract with his subjects and if a king broke that contract he could be penalised by whatever sentence was considered necessary. King Charles had failed in his trust. Cromwell and his companions justified regicide on the following grounds: 'they believed there were great occasions in which some men were called to great services, in the doing of which they were excused from the common rules of morality: such were the practices of Ehud and Jael, Samson and David'. God's dictates are revealed in such circumstances, step by step. As Professor Hill observes, Charles's death was seen as inexorable, necessary and God-willed. They could do nothing else with the man, for he had been judged 'public enemy to the Commonwealth of England'.

Bradshaw and others were well aware of precedents. They cited those previously deposed and killed sovereigns, Edward II, Richard II and Mary Queen of Scots.

Then in March a House of Commons resolution to abolish the offices of king and the House of Lords affirmed: 'It hath been found by experience that the office of king in this nation and to have the power thereof in any single person is unnecessary, burdensome, and dangerous to the liberty, safety and public interest of the people of this nation and therefore ought to be abolished.' A Council of State was elected whose members included Bradshaw the regicide and numerous anti-monarchical figures. And on 19 May 1649 England was declared a Commonwealth and Free State. The statue of King Charles was thrown down and on the pedestal the words were engraved: *Exit tyrannus, regum ultimus* – the end of the tyrant, our last king.

Some have argued that 'whatever could be said of the execution of King Charles I, that it was inevitable, even that it was necessary, it could never be said that it was right'. But Christopher Hill has pointed out that the numerous arguments both against monarchy and in favour of regicide, were not made by a 'loony left' but by wide-ranging representatives of different groups in the nation, indeed by men and women of overwhelmingly religious conviction, including John Milton. The arguments made against absolute monarchy and in favour of Parliament as the source of legislative power in the nation constitute the most fundamental legacy on which parliamentary democracy was erected. And these arguments issued from a most violent, revolutionary and at the same time honoured of moments in English history. Their thought and their actions, their violence in word and deed, directly opposed the State of King Charles I. The State that emerged from the bloodshed of civil war would never look the same again. Through violence in word and deed a step forward had been taken whereby the people as represented in Parliament constituted the State and the sovereignty of Parliament became fact. And the question that all this raises is whether any of this could have occurred without the violence of word and deed against Charles's vision of the State as absolute monarchy with the king alone as government.

Furthermore, how much historical imagination is required for us to put ourselves back into a period of civil war, disruption and cruelty for us then to agree that both civil war and regicide were the only way out of an intolerable situation?

Professor Franklin Ford, Professor of Ancient and Modern History at Harvard University and author of *Political Murder*, has argued that one cannot find many examples of political assassinations that have done even the perpetrators much good. And the backlash was always much more unpredictable and uncontrollable than expected. But in the case of Charles I we have something a bit different. His death was a measured decision, not immediately jumped to but eventually arrived at – to cut through a political Gordian knot with the headsman's axe. This was based less on a *theory* of tyrannicide, that Charles was some sort of monster – although he *was* called a tyrant and traitor. Instead, the regicide was set against an emergent body of political theory: that there are other representatives of the people who have to be balanced against the king, or whose claims must be balanced against those of divine right. That is, of course, a very different atmosphere in which to debate the question of regicide than the over-heated and abusive language of tyannicide theory. And Professor Ford insists that tyrannicide theory itself was at something of a low point in the mid-seventeenth century. Certainly the bloody wars of religion, particularly the assassination of Henry IV of France in 1610, had been greeted in a negative way, and had even been condemned by the Jesuits who had previously seemed to be fairly friendly towards the notion of selective tyrannicide in the late sixteenth century. What happened in 1649 in England was a double shock. It was, says Professor Ford, the first measured judicial decision to strike down a monarch at a time when bounty-hunting against power figures was at a very low point in popularity.

Should we then try to distinguish between regicide and tyranni-cide? And was Charles a tyrant in the way this term would have been understood in the seventeenth century?

Professor Ford argues that tyrannicide carries with it a claim of moral justification which political assassination need not. If assassi-nation is practical, there are people today in most governments of the world who will argue that a timely assassination may save other lives without saying that there is any ethical justification that raises this to a different level of behaviour other than simple physical violence for utilitarian ends. Hence regicide as political assassi-nation should be taken as the more useful term for the early modern period of European history. The utility of regicide is said to explain the situation of Louis XVI of France in 1793, a decision arrived at almost sadly on the part of the people who could not do anything else. It was thought that so long as the King lived he would be a centre for resistance to the new regime and there were national interests, of peace, which dictated his elimination. Professor Ford believes that this was perhaps the way some of the Bolsheviks viewed the Tsar during the Russian revolution. And so Ford argues that it is only at the point when one says regicide is demanded by the misdeeds or the corruption of its object that it becomes tyrannicide. We have here an appeal to ethical evaluations of the person rather than the wider category of utilitarian political calculations.

But does this take seriously enough the odd – to us – mixture of the high religious and ethical line and utilitarian calculations of seventeenth-century thinkers and actors in the dramas of the 1640s? Their language was urged on both by the necessity of settling the Civil War and raising to prominence parliamentary sovereignty, and by high moral outrage at Charles's very personal kind of abso-lutism, to say nothing of the demands for religious liberty for Puritans against the doctrines of the Anglican bishops and in parti-cular Archbishop Laud. John Goodwin, the Vicar of St Stephen's, Coleman Street argued in favour of the 'lawfulness of the present war' by warning 'of those men who are ready . . . to fall upon us, and our lives and liberties *both spiritual and civil*, upon our estates, our Gospel and Religion, and all that is, or ought to be dear and precious unto us'. The feelings against Charles as tyrant and the feelings against monarchy in general were ethical evaluations of the King's person and the very idea of a particular kind of State, that of monarchy. And in the intellectual circles of the time, the anatomy of tyranny along with possible means to its eradication were known to have a long history – as far back as the ancient Greece of Aristotle.

In 1644 when Milton wrote his famous pamphlet arguing for freedom of the press, *Areopagitica*, he likened the English Parliament to that democratically elected supreme court of the Athens Socrates would have known named after Areopagus, the hill on which it met. Parliamentary censorship of the press was a piece of reactionary legislation unworthy of a country engaged in a struggle for a free commonwealth. As in ancient Athens so too in England, 'Truth and understanding are not such wares as to be monopolised and traded in by tickets and statutes and standards'. If, to seventeenth-century thinkers, a democratic, ancient Athens stood for freedom of thought and expression then it also reminded them of tyrants of old and the means to their elimination.

Aristotle, perhaps more than anyone else, in his *Politics* and in his *Constitution of Athens*, tried to define tyranny as a category of government. The implication that a tyrant should or could be overthrown legitimately is also there in Aristotle. He outlines *three* forms of tyranny but it is the third which is the most extreme. It is 'any sole ruler who is not required to give an account of himself and who rules over subjects all equal or superior to himself to suit his own interest and not theirs. This kind of rule is endured unwillingly for no one willingly submits to such rule if he is a free man' (*Pol.* IV. 1295 a 17).

Tyranny generally is the rule of one for the benefit not of the ruled but for himself. Indeed it is monarchy (the rule of one) for the benefit of the one. It does not aim to be of profit to the common interest (*Pol.* III.vii). It is a monarchy exercised like a mastership over the association which is the State (III.viii). Now Aristotle tells us that there are certain kinds of kingship, among non-Greeks or among the Greeks of old, which are legally established and even ancestral. Their legality and ancestral status make them relatively safe and stable because such tyrannical kings rule over *willing* subjects. Even those monarchies that were *elective* dictatorships, as among Greeks of old, although not ancestral still were subject to law. We would call him an absolute king if he ruled over *willing* subjects *according to law*, but he is a tyrant if he rules over unwilling subjects without being subject to the law (III.xiv). The crucial issues for Aristotle seem to be that tyranny is kinglike when the subjects are willing and when his sole rule is according to law (IV.x). The tyrannical nature of such kingship lies in rule being exercised as by a master according to his personal decision.

Aristotle then goes on, it is not clear with how much irony, to provide tips for tyrants who wish to stay in power. These include flattery, deceit and perhaps most importantly that a tyrant ought not to *appear* to be one in the eyes of his subjects. If the tyrant wishes to remain in power he must, for his own benefit, gradually take on the attributes of kingship, which is ruling for the benefit of the ruled. But tyrannies not so inclined have characteristics which Aristotle outlines and he says, 'they are utterly depraved' (V.xi). What is more, they never last long (V.xii).

This raises some questions about Charles I. Was he a tyrant according to any of Aristotle's definitions? His kingship was ancestral and *he* believed he ruled according to the laws of England. But did he rule over willing subjects and did they agree that he ruled according to the laws of the land? And if the debate in the 1640s was over whether the King was above Parliament or Parliament above the King, then those who argued for the latter would surely say that Charles was a tyrant in the third category, a sole ruler who is not required to give an account of himself and who rules over subjects all equal or superior to himself (when assembled in Parliament) to suit his own interest and not theirs. This kind of rule is endured unwillingly, said Aristotle, 'for no one willingly submits to such rule if he is a free man'. Were Englishmen free men? And if, as Cromwell insisted, kingly government was a contract then in not fulfilling his side of the contract Charles was no longer legitimate as king. Following this line, Charles could not even be demoted to those forms of absolute monarchy that were tyrannical because according to Aristotle such tyrannical monarchy ruled over *willing* subjects, were *legally* established or were *elected* dictatorships. Hence by 1649 Charles was perceived by some to be ruling over *unwilling* subjects and *not* according to the law as made in Parliament. He was a tyrant.

When the political theorist Thomas Hobbes wrote his *Leviathan* (1650) to justify absolute sovereignty he insisted that the king, if there was one, was alone in England the representative of the people. According to Hobbes, in a monarchy the person representative of all is sovereign and that is the king. Sovereign power is indivisible. In a monarchy it is the king's alone. 'And I know not how this so manifest a truth should of late be so little observed: that in a monarchy he that had the sovereignty from a descent of 600 years was alone called sovereign and was unquestionably taken by them for their king.' In such a situation, says Hobbes, we must be careful of not using the word 'representative' of those who 'were sent up by the people to carry their *petitions* and give *him*, if *he* permitted it, their advice'. Advisers are not sovereigns and do not represent the people. This 'may serve as an admonition for those that are the true and absolute representative of a people, to instruct men in the nature of that office and to take heed how they admit of any other general representation upon any occasion whatever, if they mean to discharge the trust committed to them'.

And so, says Hobbes, the monarch bears the person of the people. 'In his politic person he procures the common interest *but* is no more or no less careful to procure the private good of himself, his family, his kindred and friends. And if the public interest chance to cross the private', well then the monarch prefers the private, 'because in monarchy private interest is the same as the public interest'.

For Hobbes, 'men who are in absolute liberty may, if they please, give authority to one man to represent them every one . . . and consequently may subject themselves if they think good to a monarch as absolutely as to any other representative'. Did the Civil War place such Englishmen in a position of absolute liberty so as to enable them willingly to subject themselves to a sovereign monarch? Or was Hobbes referring to that period before the beginning of the 600 years in English history of sovereignty from descent when Englishmen agreed to call sovereign their king?

According to Hobbes, once you had a king on the throne, you could not judge his performance. You could not justify rebellion by shouting 'tyrant'. For Hobbes, the only difference between commonwealths is whether sovereignty is in one man, or in an assembly of a part, or in an assembly of all that will come together. The first is monarchy, the second aristocracy and the third a democracy or popular commonwealth.

As for tyranny, Hobbes says 'there be other names of government in the histories and books of policy: as tyranny or oligarchy. But they are not the names of other forms of government but of the same forms MISLIKED. FOR THEY THAT ARE DISCONTENTED UNDER MONARCHY CALL IT TYRANNY'. Such 'mislikers of monarchy' may not instigate its overthrow. The much misliked Thomas Hobbes was the man who sought to bury the legitimisation of tyrannicide!

But had the sovereign king Charles 'discharged the trust

committed to him'? If one could not remove Charles because he was a tyrant was there any other way of getting rid of him? For most Englishmen of the time there was no question about his legitimacy. Nobody questioned that he had come to the throne legally so that it was not a fight over title as it would have been the case for many of the rulers in Italy of whom Machiavelli wrote in the sixteenth century. In Italy the founders of new princedoms had no right to their position. In Charles's case, it had to be a judgement of his performance on the throne and Professor Ford believes this stopped short of the more effusive charges of 'monstrous behaviour'. When it was not encumbered with religious factionalism and with the charge that he was misinterpreting his role as God's representative in England, it was narrowed down to Charles having made war against his own people. From the time he had raised the royal banner, Charles had been seen to have committed treason against the nation of England. But since when could a king commit treason against his people? Treason as defined by monarchs was rather the act of a subject against the king! This argument of treason could not and, in the end, did not stand. Hobbes, however, went one step further.

Hobbes said that so long as the king protected his people and in that protection provided that function of sovereignty, he could not be resisted. The question now was, had Charles performed his sovereign function in maintaining the peace of the realm and protecting his subjects? Professor Ford interprets Hobbes as saying that when Charles fled or even considered fleeing, when he lost control of the physical order of England, he had surrendered what for Hobbes was the real claim to sovereignty.

But these are all legal or logical arguments. Did no one take the doctrine of a king's divine right seriously? The answer is, very seriously indeed. How could religious men justify a right of resistance to a king divinely ordained and anointed? Here the Bible and its rich legacy of divinely sanctioned killings of false rulers came into its own. Particularly in the Old Testament Books of Judges and Kings, Professor Ford points out, there is 'a bloody chronicle of theological justifications of divinely inspired resistance to tyrants. Grafting biblical justifications on to the Aristotelian anatomy of tyranny and its solution produced the rich mixture of a Christian justification of tyrannicide from the Middle Ages into the early modern era'.

And yet medieval thought on the whole is not friendly to tyranni-cide especially if one reads the great Catholic scholastic theologian Thomas Aquinas who advised caution. But then that extraordinarily well-travelled adviser to archbishops of Canterbury, John of Salis-bury, wrote a vast work, the *Policraticus*, in the twelfth century. He analysed tyrants throughout history and praised those who rid their societies of such pestilence. But did he offer a justification of tyran-nicide? It is still the subject of much debate today, but there is little doubt that in the medieval and early modern periods it was believed that he had. John of Salisbury wrote: 'Though treason takes many forms there is none more deadly than that which is aimed against the very body of justice. The whole state has a case against tyrants and were it possible, even more than the whole state. For if it be permissible that all prosecute those charged with treason, how much more then, those [tyrants] who trample down the laws which have the right to rule over rulers themselves! Truly there will be no one to avenge a public enemy, and he who does not prosecute him sins against himself and against the whole body of the state.'

So rather like the Bible, so too past authorities could be and were mined for justifications of behaviour in the 1640s.

Was Charles a tyrant in the sense that he cruelly oppressed and persecuted his subjects? Christopher Hill describes Charles's government in the 1630s as 'pretty nasty' especially under Arch-bishop Laud although Charles was ultimately responsible. Crom-well finally saw it as a cruel necessity to get rid of him. From the point of view of the people who were responsible for his death, it was probably a political mistake which certainly alienated many people who up till Charles's death were sympathetic to the cause of the Army. But it must be said that the rhetoric of tyranny came far behind the legal argument. The regicides, those actively engaged in trying Charles and killing him, were particularly anxious to empha-sise that everything had been done in public before the face of all men and all nations. Thereafter, did people like Milton feel full of guilt or could they see the kind of beauty of the logic that had brought it about?

Professor Hill tells us that Milton certainly did not feel guilty about it. Before the trial and execution he wrote a pamphlet justi-fying kings being called to account by their peoples. Milton anticipated Charles's death. And Milton's political views, like those of so many other people at the time, were shot through and through with millennial hopes. Parliamentarian propagandists made a great play of God's Englishmen fighting to bring about his kingdom on earth by getting rid of rulers who, like Charles I, were smeared with popery. As we saw in the previous chapter on millenarians and utopians, the 1650s were agreed on as the times to be expected and it was understood that before the arrival of the millennium there would be troubled times of war. King Charles would be succeeded by King Jesus. Professor Hill insists that millenarian views were not 'loony' views – they were scholarly views which had been spread among the multitudes. Indeed 'any Member of Parliament had had millenarian sermons preached to him at least once a month for eight years prior to 1649. And Cromwell clearly believed that something important was going to happen in his lifetime.' With a large number of people having lost their property during the Civil War, with bad harvests and great poverty, with people starving in the streets in the winter of 1648–9, people were prepared for extremist hopes and dreams. Quakers like George Fox could say that 'Christ and his saints, of whom I am one, shall judge his and their enemies'. History gave such people a role to play and they took it. Professor Hill makes it clear that extraordinary things seemed possible, and that was what the execution of Charles was. For some people it was a great shock or a great wickedness. For others it could have been the door to something absolutely different and enormously better. Christian millenarianism fed into the debates on regicide and commonwealth government. But while a future saintly commonwealth fired imaginations, it did not obscure what was then and still remains the central issue at stake: that sometimes violence, and indeed regicide, is necessary and makes serious claims on our understanding. As Milton wrote in 1649, in the *Tenure of Kings and Magistrates*, when he urged the justice of tyrannicide:

> it is lawful and hath been held so through all ages, for any who have the power, to call to account a tyrant or wicked king, and after due conviction to depose and put him to death, if the ordinary magistrates have neglected or denied to do it . . . Surely they that shall boast, as we do, to be a free nation, and not have in themselves the power to remove or to abolish any governor supreme, or subordinate, with the government itself upon urgent causes, may pleasure their fancy with a ridiculous and painted freedom fit to cozen babies; but are indeed under tyranny and servitude, as wanting that power

which is the root and source of all liberty, to dispose and economise in the land which God hath given them, as masters of family in their own house and free inheritance. Without which natural and essential power of a free nation, though bearing high their heads, they can in due esteem be thought no better than slaves and vassals born, in the tenure and occupation of another inheriting lord, whose government, though not illegal or intolerable, hangs over them as a lordly scourge, not as a free government – and therefore to be abrogated. . . . Though perhaps till now no protestant state or kingdom can be alleged to have openly put to death their king, which lately some have written and imputed to their great glory, much mistaking the matter, it is not, neither ought to be, the glory of a protestant state never to have put their king to death: it is the glory of a protestant king never to have deserved death. And if the parliament and military council do what they do without precedent, if it appear their duty, it argues the more wisdom, virtue and magnanimity, that they know themselves able to be a precedent to others [who] . . . in future ages . . . may learn a better fortitude – to dare execute highest justice on them that shall by force of arms endeavour the oppressing and bereaving of religion and their liberty at home: that no unbridled potentate or tyrant, but to his sorrow, for the future may presume such high and irresponsible licence over mankind, to havoc and turn upside down whole kingdoms of men, as though they were no more in respect of his perverse will than a nation of pismires.

What happened in 1649 wasn't assassination at all. Professor Hill insists 'that was the whole point: the legal forms were very carefully gone through. There was a court, there was a President of the court, legal forms were pursued at every turn and evidence was heard. It was a show trial. But the whole point was that it should be seen to be the People of England sitting in judgement on their king.'

Where then is the State? If you have executed the king who was head of State, have you somehow built yourself a state almost as his scaffold so that when he goes, it is all still there and intact? There is not much evidence that men approached this in such theoretical terms. But one man who did was Gerrard Winstanley, the communist Digger whom we met briefly in the previous chapter. He said kingly power is something different from the king. He insisted that kingly power went on existing in England though you had cut off the

King's head. The State is still there and has not changed. Indeed what is so interesting is that when England was proclaimed a free state and a commonwealth on 19 May 1649, monarchy had already been abolished along with the House of Lords. Everybody knew what a commonwealth was – the people as opposed to the king, the people of England as superior to the king. The word 'commonwealth' was a common term in political discourse. But to have a commonwealth not only superior to but *without* a king is what was new. And some did indeed believe that from then on it was goodbye to all kings. But how many? Professor Hill believes that very few of the Members of Parliament who set up the Court to try the King were republicans, very few indeed.

So were those responsible a small core of dissident people or was there a great bubbling of discontent in the nation making it happen? Discontent was widespread, but how many people actually supported Charles's death and the way it was done is yet another question to which we do not know the answer. But we do know that the Army was finally responsible for it and the Generals of the Army were the people who were the conspirators. Cromwell kept in the background until the last moment. His concern was to preserve the unity of the Army, and there certainly was seething discontent in the ranks. They had defeated the King in civil war; the Army took him into their power, away from Parliament, and were negotiating with him when he escaped from their custody and started a second civil war. That second civil war involved the Scots coming into the country. And throughout the whole of 1648 the Army was marching backwards and forwards across England. There was trouble in Wales, trouble in Kent, trouble in Lancashire, and so on. Professor Hill describes it as a very wet, nasty summer and the army rank and file just got fed up. The Man of Blood had to be called to account.

How many ordinary people really thought in January 1649 that Charles must be put to death is not certain. A ploughman in Yorkshire, Professor Hill observes, did not know what was going on in London. And yet, so many churches were effectively political cells and were clearly antimonarchical in principle. John Bunyan (1628–80), the pastor of a church in Bedfordshire, did not want a king and did not want Cromwell to accept the crown either. And when the monarchy was restored in 1660 with Charles II on the throne, Bunyan regretted the Restoration. He says this in covert forms especially in his *Pilgrim's Progress*.

One of the objects of the Restoration of 1660 was to stop ordinary people from getting together in congregations like Bunyan's and expressing political views. Indeed, the sort of sermons Bunyan preached were rabble-rousing attacks on the gentry and the rich. Using the parable of Dives and Lazarus, Bunyan preached that more servants than masters, more tenants than landlords would get to the kingdom of heaven. Bunyan was regarded with good cause by the gentry to have been a pestilential fellow who preached sedition. He was certainly seditious against the Restored monarchy. And Bunyan was by no means unique. Professor Hill says that it is now known that there was much more widespread plotting against the Restored monarchy among the congregations than was previously thought. But although people were plotting and planning, it seems they could not agree among themselves. The Restoration of Charles II to the throne was a parliamentary construction which emphasised that England was governed by king in Parliament. Hence the focus of any opposition could no longer be the king alone because the Restoration meant Parliament and king coming together. The year 1660 was supposed to bring the two sides, Parliament and king, into a compromise. This did not last long. And we are soon on our way to 1688 and the 'glorious' revolution.

But what of the regicides? People did not think one single thing about them but many things. In 1660 Parliament passed an Act of Oblivion for all the earlier troubles with the exception of the regicides. Milton's name was on the list for a long time and it is not clear how he escaped the scaffold when others who were involved directly in Charles I's death did not. The number of regicides who were actually executed was quite small, fewer than ten; most of the others escaped overseas. But what impressed contemporaries was that they met their deaths well. All the speeches of the regicides at their execution were defiant. The cause had been a glorious one and they were certain it would revive.

Some have argued that the period 1640–60 was the real turning point in English history, a period in which the true ancestors of the reformers of the Industrial Revolution could be found. In the 1840s the historian John Foster said it was 'a grave reproach to English political biography that the attention rightly due to statesmen who opposed Charles I, in themselves the most remarkable men of any age or nation, should have been suffered to be borne away by the poorer imitators of their memorable deeds, the authors of the imperfect settlement of 1688'.

Others have called the regicide of 1649 'the great political blasphemy of the 17th century'. Blasphemy or not, we have often been given to understand that English history has been remarkable because of its reasonable and slow evolutionary process, shunning violence and sedition. What then do we make of the 1640s which ended in legally justified tyrannicide? What do we make of the church wardens of Little Horstead in the Sussex Weald who said: 'What care we for his majesty's laws and statutes?' In 1642 the men of Chelmsford said 'Kings are burdens . . . The relation of master and servant has no ground in the New Testament. In Christ there is neither bond nor free. Ranks such as those of the peerage and gentry are ethnical and heathenish distinctions . . . Gentlemen should be made to work for their living or else should not eat.' And in warning the House of Commons in 1646 that compromise was not what men desired, the Leveller Richard Overton put the argument against Charles and kings in general in words that defy our historical amnesia:

> Have you shook this Nation like an earthquake to produce no more than this for us; is it for this that ye have made so free use and been so bold both with our persons and estates? And do you conceive us so sotish as to be contented with such unworth returns of our trust and love? No. It is high time we be plain with you [the House of Commons]. We are not nor shall not be so contented. We do expect according to reason that ye should in the first place declare and set forth king Charles his wickedness openly before the world and withall, to show the intolerable inconveniences of having a kingly government, from the constant evil practices of those of this nation. And so to declare king Charles an enemy and to publish your resolution never to have any more, but to acquit us of so great a charge and trouble forever, and to convert the great revenue of the Crown to the public treasure to make good the injuries and injustices done heretofore and of late by those that have possessed the same. And this we expected long since at your hand and until this be done, we shall not think ourselves well dealt withall in this original of all oppressions, to wit, KINGS.

Professor Franklin F. Ford has argued that when regicide is justified in terms of the misdeeds of its object it becomes tyrannicide. In the last two centuries tyrannicide has become a veneer which justifies political assassinations carried out for any number of reasons. Where Ford believes that the killing of those in power has hardly ever achieved anything in all of history, we stop and think of recent events in Romania where the Ceausescus were held to be the embodiment of illegitimate force, and were violently removed.

On Boxing Day 1989 we heard the news of the assassination: the dictator was dead. And the citizenry was on edge.

Jonathan Ayal, Assistant Director of the Royal United Services Institute for Defence Studies, believes Ceausescu epitomised everything that was wrong in Romanian political culture for the last one hundred years: the high level of corruption, secrecy, the clique of rulers, the personality cult. Ceausescu thought he *was* Romania and completely associated the affairs of State with the affairs of his family. The Ceausescus engaged in an excess of violence and control so that the majority of the population came to believe it was better to die now than slowly over one's lifetime. And when that point is reached, a tyrant has to confront the entire population. The future held no promise. The trial on Christmas Day and the tyrant's immediate execution were dictated by the consideration that without the death of the dictator his security service would continue to fight in the hopes of their success. His death was dictated by necessity. 'A cruel necessity', as Cromwell had put it. But will it be effective and long lasting? Not if past experience is any guide. Should the people have waited him out as Professor Ford advocates? Jonathan Ayal believes they could not have waited. However, intellectuals in Romania have already begun to doubt whether the Ceausescus got a fair trial. Others are keen to show that the trial was a proper one and that a judicial murder had been carried out. In two years from now, in two centuries from now, perhaps doubts will be raised as they are today over the execution of Charles I.

Reflecting on seventeenth-century English history Jonathan Ayal believes that the events of 1649 were 'the triumph of an idea, a triumph of one framework of rule – parliamentary government, over another – absolute monarchy'. In Romania, the revolution 'was the triumph of the most basic wish of every individual in every country: food, some amenities and freedom'.

Compare and contrast, as they say.

CHAPTER SIX

REVOLUTIONS

A ccording to Professor Ted Honderich of University College, London, and author of *Violence for Equality*, revolution is a fundamental political change and is often accompanied by violence and terror. But it is not easy to define, let alone explain *in general*. Revolution occurs most often when the system of government has broken down, when people are in a state of very considerable grievance and when they are frustrated in achieving their fundamental desires. Professor Honderich lists six such basic desires: a decent length of life, material goods, respect or self-respect, freedom and power, human relationships of various kinds within a society and more personally, and a recognition of culture including religion. When these basic desires remain unrequited, then crises mount up unremedied and may only be surmounted by revolution.

Our purpose here, though, is not to speak of revolution in general but to look at the events that led up to England's Glorious Revolution and then to consider the consequences of 1688. We will then be in a better position to judge whether England's revolution was in any sense a model for the French Revolution one hundred years later. This is not an attempt to tell a story that is of interest only to historians. National identities are at stake. This is because it has been said for centuries that the Glorious Revolution was a landmark in British constitutional history which marked Britain out as unique in having come to a constitutional settlement in a non-violent and bloodless manner. As a consequence, we have come to believe that violent revolution itself is precluded by the structure of English institutions. We even find it hard to believe that in Britain political beings ever have thought or acted in a revolutionary manner to achieve their aims, of which we are the beneficiaries. But we have unknowingly been the heirs of what is called a Whig interpretation of British history. In 1931 the distinguished historian Herbert Butterfield warned us to be suspicious.

Today, debates on British democracy seem to take for granted that the revolution of 1688 was peaceful and bloodless. But an investigation uncovers secret plots, militant popular uprisings, aristocratic conspirators who planned regicide (again), political martyrdom, and the greatest and most radical political treatises of the time, *Two Treatises of Government* (1689), written by an English philosopher, John Locke. As the centuries have passed we have forgotten the sedition and rebellion that marked the 1680s. And Parliament's small exhibition in the Banqueting House in 1988 somehow ignored the Irish dimension of the Glorious Revolution: the extraordinarily bloody consequences in Ireland of this 'peaceful revolution' seem to have escaped the historical memory.

For generations we have been taught that Locke's *Second Treatise of Government* was an unproblematic hymn to the Glorious Revolution and to the establishment of William and Mary on the English throne. No professional historian believes this any longer. But nineteenth-century biographies of key figures in the events that led up to 1688, many written by descendants of those involved, have successfully insulated Locke and his associates from charges that he and they were engaged in a regicidal plot against King Charles II and James, his brother. As the great historian Macaulay put it, it had to be assumed that Locke's temperament as a philosopher 'preserved him from the violence of a partisan'. But we now know that Locke and a host of articulate men of high and low degree went much further towards bloody and violent revolution and treason than any of his earlier biographers knew or would admit. As we shall see, Locke along with many noble and more humble associates saw the revolutionary *dissolution* of government as glorious. And they saw the eventual constitutional settlement as a compromise that was something less than glorious.

In effect, there were two Glorious Revolutions, the first radical, the second conservative, both of which describe the erratic career of the Whig 'party' from 1660 to 1690.

If we want to discuss what happened in that earlier period we must first define our terms. What was a 'revolution' in the seventeenth century, and was the Glorious Revolution one of them?

Professor Richard Ashcraft, a visiting fellow from UCLA at All Souls College, Oxford, points to the difficulty for modern historians in defining the term 'revolution' and then applying it to historical circumstances. What revolution means in the twentieth century is not what it meant in the seventeenth. It had more to do with the closing of a circle than anything else. In addition, we need to distinguish between the intentions of the seventeenth-century revolutionaries and the unintended or unforeseen consequences of their acts.

In his book on the French Revolution, *Citizens*, Professor Simon Schama of Harvard University makes the point that revolution, in its early usage, was a metaphor drawn from astronomy, referring to the periodic turning of the spheres. It implied predictability and the preservation of order. Contemporaries had referred to the Restoration of the monarchy in 1660 as a revolution, a revolving, a return to some previous point, and specifically a bringing back of the king and the restoration of a previous form of government. Charles II had been 'restored' to the throne in 1660 by both royalist and parliamentarian gentry who had watched the events of 1640–60 in horror, as pro-royalists had their lands confiscated. Families that had directed county affairs for generations had been replaced by upstarts, soldiers, militant 'mechanics'. During the Restoration period there none the less remained many who had been prominent in the Civil War and during the Commonwealth period, or who were the direct heirs of the Civil War republicans. In the last resort these men would have preferred to abolish monarchy altogether because they saw it as given to arbitrary rule. They were admirers of classical republics and of modern republics like Holland and Venice. Their hostility to the monarchical authority of the Stuarts had led them to risk their lives for a vision of English liberties which they took to be a birthright, and many men had died violently for this vision. But by 1660 the total abolition of monarchy could be nothing more than a distant dream. The chaos of the interregnum between Charles I's death and 1660 had dampened any widespread faith in constitutional novelty. But those men whose attitudes had been formed during the 1640s and 1650s did not just disappear. Those who had not made their peace with the establishment went underground and bided their time. They were to reappear in the late 1670s and early 1680s.

In 1660 Presbyterians had intended to restore Charles to a

monarchy that would be strictly limited by the conditions that had been offered, and rejected, by Charles I. They failed. Though whether Charles II actually had the same powers as his father or not is debatable. He certainly gained control of the militia, the Church and the town corporations, and was able to exercise possibly even more power than his father. In such conditions those who inherited the ideals of the earlier tradition to alter the country's Constitution from a monarchy to a republic now opted for the more pragmatic image of a mixed monarchy – King and Parliament – which sought to transfer constitutional power from the Crown to Parliament. It seemed more pragmatic to attempt to limit the prerogatives of the Crown than to abolish it entirely. But there still was a fear among moderates that with Charles restored, his brother the Duke of York, James, could succeed him. James was a practising Catholic whereas Charles had been perhaps a secret Catholic, and it was believed with some justification that a fundamental tenet of Catholicism at that time was absolutist monarchy. (The Renaissance papacy until the early seventeenth century had shown itself to be a powerfully effective absolutist State with a well-developed bureaucracy and foreign policy, indeed the very model of an absolutist State for Europe.)

Protestants who were gripped by the anti-Catholic hysteria of the seventeenth century were troubled by what could happen if a Catholic monarch came to the throne. In fact, the 1680s was a decade marked by a pervasive fear of Catholicism and a widespread belief that a conspiracy existed to reestablish that religion in Protestant England. This seemed evident from the practice of severe repression directed against non-Anglican Protestant dissidents and nonconformists who were identified as politically motivated.

Charles II was cousin to the Catholic Louis XIV of France. He had only to look across the Channel to see Louis as the very image of a king who demanded and received absolute obedience from his subjects. It seemed clear that at least part of Louis's success was due to the assistance he received from the doctrines and practices of Catholicism. All seventeenth-century princes recognised an identity between Catholicism and absolutism. And Charles tailored his foreign policy accordingly. As more than one historian has noted, secrecy, popery and despotism became the watchwords of the decade.

Indeed the decade had begun with the signing of the secret treaty of Dover between England and France. This first, secret, treaty contained clauses in which Charles promised to declare his adherence to the Roman Catholic religion, and he received a payment of £200 000 and French troops from Louis to assist him in the execution of his 'grand conversion'. A second, public, Treaty of Dover, made no mention of Charles's Catholic cause and instead conveyed a commercial and military purpose: the prosecution of a joint war against the Protestant Dutch republic, that refuge of regicides, rebels and republican plotters. From the signing of this treaty, it was seen by many to be only a matter of time before Charles subverted the constituted religion and political order of the land.

But why were so many Englishmen anti-Catholic? There was a deeply rooted fear that went back into the sixteenth century, certainly back to Elizabeth's reign, when she had been excommunicated by the Pope. This meant that no Catholics thereafter had a legal obligation to obey her and Catholics were therefore all potentially subversives. Furthermore, the standard view in the seventeenth century was that Catholics were not required to keep agreements and contracts with heretics. And to the Catholic Church, Protestants were heretics. Hence you could never trust any agreement between a Catholic and a Protestant and this was magnified in the case of a Catholic king and his Protestant subjects. If, as was argued by many Protestants, government was itself a contract between the ruler and the ruled, then no such contract between a Catholic monarch and his Protestant subjects was binding! How can Protestant subjects trust the intentions of a Catholic king if a Catholic owed no obligations to heretics? Indeed, some continental Protestant monarchs in the sixteenth and seventeenth centuries had been assassinated by Jesuits. And during the reign of Queen Mary ('bloody Mary') Protestants had been put to the stake while others had fled to Geneva and elsewhere in Europe.

But anti-Catholicism was only one item on the political agenda of the political opposition to Charles II and James, Duke of York. Protestants were themselves divided by differing religious tenets and their political consequences.

The leading opposition personality in these days was the radical Whig, Anthony Ashley Cooper, the first Earl of Shaftesbury. Opposition Whigs believed they were defending the ancient constitution against what they took to be Charles II's attempts at its subversion. The first Whigs were a faction of those former Presbyterians who had unsuccessfully sought an alliance between High Church Anglicans and dissenting Protestant groups in order to limit the Crown's patronage. They also appealed to the antiquity of the House of Commons and sought to safeguard parliamentary gains against the use of royal prerogative. The battle between High Church Anglicans and those with dissident religious views was also a political battle centred on a debate over the location of authority and sovereignty.

In 1669–70 there had been a sharp and perceptible turn towards political repression of religious dissent. This helped to crystallise the intensity of an active opposition to the Anglican Church and the Court. In 1669 Charles had proclaimed against all dissenters and there was an abundance of persecuting activities. But after issuing an anti-dissenter declaration, Charles had then used his prerogative to pardon the fines levied against some nonconformists. In 1670 Parliament had come to the aid of the Anglican Church by enacting a second Conventicle Bill which identified religious conventicles with a riot, thereby merging the notion of religious nonconformity with political sedition and disorder. As finally passed the law did not go quite this far but it was attacked for the arbitrary power it gave to a single magistrate against whose judgement a defendant had no appeal. This law went into effect one week before Charles signed the secret Treaty of Dover.

Charles's own position was complicated. It seems that he first tried to gain the Anglican Church's support for the absoluteness of royal authority through the prosecution of nonconformists, but then, once this had been achieved, he used his prerogative to pardon dissenters and thereby win dissenter support for his supremacy in religious matters, granting them toleration through his prerogative. He legislated against religious intolerance but used his prerogative to grant selective tolerance. And in using his prerogative indulgence to nonconformists he also included a toleration of Catholics.

Anglican clergymen like Samuel Parker argued that Protestant nonconformists and dissenters were the worst and most dangerous enemies of all forms of authority so that enforcement of penal codes against nonconformists was to be encouraged. He insisted that religious dissidents were also political dissidents. Whatever such nonconformists proposed in religious terms was essentially an anti-authoritarian political argument. Their so-called religious concern for the liberty of an individual's conscience was really a cloak for their true aim: liberty of practice. For Parker and other Anglicans, those in authority in Church and State were more competent judges of laws and policies than anyone else. In contrast, those Whigs around the Earl of Shaftesbury argued:

> That a few leaders of the Church of England should monopolise to themselves the name of rational divines, is simply an expression of their overblown pride.

> For men to be tied and led by authority as it were with a kind of captivity of judgement, is brutish. To resign ourselves to the command of superiors on the basis of their appeal to authority is to say that God would have us lay aside our reason which He has given us for a guide.

Here was the heart of the religious and political debate. Was man as created by God sufficiently rational to make his own decisions both in matters of faith and in matters of community governance? Protestant dissenters were convinced that God had created an ordered world, an unbroken chain of reason within which man must himself discover his place. Hence to rely on the authority of civil magistrates as a substitute for an individual's use of reason in the performance of moral obligations, was not only lazy and impious, but it signified a failure to recognise the Protestant as opposed to Catholic emphasis on the individual's relationship to God. Individuals, said nonconformists, were rational individuals, having been created in a state of equality and freedom. It is common to all men not to be subject to the absolute will of any other person. And such rational and responsible individuals constituted a natural, moral community with moral obligations owed to each other and to God. Reason enabled them to discover those obligations to others. There was already a law in nature which rational men could discover through their own use of reason applied to their moral responsibilities. And just as this law of nature imposed duties, so it confirmed the rights of individuals, including the right to follow the dictates of one's own conscience. The exercise of rational choice was a natural right, which enabled men to provide for their own welfare. It is obvious that this religious nonconformist Protestant view was not politically innocent: it queried the basis on which authority was erected and maintained over rational and responsible men. The fear of James, as a Catholic, succeeding Charles on the throne, was a real one for men who, on religious grounds, could not resign themselves to the command of superiors simply on the basis of such superiors' appeal to authority.

At the beginning of the 1680s there was a concerted attempt to prevent a Catholic from attaining the throne as well as an attempt to ensure a freely elected Parliament whose will would somehow be translated into law. In 1680 the House of Commons passed the Exclusion Bill which would prevent James from ascending the throne. But the House of Lords would not exclude him and, among many others, the bishops rejected it. The more radical Whig policy – which was to attempt to promote limitations of the royal prerogative – was now subordinated to a much less radical belief: that excluding James from the throne would suffice to secure the birthright of Englishmen. Instead of limiting monarchy in general, some now said that all that was needed was to change the person of the monarch. But adherents of a commonwealth persuasion in both Houses continued to argue for the more ambitious goal of limitations to the point that it would hardly matter which king was on the throne, even a Catholic, were he suitably circumscribed.

However, neither monarchical circumscription nor Catholic exclusion could be achieved. And this was because there were two opposing but powerful views of monarchy adopted by men of political power and influence.

For Whigs, monarchy was a traditional *human* institution whose power could be limited because it existed for the benefit of the ruled. Monarchy served the people by dispensing justice and protecting subjects from violence at home and attack from abroad. If a monarch misused the powers of his office, or threatened to do so, his powers should be restricted or, in the last resort, he should be removed or deposed. Subjects had a right to resist a king turned tyrant. While most Whigs avoided a clear exposition of a subject's *right* to resist a monarch's commands, they did argue that the subject's *duty* of obedience was not unconditional: it could be overriden by his prior right of self-preservation. Following on from the Protestant nonconformist argument that each man was his own rational authority and not simply resigned to the unquestioned command of authoritative superiors, the question was, under which, if any, conditions did a subject have the duty if not the right to resist? The answer was that in certain conditions in which a king ceased to act as a king, he could be considered to have forfeited kingship, returning to the status of a private individual. Thus one Whig argument focused not on the explicit right of resistance but rather on the question of what kingly authority was. When does a king cease to be king? Since, it was argued by John Locke, a king's authority is given him only by the law, he cannot empower anyone to act against the law or justify him by his commission in so doing. The commission or command of any magistrate, where he has no authority, is void and as insignificant as the command of a private man. Therefore, subjects cannot exercise power over a king *unless* he does something that makes him cease to be king. And if he becomes merely a private man he has no public authority, an authority given him only by the law. This can occur if the king tries to overturn government or has a design to ruin the kingdom and commonwealth. But this resistance theory is not opposed to a strong acceptance of *rightful* authority.

Tories, however, argued that monarchy was hereditary, that royal authority was sacred and that subjects had a duty not to resist the king. If any of them feared royal tendencies towards Catholicism, they none the less looked with even greater horror at the possibility of a popular debate concerning the issue 'when does a king cease to be king?' Who was in a position to judge? Surely not the common man. Tories argued that according to the anti-monarchical dissenters, all men by native right are equally born with a like freedom but, they said, even if this were accepted as true, it would make the people nothing more than a headless, disordered multitude. What could the nonconformist Whig language of natural rights, equality and popular sovereignty mean except a defence of the sovereignty of the rabble or the dregs of mankind? To grant the individual the right of being his own judge and asserter of his own privileges would produce, according to them, an independent herd of licentious and ungovernable men. It would not produce a compact body of citizens united together.

'Tis insufferable for the multitude whose duty it is to be governed, to concern themselves in public affairs, as if they were sharers in the government itself'. And so Tories asked Whigs whether they really meant to lodge this ultimate power 'with every pert tradesman . . . or every capricious brain and vulgar understanding?' And most Whigs replied 'No'!

When Parliament sat in Oxford in 1681 Charles had to face the most hostile and radical group of legislators he had yet confronted throughout his reign. Three elections had been won by the Whigs with increasingly larger majorities. After six days with the resultant

Parliament, Charles sent them home. He dissolved Parliament with a resolution never to call another. He conveyed this in private, but Shaftesbury and others were now convinced that Charles had attempted to defeat the purposes of representative government by preventing Parliament from carrying out its constitutional duties regarding redress of the people's grievances. Indeed, Shaftesbury was arrested soon afterwards but a jury had him released because there was insufficient evidence.

Out of this royal proroguing of Parliament grew the theory of revolution and revolutionary acts that led to 1688.

Some continued to argue that the king did, of course, have the prerogative to call Parliament and dissolve it, but that this power was a fiduciary trust and not an inherent attribute of monarchy. It was not an arbitrary power of the executive, the king, which merely depended on his good pleasure. Rather the king had to make use of this prerogative for the public good, for the good of the nation as the exigencies of the times should require. This was the basis of John Locke's argument.

Others argued that parliaments should be called annually to avoid any dependency on the king's judgement to use his prerogative to call Parliament at a precise time, place and for a stipulated duration. If it remained the royal prerogative, who was to judge whether he made the right use of it? And what should be done if there were to be a conflict between the royal executive and the parliamentary legislature?

From Shaftesbury's circle came the following radical answer to this question, penned by the man who was probably his closest friend and personal political adviser for over sixteen years: John Locke. 'Between an executive power in being with such a prerogative, and a legislative that depends on his will for their convening, there can be *no* judge on earth. The people have no other remedy in this as in all other cases where they have no judge on earth, but to appeal to heaven.' The appeal to heaven meant revolutionary resistance! The King's actions in preventing Parliament from meeting to redress the grievances of the people (especially regarding James's succession) was, for Locke and others, a violation of the original constitution. If it were now asked: 'When does the king cease to be king?' the answer was returned: 'Right now', because he had tried to overturn the government by preventing Parliament from exercising its constitutional function. Many were convinced that Charles had no intention of calling another Parliament. More than that, he wished to rule without it.

This argument for resistance, then, was grounded in the constitutional principle that people had a right to a redress of grievances by elected representatives.

And now those whose attitudes had been formed during the 1640s and 1650s reappeared. Professor Ashcraft points out that one of the interesting things about the 'resistance movement' of the 1680s is that most of the people who participated in it were in their fifties and sixties. And men like John Locke, a medical doctor and political philosopher, actually appear to have become *more* radical as they grew older. Professor Ashcraft notes that this sounds counter-intuitive to us because we tend to think of radicals and revolutionaries as being relatively young individuals. Here we have an older generation of radicals – not only with political experience but also of an aristocratic stamp.

In the past it was common to attribute such radical views to obscure hotheads like Robert Ferguson. But even in Ferguson's message we hear the nonconformist Protestant themes that penetrated so much of the radical Whig policy: 'Our lives and our estates are not to be subjected to the arbitrary and despotic pleasure of a sovereign. In acting against the law, the king cancels all bonds by which subjects are tied to their prince. And whenever laws cease to be a security unto men, they will be sorely tempted to apprehend themselves cast into a state of war. They do not rebel. Rather the king has rebelled against them. Hence they are justified in having recourse to the best means they can for their shelter and defence.'

One need not have been a republican desirous of changing the constitution, to argue as some did, namely Shaftesbury's circle, that given the mixed monarchy itself, the King had subverted the existing constitution by dissolving Parliament and calling no other. The injury to the people under the existing constitution was the loss of their legislative power. And they argued that such a loss automatically dissolved government which could only be recovered when the legislative was reinstated and the aggressor, who had turned himself into a private man, was punished. Charles had put himself in the position of an aggressor against the people. Every man knew that by natural law, and with government dissolved, individuals had the right to associate together to provide a mutual defence.

Hence it is appropriate that the people be seen as resisting rather than rebelling.

To some, then, government had been suspended after the dissolving of Parliament of 1681 and the King's intention not to call another. The punishment of the aggressor was now to be prosecuted.

For more than 200 years historians have attempted to deny that Whigs were ever engaged in a conspiracy against the government, let alone that they plotted to kill both Charles II and James. But the research of Professor Richard Ashcraft and others has shown that more than a few individuals were involved, and that what is called the Rye House conspiracy encompassed a scheme for widespread general insurrection as well as a plan for a royal assassination. The number of persons who did know about the plot against the King is far greater than has been generally assumed. This means that a large number of people were guilty of treason. It does not mean that, when the plot was discovered, the government correctly identified the conspirators, nor does it mean that the prosecutions and executions were correct.

But what is important for our investigation of people against the State is the fact that hundreds of individuals were participants in and many more sympathisers with an organised attempt to resist Charles II in what they believed were his designs to institute Catholicism and an absolute monarchy in England. Let us look at the events which led to the Rye House conspiracy.

With the dissolution of Parliament it seemed the radical Whigs, centred round Shaftesbury, had contingency plans to block the succession of James in the event of Charles's death. Could they not repeat the regicide of 1649? It seems that Shaftesbury never had the kind of support to cut off Charles II's head. But Professor Ashcraft says that a plot was afoot, and as soon as you start this kind of plotting, you find out who your friends are. Some Whigs had retired into the countryside to live 'quiet lives of desperation'. William Penn, for example, had previously been involved in the electoral aspects of Whig policy. Shaftesbury was left with a relatively small group of supporters of note, among them members of the aristocracy, and a larger group comprised of former commonwealth officers, colonels and majors from the Civil War days, along with members of the clergy, tradesmen and artisans. They allied themselves with the illegitimate son of Charles II, the Duke of

Monmouth, who campaigned to acquire the throne on the back of popular uprisings especially in the West Country. But now the aim was not simply to replace one royal personality with another.

It was well know that Charles loved the horse races. And so the immediate plan was to kill both Charles and James on their return to London from the races at Newmarket. Professor Ashcraft tells us that £600 had been raised by Shaftesbury and this sum had been deposited in an assassin's hand for the doing of the deed. The assassination was to be carried out by people who were, by and large, from the lower classes with protection from Shaftesbury and Monmouth. A general insurrection involving the Scots, the West Country and London was planned. And the conspiracy involved radicals from the highest to the lowest in society.

The plan was that Charles would take a certain road home from Newmarket to London and would pass by a public house that was owned by one of the plotters. There was a narrow bridge that had to be crossed. When the first part of the army escorting Charles's carriage had crossed the bridge they would drag a cart across the bridge and block the way back for the front group of soldiers. Then they would attack the rear and murder Charles and his brother James. Professor Ashcraft says that this was a plot that possibly could have succeeded. But they never acquired enough men and arms to execute it, and Charles's 'day at the races' had, for other reasons, been altered.

Although the radicals had been fairly successful in maintaining a high degree of secrecy, writing in cypher and metaphor, and meeting in safe houses, the government had been on the look-out and came close to discovering their purpose. And then they were informed on by a co-conspirator who got cold feet.

On 14 June 1683 the Secretary of State, Jenkins, held an interview with the conspirator, Keeling, who presented him with evidence of the plot. The government issued warrants for the arrest of the conspirators on 21 June. Some like Algernon Sydney and Lord Russell were caught and executed. Hundreds of others fled into exile. John Locke hastily left London on the eve of Keeling's confession and slipped out of the country for Holland, taking with him the unfinished manuscript of the *Two Treatises of Government*. He stayed abroad for six years, in hiding.

Both Anthony Wood and Humphrey Prideaux reported that after the Rye House conspiracy was discovered, Locke had taken with him several letters and writings without being searched. But if these texts had been confiscated, they argued, they would have revealed Locke's involvement in the conspiracy. Prideaux had been spying on Locke since 1681 and he said: 'our friend John Locke [like the other Rye House conspirators now caught], is likewise become a brother sufferer with them; as soon as the plot was discovered he cunningly stole away from us and in half a year's time no one knew where he was'.

At the trial of Algernon Sydney, the Attorney General said that his *Discourses* had been aimed at persuading the people that the King was introducing arbitrary power, that he subverted all their rights, liberties and properties, so that the very purpose of this tract was 'to persuade the people of England that it is lawful, nay that they have a right to set aside their prince in case it appears to them that he hath broken the trust laid upon him by the people'.

The exiled plotters did not give up. They continued to plot against the regime, and when James came to the throne in 1685 they launched a two-pronged invasion, one in Scotland and the other in the West Country – Monmouth's rebellion. These were crushed. This meant that those people who were the most radical already had two failures before William of Orange's invasion of 1688. William was not to be their first choice, as we shall see, but his would be, as Professor Ashcraft puts it, 'the only revolution in town'.

After the spate of trials and executions of known conspirators in the Rye House plot James used his prerogative to pardon others. Gradually James, like Charles before him, developed a policy directed at winning dissenters' support through his use of pardons, indulgences and propaganda. Indeed his policy of religious toleration was aimed at dividing the radical Whigs into those who accepted toleration and those who remained in Holland and who moved closer towards William of Orange. William now appeared to them as the only means by which they would see England again, after it had been released from the threats of 'popery and slavery'.

Like Charles, James's policy of toleration of nonconformists included Catholics, and this to an even greater degree. In 1687 all corporations and offices of every kind were thrown open to Catholics and some branches of government were taken over by them. James replaced Protestant deans and chancellors of universities with Catholics, and to the radicals this meant nothing other than a long-term strategy to restructure the social and political institutions of England in conformity with Roman Catholicism and absolute monarchy. And like Charles, James too attempted to rule the country without Parliament. He was determined to make himself financially independent of Parliament by manipulating the means by which men got elected. He issued *quo warranto* proceedings against corporation and borough charters so that the requirements and privileges of parliamentary representation were redefined and restructured. He drafted new charters to ensure a pro-monarchical Tory dominance in both municipal affairs and parliamentary elections and gained greater control over the internal affairs of many boroughs than ever before. By this means he influenced the composition of the House of Commons, packing the House, restricting suffrage and tightening the links between his appointments and removals of local magistrates. He was determined to use Parliament and secure the results of elections in his favour. In Scotland he explicitly ordered all towns not to hold elections before his royal nomination of the candidates!

And then, in 1685, James dismissed Parliament. He might have ruled without it for the rest of his reign but for one problem. He wanted the laws against Catholics (the Test Act) removed from the statute books and this could only be done through legislation. Along with his previous violation of charters and his removal of Protestant magistrates in favour of Catholics, this was interpreted as a regular plan for the institution of popery and hence absolutism. Another red light of warning!

Now we reach the last phase in our story and that momentous year 1688.

William of Orange was married to James's Protestant daughter, Mary, and he was interested in ensuring that she would eventually succeed to the throne. But with the pregnancy of James's queen and the very good prospect that James would have a male heir who would be raised as a Catholic, which indeed came to pass, a Catholic succession seemed likely. William realised the urgency of Mary's interest in a Protestant succession. When he decided to come to England, he did not say he was coming for the crown. Instead he publicly declared throughout Europe that the only reason for his coming was to promise a freely elected Parliament that would decide what to do about any matters of controversy. But did this mean he was criticising only James's impeding of Parliament or did he include a wider condemnation of Charles's behaviour as well?

Radical Whigs wanted the grievances of previous reigns taken into consideration in any final constitutional settlement. They had lost too many friends over the past decade as martyrs to their cause and resented recent converts to William's cause putting themselves into a position of managing William's invasion. But if William was not the first choice of many radicals to deal with England's problems his was the only practical revolution. Many now went along with him. Many exiles sailed with him and were in a sense appendages to a much larger and much more efficiently organised and much more conservatively operated enterprise than any previous opposition to James had been. The radicals, who had launched the whole opposition movement, were not to be satisfied with the outcome, however. William used them to manoeuvre himself into position. He did not see them as reflecting his own views, nor did radical views now represent those of the nobility and gentry at large. A compromise was finally worked out which rejected the radical view of how the Glorious Revolution had occurred in the first place.

William invaded England and on 18 December 1688 King James fled London 'for his own safety' and arrived at Rochester. On the night of the 22nd he slipped away from England to land in France on Christmas morning. Because Parliament had already been dissolved, it led to a situation in which separate assemblies of peers and former members of the Commons now known as 'the Convention' invited William to take over the conduct of government for the time being. Starting in 1689 William was performing many of the functions of a king, commanding the armed forces and directing civil government. Given that his mother had been a Stuart and that he was married to the Protestant Mary who was James's daughter, should he now be recognised as king? The debate that ensued raised fundamental problems concerning both political principle and practice about the origin and nature of monarchy, the origin and nature of sovereignty and, perhaps most importantly, it decided the issue of who in England had the right to declare on such problems. Just what did the flight of James mean?

At the Convention the radicals argued that James's tyranny even before his departure from England had put an end to his authority as king. James had forfeited his right to be king well before William had landed. Whether James had left England or not was irrelevant.

Although the Convention refused to accept this, some Whigs and Tories did agree that the *consent* of all *substantial* citizens with rights and liberties was the basis of political authority and it was the task of government to preserve such rights and liberties. They also agreed that some kind of *contract* with a quasi-legal status existed to restrain a king's actions, because the king was a trustee who ruled upon conditions. Any breach of these conditions constituted a breaking of the contract and forfeiture of the crown. But they withdrew from accepting that if power was returned to the people, it was returned to the *multitude*. Instead, in the event of constitutional subversion, it was the *representatives* of the community who were free from allegiance and it was they who assumed the right to retain or depose the monarch.

A majority of MPs at the Convention wished to offer the crown jointly to William and Mary. And they wished the parliamentary convention to lay down conditions upon which the offer was to be made. Lord Falkland wanted clarified just 'what powers we ought to give the crown'. And so it was resolved: 'That King James II having endeavoured to subvert the constitution of the kingdom, by breaking the original contract between king and people and by the advice of Jesuits and other wicked persons having violated the fundamental laws, and having withdrawn himself out of this kingdom, has ABDICATED the government and that the throne is thereby vacant.' The Convention compromised on the meaning of James's flight but not on the contractual nature of rule.

The debate in Whig circles centred around two principles that were not necessarily reconcilable: on the one hand was the ancient constitution and on the other was the language of rights and resistance. If there was an immutable constitution, was it also possible to argue that the principle of common good was *higher* than this and in certain circumstances could liberate the community from the constitution? Could this higher principle of the common good allow the people to refashion the constitution as they saw fit? A commitment to an immutable ancient constitution made it difficult to deny the historical fact of the King's supremacy over Parliament. This would mean that the right of resistance had to appeal to a theory of sovereignty *beyond* history and the ancient constitution. This would be an appeal to some prior natural or divine right that might be exercised by the community *outside* the frame of any constitution.

Furthermore, just what was this Convention of Parliament? It was not a proper Parliament since it had not been called by the King. Some argued it was precisely a wider repository of the community's right to make and unmake constitutions. But few Whigs and Tories, in the last resort, were prepared to rebel or resist and in some wholesale fashion reconstruct civil government. And even with the ambiguous legal situation in which they were placed by James's flight – that of a kingdom without a king – the conservative Whig view prevailed: the constitution was held to be static and immemorial and the only visible alteration had been James's subversion of it by which he, personally, forfeited the crown. The Convention, according to this more conservative view, was held to be no more than an ordinary Parliament – imperfect only in the absence of the King. It exercised an extraordinary power as it was historically entitled to do, by merely filling the royal vacancy. James's kingship had been dissolved but the constitution had not.

And because the more conservative view prevailed that the Convention could not create new laws until the new monarch gave his consent, they chose (against the radical concern to set down the limits of monarchy) to instal the new king first. They rejected what they took to be alarming consequences of proclaiming that James's flight was equivalent to his deposition because this would mean that England had an elective monarchy. So they modified what was meant by his flight to mean his abdication and their allegiance to a *de facto* monarch, William. The radical view, that both Charles's and James's tyrannical behaviour dissolved parliaments and consequently returned sovereignty to the people who exercised their right of resistance, leading to a suspension of the constitution itself, was rejected. But only after considerable struggle.

As the work of Dr Mark Goldie has shown, during this period of intense debate in the Convention numerous radical pamphlets were produced arguing that the new king must be visibly elected and that the citizens must express their formal consent through a universal oath of allegiance to the new regime. Subjects would be accorded the right to exercise their rights of resistance by a right to bear arms and through their membership in the militia. Widespread political education in consensual principles was foreseen with a suppression of absolutist principles. All the pamphlets spoke of the constitutional shift in powers in a detailed manner. The royal prerogative of vetoing and dismissing parliaments was to be removed. Control of the militia, the declaration of war and the appointment of judges were to be transferred to Parliament. The Crown's revenues were to be reduced drastically to prevent the possibility of a royal standing army and to make regular parliaments unavoidable. Monarchy was to be very limited. And many of these radical pamphlets argued that the revolution had produced a total dissolution of the Constitution. James had not abdicated but had been deposed. 'The departure of the king amounts to such a desertion as dissolving government. This means that power has necessarily reverted to the people who may erect a new constitution, either according to the old model if they like it so well, or any other that they like and approve of better.' 'The interregnum of January 1689 had created a state of liberty in which the people could foist a new constitution on the king, and if they do it not now, the ages to come will have occasion to blame them forever!'

Hence, for the radical Whigs, it was the *interregnum* between James and William that was the Glorious Revolution and not the ascension of William and Mary to the throne!

The radical position pragmatically recognised that the parliamentary Convention would place William on the throne but they had no illusions as to his political virtues. If one person were to replace another as king, then the terms of the new contract with him must be ensured. Lord Delamare referred to 'the new elected prince', while others referred to the king as 'high sheriff' of the nation.

The Convention did not pursue a change of constitution so that England would become a republic rather than a mixed monarchy. But *many* of its leading speakers and active committee men were, while not necessarily republicans at all, of a radical persuasion. Perhaps the most notable was John Wildman, one of the Rye House conspirators and a veteran of Leveller campaigns during the Civil War who now sat in the Convention. Disraeli astutely described him as the soul of English politics from 1640 to 1688. Wildman and other active radical publicists had important friends in the House of Lords where there was a group of militant Whigs: Mordaunt, Delamare, Macclesfield, Lovelace, Wharton and Bolton. Some were friends of John Locke.

Beyond these aristocrats there was a network of lesser men who constituted the extensive radical underground during the Revolution years with ties to London politics. And they had support from dissenting clergy with publishing connections.

Sir Robert Howard, formerly active in the Exclusion crisis of 1680, now argued: 'In my opinion the right is therefore wholly in the people who are now to new form themselves again under a governor yet to be chosen.' Sir John Morton and Sir Henry Capel agreed. Hence the resolution that was passed said that James had broken the original contract, had violated the fundamental laws and withdrawn himself from the kingdom, such abdication leaving the throne vacant. And with the declaration secured, the radicals now tried to delay proceedings in order that the terms of the new contract could be determined.

But William made it clear he wanted no conditional limitations. And the Williamite Whigs emasculated the Convention's declaration so that the crown was not now made conditional on even those weak stipulations that remained. Indeed, the final Bill of Rights dropped the phrase 'The original contract' between Crown and people. And when the Declaration of Rights was read to William and Mary in its watered-down version, it stipulated how the crown was to pass to Mary and her heirs, then to her sister Anne and hers, and finally to any heirs William might have by a later marriage. A hereditary principle of sorts was thereby maintained.

Effectively, the Tory attachment to divine right monarchy as hereditary was not destroyed in 1688, and what was adopted was a fiction that James had abdicated. This enabled him to be removed but not deposed. The legal status of the Declaration of Rights, which was originally intended 'to tie [William] up to a strict observance of conditions more than other princes before him', in the end, was ambiguous. And William never promised to abide by its terms anyway. William simply said he had no other intention than 'preserving your religion, laws and liberties and [he] would endeavour to support them'. The Declaration, which spoke of the abuse of powers of Charles and James, was not an explicit contract between William and Mary and their subjects. When the Declaration was turned into a Bill of Rights, what was new in it was that no Catholic could gain the English throne. It did not question royal prerogatives themselves. It only referred to earlier abuses. What was also new was that the raising of or keeping of a standing army within the kingdom in peacetime was against the law unless it received the consent of Parliament. And when the Bill vaguely referred to the election of MPs being 'free', it made no attempt either to define that freedom or to provide a mechanism for the enforcement of its stated objectives.

In the end, the defeat of the more radical elements in the Convention was achieved by conservative Whigs themselves. The people who really managed the revolution, basically the leading members of the landed aristocracy, probably did achieve what they wanted from all this. But the radicals who had in a sense launched the whole opposition movement were less satisfied. A distinctive number of people felt that the opportunity to rethink and perhaps rewrite the English constitution in 1688 was missed. It was missed because the people who were in the Convention Parliament treated it as though it were just a temporary lapse in the regular exercise of authority and they regarded themselves as just a regular Parliament, there to patch things up. But as Professor Ashcraft says, the radicals really wanted people to think more seriously about what the opportunity of the Interregnum presented to them and what it allowed them to do in terms of the English constitution. And so, when William began to bring back the same Tories who had been James II's advisers, the people asked what the revolution had really amounted to if the same people were in power who were there before.

This did lead some to say that this was an inglorious revolution. They framed their disappointment quite openly, writing pamphlets that threatened William with the same consequences that James had paid. But by the 1690s they were a small minority.

By the time the Convention was dissolved a succession of radical causes had failed. Out of the revolution that caused the debate in the first place, two rival traditions of Whiggism were born and were to endure throughout the next century. Only with recent historical scholarship has one of those Whig explanations as to what happened at the Glorious Revolution been balanced by contemporary Whig alternative interpretations. Both effectively agreed that the final settlement was hardly revolutionary at all but, as we have seen, for very different reasons.

And what of the unintended consequences of the revolution? With hindsight the real revolution was in the changed relation of Parliament and Crown. And the origins of this were not in the minimal constitutional changes but in the financial settlements. The King was given a revenue adequate only for his civil expenditure. The great changes brought about by the revolution's aftermath owed far more to the impact of the financial settlement compounded by the subsequent war with France than to the change of ruler or the limited Bill of Rights.

The failure to grant William an adequate independent income seems to have been the only deliberate and pragmatic solution to the concern to prevent him from abusing royal power. The financial settlement achieved this without resolving the issues of principle which were at the heart of the Glorious Revolution in the first place. With Parliament meeting regularly to deal with financial issues, it became a permanent institution whose sessions were determined by the need to complete money bills for the year.

The changes that followed in the wake of the constitutional settlement were therefore limited, conservative and wiped clean of the projected more radical coherence that had originally been intended to secure the sovereign rights of Englishmen and to limit royal prerogatives. There was nothing in the *final* settlement like the sort of logic which underlay either France's administrative revolutionary restructuring in the 1790s or the Napoleonic Code. The settlement defined in a *negative* sense the future relationship of Crown and Parliament. The Crown's prerogative was effectively curbed through the financial weakness of royalty. But the Crown's influence in controlling Parliament by means of places and pensions could still be even more threatening than prerogative. Of the legislative proposals listed for the Convention's discussion, few reached the statute book. The King still had power to call and dismiss Parliament at will, subject from 1694 to Parliament's need to be kept in session to complete money bills. The King could still choose ministers, direct administration and formulate policy modified only by his need for money. And it was precisely this pragmatic need for money that gradually ensured parliamentary cooperation that went beyond taxation and allowed for government borrowing. The original radical proposal for annual parliaments came to be seen as a necessity. Meeting annually, Parliament strengthened the credit system through the investment in a national debt, a system that continues today.

In 1694, when a loan of £1 200 000 was raised at 8 per cent from subscribers who were incorporated as the Bank of England, empowered to deal with bills of exchange, the national debt became a permanent institution and a secure investment. And so the 'revolution' of 1688 was effectively secured by the foundation of the Bank of England and a system of public finance that encouraged investment in a future regime, stimulating growth in British prosperity and power.

The *financial aftermath* of the Glorious Revolution was the real turning-point in British history and it was this financial revolution that made Britain into a major European, indeed world, power, where new monied men, both British and foreign, who were not traders or landowners, were gradually recognised as bearers of immense political power through their power to lend money to the government.

And yet another unintended consequence emerged from the settlement. Professor Ashcraft notes how people sometimes think that toleration is a consequence of the growth of reason, science and civilisation but it was nothing of the kind. The object of religious toleration was to bring as many Presbyterians and Independents into the Anglican Church as possible. This was called 'comprehension'. If you could only suspend some of the 39 articles of faith of the Church of England to which people were required to swear allegiance, then perhaps you could get most dissenting Protestants into the Anglican Church. So a Bill of Comprehension and a Bill of Toleration were introduced. The assumption was that this toleration would only last for a short period because if most of the dissenters found themselves in the Anglican Church, the pressure to conform would increase. But as it happened, the Bill of Comprehension was derailed in the process of legislative objections while the Bill of Toleration was passed. This was precisely the opposite of what people intended. Most dissenters remained outside the Anglican Church and many others were drawn away from Anglicanism towards dissenting. Gradually, the practice of toleration made people realise that it wasn't such an awful thing, and disaster and chaos did not result. The Act of Toleration led to the conviction that, in fact, it was a good thing.

It has been suggested that those Whigs who served as apologists for the revolutionary *settlement* and who had argued that government had *not* been dissolved, that traditional institutions retained their authority and that actions taken were taken and justified by reference to known law, used history in a convenient way. Their account of the events of 1688–9 ignored the substantial groups of Whigs who believed that government had been clearly dissolved and that the Convention was more than just another Parliament but one that looked towards a radical remodelling of the constitution. Many indeed claimed that the settlement had failed to effect even the restoration of what was taken to be an ancient constitutional liberty. Tories accepted the settlement on the grounds that the ancient constitution had been set aside *this once*, as an act of necessity rather than of right. And they struggled to add that a *de facto* government under William had been erected until time should remedy the situation and reestablish hereditary monarchy. Ruling Whigs justified the settlement as an act carried out *within* the structures of the ancient constitution and was designed to preserve it. It was these men whom the 'revolution' enabled to continue as rulers. In the eighteenth and nineteenth centuries the Whig Member of Parliament Edmund Burke and the historian Macaulay struggled to reconcile these Whig and Tory interpretations. But as we have also seen there were many who said James *had* been deposed, the government dissolved, and that power had reverted to the people, indeed, that William had been *elected* and James 'cashiered' and that Englishmen could do this again should the need arise.

This was the argument that the Unitarian preacher Richard Price and others used and which Edmund Burke attacked in his *Reflections on the French Revolution* in 1790, a hundred years after the 1688 revolution and after the French Revolution had begun.

His magnificent analysis of the constitutional settlement of 1688–9 paradoxically used the Tory argument of the settlement: that the English revolution had been an act of necessity and had not established any general right to repeat the cashiering of governors. To avoid the extremes of arguing that the revolution had established a right of deposition *or* that it set up merely a *de facto* regime, Burke had to take the Tory line that the act of necessity had been performed within a framework of historical constitutionality and that the frame had not been dissolved. He too argued that the British constitution was immemorial and prescriptive so that the men of 1688 had acted within its frame. This meant that Britain's history was a story of gradual adaptation of and piety towards precedents, an adaptation that was natural, prudential and undynamic. It had nothing to do with what was occurring in France. It did not serve either as a model for French revolutionary acts or as a justification of them. Unlike the French, Englishmen could not speak of natural rights being disregarded by the constitution, because Englishmen had never had such abstract natural rights nor do any other men.

After 1689, with William and Mary enthroned, England had enjoyed a relatively wide religious liberty *for Protestants*, a comparatively free press and a large measure of political freedom. The other side of this liberty was the increasingly severe penalties for infringements of the sanctity of property that were enacted, where more and more offences against property carried the death penalty. A pick-pocket who stole a shilling could be hanged. This obsession with the protection of private property underlies the fact that the main bene-ficiary of the revolutionary settlement was the landed élite whose members came increasingly to dominate the politics of succeeding generations. By the reign of Queen Anne, property was acknow-ledged to be the social basis of personality. But it was the emergence of classes whose property consisted not of land or goods or even of gold bullion, but of paper promises to repay in an undefined future, that is, stockjobbers, political adventurers and investors in public credit, that signalled a real revolution. For such monied men heral-ded new types of personality with political power: they were seen as unprecedented, dangerous, unstable and often foreign. But they would guide Britain's imperial destiny.

When, on the eve of the French Revolution some Englishmen who were members of the Revolution Society in London took up the seventeenth-century radical Whig argument that by the principles of the Glorious Revolution the people of England had acquired the *rights* to choose their own governors, to cashier them for misconduct and to frame a government for themselves, Burke said 'No'.

> This new and hitherto unheard of Bill of Rights, though made in the name of the whole people belongs to [those members of the Revolu-tion Society] and their faction only. The body of the people of England have no share in it. . . . If the principles of the Revolution of 1688 are anywhere to be found, it is in the statute called the Declar-ation of Right. In that most wise, sober, and considerate declaration, drawn up by great lawyers and great statesmen, and not by warm and inexperienced enthusiasts, not one word is said, nor one sug-gestion made, of a general right 'to choose our own governors, to cashier them for misconduct and to form a government for ourselves'.

Indeed, for Burke, the Declaration settled the succession of the crown. And to Burke the Declaration of Right and the Bill of Rights of 1689 demonstrated 'how totally adverse the wisdom of the nation was from turning a case of necessity into a rule of law'. In that phrase, 'wisdom of the nation', John Locke, the Earl of Shaftesbury, Algernon Sydney, John Wildman and other seventeenth-century political agents were written out of England's history. They were nothing but warm and inexperienced enthusiasts.

For Burke, William had been 'a small and temporary deviation from the strict order of a regular hereditary succession' but a principle of jurisprudence is not drawn from a law made in a special case. 'If ever there was a time favourable for establishing the principle that a king of popular choice was the only legal king, without doubt it was at the Revolution. Its not being done at that time is a proof that the nation was of the opinion it ought not to be done at any time.'

This act of necessity was the only case in which Parliament departed from the strict order of inheritance in favour of a prince who, though not next, was, however, very near in the line of succession.

'The two Houses did not thank God that they had found a fair opportunity to assert a right to choose their own governors, much less to make an election the only lawful title to the crown. Their having been in a condition to avoid the very appearance of it as much as possible, was by them considered as a providential escape.' 'Though a king may abdicate for his own person, he cannot abdicate for the monarchy.' And in the case as this was, of extreme emergency where monarchy was not destroyed but William exchanged for James, 'this was effected without a decomposition of the whole civil and political mass for the purpose of originating a new civil order'. When England found itself without a king its constitution was not dissolved. Instead, they regenerated the deficient part of the old Constitution. Indeed, 'King James, was a bad king with a good title'. In writing to a French friend as France underwent its revolution, Burke vented his dislike of revolutions that began with abstract, first principles of human rights, divorced from tradition and a constitution. Such revolutions had, he said, so often been signalled from pulpits. He rejected 'the total contempt which prevails with you [in France] and may come to prevail with us, of all ancient institutions'. To Burke, change and reform were like the growth of a coral reef, the growing on itself through the perhaps boring procedures of law, Parliament, and of the day-to-day pragmatic exchange of interests in the political world. One might then expect a reference to the wide-ranging and oppositional debates of the 1688 Convention of Parliament. But no. That contemporary Englishmen, like Dr Price and his Revolutionary Society, sought to export principles of revolution 'as raw commodities of British growth', '*though wholly alien to our soil*, or order afterwards to smuggle them back again into this country manufactured after the newest Paris fashion' was anathema to him.

> The people of England will not ape the fashions they have never tried, *nor go back to those which they have found mischievous on trial.* They look upon the legal hereditary succession of their crown as among their rights, not as among their wrongs, as a benefit not as a grievance, as a security for their liberty not as a badge of servitude. They look on the frame of their commonwealth such as it stands, to be of inestimable value; and they conceive the undisturbed succession of the crown to be a pledge of the stability and perpetuity of all the other members of our constitution.

According to Burke, James's abdication was grounded in nothing less than a design confirmed by a multitude of illegal overt acts to subvert the Protestant Church and State and their fundamental, unquestionable laws and liberties. 'They charged him with having broken the *original contract* between king and people' although the reference to that original contract had been, we observed, dropped from the Declaration of Right presented to William and Mary. And hence

> their trust for the future preservation of the Constitution was not in future revolutions. The grand policy of all their regulations was to render it almost impracticable for any future sovereign to compel the states of the kingdom to have again recourse to those violent remedies. They left the crown what in the eye and estimate of the law it had ever been, perfectly irresponsible. In order to lighten the crown still further, they aggravated responsibility on ministers of state. . . . They secured soon after the frequent meetings of parliament by which the whole government would be under the constant inspection and active control of the popular representative and of the magnates of the kingdom. They did not declare a right to cashier their governors. Indeed the king is not distinguished from the Commons and the Lords who in their several public capacities, can never be called to an account for their conduct.

To Burke, the views of the Revolution Society were not consonant with British history as he read it, for they argued – as we have seen that many in the seventeenth century had argued – that 'a king is no more than the first servant of the public, created by it and responsible to it'.

But if a dethroning, 'or if these gentlemen like the phrase better

"cashiering kings" will always be, as it has always been, an extraordinary question of state' and if this extraordinary emergency had
been taken on board in 1688, why, for Burke, had the similar,
once-and-for-all cashiering of Louis XVI and Marie Antoinette not
been a similar necessity? The reason was that the French argued that
sovereignty had fallen back to the *multitude* to form a *new* constitution and this would be a republican one rather than a mixed
monarchy. The *wisdom of the nation* in 1688 sought to maintain
monarchy. For Burke the wisdom of the French nation was nowhere
to be found because the Estates General effectively had an overwhelming majority of members of the third estate!

> Judge sir of my surprise when I found that a very great proportion of
> the Assembly was composed of practitioners in the law. It was
> composed not of distinguished magistrates who had given pledges
> to their country of their science, prudence and integrity, not of
> leading advocates, the glory of the bar, not of renowned professors
> in universities, but for the far greater part . . . of the inferior, unlear-
> ned mechanical merely instrumental members of the profession. . . .
> The general composition was of obscure provincial advocates of
> stewards of petty local jurisdictions, country attorneys, notaries and
> the whole train of the ministers of municipal litigation. . . . *When the
> supreme authority is vested in a body so composed it must evidently produce
> the consequences of supreme authority placed in the hands of men not taught
> habitually to respect themselves* . . . Nothing can secure a steady and
> moderate conduct in such assemblies but that the body of them
> should be respectably composed, in point of condition of life, or
> permanent property, of education and of such habits as enlarge and
> liberalise the understanding.

Instead the revolutionary French Assembly was peopled with
'country clowns . . . some of whom are said not to be able to read
and write', and along with them are traders who '. . . had never
known anything beyond their counting houses'. For Burke there is a
natural aristocracy of governors with landed property as surety,
while 'the property of France does not govern it. Of course property
is destroyed and rational liberty has no existence. All you have got
for the present is a paper circulation and a stock jobbing constitution', precisely what had been produced by the expansion of
public credit in the aftermath of England's Glorious Revolution and
which Burke both feared and disdained.

Handing the English over not to the events of their history but to a magisterial interpretation of that history, Burke asks us to observe that

> from Magna Carta to the Declaration of Right it has been the uniform policy of our Constitution to claim and assert our liberties as an entailed inheritance derived to us from our forefathers and to be transmitted to our posterity – as an estate especially belonging to the people of this kingdom without any reference whatever to any other more general or prior right . . . We have an inheritable crown, an inheritable peerage and a House of Commons and a people inheriting privileges, franchises and liberties from a long line of ancestors. . . . We receive, we hold, we transmit our government and our privileges in the same manner in which we enjoy and transmit our property and our lives.

Burke says that the French should have built on their old foundations. But the country clowns in the Estates had no understanding of just what those foundations were. By allowing the third estate such power, the French constitution was placed in the hands of 'men destined to travel in the obscure walk of laborious life' and their vain expectations of liberty, fraternity and equality served 'only to aggravate and embitter that real inequality which it never can remove and which the order of civil life establishes as much for the benefit of those whom it must leave in an humbler state as those whom it is able to exalt to a condition more splendid, but no more happy'.

The real rights of men consist, for Burke, in their right to live by the rules of civil society and not a right to make those rules anew.

> Whatever each man can separately do, without trespassing upon others, he has a right to do for himself; and he has a right to a fair portion of all which society, with all its combinations of skill and force, can do in his favour. In this partnership *all men have equal rights but not to equal things*. He that has but five shillings in the partnership has as good a right to IT as he that has five hundred pounds has to HIS LARGER PROPORTION; but he has NOT A RIGHT to an equal dividend in the product of the joint stock. And as to the share of power, authority and direction which each individual ought to have in the management of the State, that I must deny to be amongst the direct original rights of man in civil society. [Rather] it is a thing to be settled by convention.

Burke has provided us with a powerful reading of some of the *consequences* of the Glorious Revolution. In other words, what Burke has described is not the events or debates that led up to and which constituted the Glorious Revolution, but what men in power made of the constitutional settlement. And for Burke there was nothing about the Glorious Revolution that could conceivably inspire the French in their revolutionary ardour.

Modern historians read the situation somewhat differently. If we pose the question of whether the events of 1688 inspired other revolutions, many historians answer by saying that it depends on how you interpret that revolution. Professor Ashcraft has argued that if we go back to the role of Locke, we see that the later, classic Whig view interpreted Locke's *Two Treatises* as a commonsensical compendium of Whig beliefs justifying the Glorious Revolution *as a settlement*. But that view has pretty much subsided in the face of more recent scholarship. The fact is that Locke's view was much more radical than most Whigs were willing to accept. He believed that power devolved to the *people* in the absence of legitimate government, and that the people could constitute an entirely *new* system in accordance with their desire to see the common good realised; and he certainly believed in a toleration that went far beyond the Toleration Act. He may even have believed in something as radical as the right of all men to vote. The kinds of arguments put forward in the *Two Treatises* are much more radical, and were recognised as such by contemporaries in the 1690s when they were published, which is why many orthodox Whigs simply shied away from referring to Locke as a source. Locke was a seventeenth-century revolutionary in that he wished to see Parliament as the important institution of government, and Parliament as an elective, legislative, representative body. He wanted to defend the right of people to have their grievances heard and redressed by that institution. The more events seemed to be moving towards an absolute monarchy, the more revolutionary did Locke's position appear. Certainly in his own context and circumstances Locke was a radical and revolutionary.

So here the question of the influence of the 1688 revolution can be answered in two ways: Locke's argument with respect to revolution did inspire later revolutionaries in America and even in France. The Glorious Revolution in that larger sense played an historical role in the future histories of revolutions.

But talking about what the people who gained control of the Glorious Revolution thought, and the more or less specific practices that they instituted afterwards, then probably Burke was right, when he referred back to the revolution as a minor, sensible transition, not likely to inspire revolution and indeed in contrast with the French Revolution.

Those people who have thought of the Glorious Revolution in terms of the *principles* of the right of people to change the government if their leaders betray their trust, a trust endowed on them by the people, have been more willing to see the Glorious Revolution as an inspiration for other events. But those who look at the Glorious Revolution as an historical set of actions carried out by individuals who actually managed it, have been inclined to see it, according to Burke's recent biographer, Stanley Ayling, as a rather conservative and minor defensive set of actions.

The French Revolution is often sung as a hymn to the violent overthrow of consummate injustice in the name of universal principles: the liberty, equality and fraternity of all men. From 1789 onwards, revolution was to mean an inauguration of new beginnings. It aimed to create a new man and the message was for all of humanity. The French Revolution did create a new fraternal nationalism, according to Professor Simon Schama. As a symbol of that great moment when sovereignty was supposedly handed back to the people, the French Revolution was to mean something new. Never was there to be a return to the aristocratic abuses previously experienced. Professor Schama describes the French Revolution as a kind of millenarian convulsion, a religious war akin to the Protestant Reformation in which people were shriven and forcibly displaced into a new political world. Even though Professor Schama has decried the violence in the Revolution and during its aftermath, the Terror, he does not deny that there were true gains. The feudal regime of taxation ended and a new political order was established in which people were represented to themselves as Brothers and Citizens whose political acts were meant to fill hungry bellies. And yet the intensity and variety of the divisions that raised the Revolution to a pitch of extreme, even gratuitous mob violence also left France riddled with internal dissension that has lasted until the present day. Did they have to aim at the obliteration of everything before they could build a new house?

The American Revolution which had just preceded that of the

French helped to confirm that oppressive systems of government could be got rid of through violent means. From the late eighteenth century onwards, both revolutions sparked an impatient excitement that led to a demand to change the world in one great trans-figuration. Crucial to an understanding of modern revolutions is the idea of freedom coinciding with the experience of a new beginning. Revolutions produce spontaneous forms of action. They are demands for participation, not representation. But as the twentieth-century political philosopher Hannah Arendt has said: '[their] fatal mistake has always been that they themselves did not distinguish clearly between participation in public affairs and administration or management of things in the public interest'. Revolutions are momentary events. While they are good for overthrowing tyrannies and establishing freedom they are not a system of government. If every modern revolution begins with a burst of high voltage, to borrow Professor Schama's term, the next stage, as today in Eastern Europe, has to switch to low voltage in the making of a constitution, the institutionalisation of the daily living of that first spectacle of explosive liberty. Life cannot be lived poised on the edge of our revolutionary seats. Pragmatic politics must come out of revolution-ary fervour. But does this deny the legitimacy of revolution in certain circumstances as the first step to a subsequent calming down of what is, none the less, a new world? In retrospect, what seems to matter more than the motives of the revolutionaries, as Professor Richard Ashcraft insists, is the consequences of their actions, conse-quences that may be wholly unintended or unforeseen.

Let us consider the following moments in our recent history. At the celebrations of the French Revolution in Paris, Mrs Thatcher

> compared the French festivities to the 'discreet' celebrations in Britain to mark the 300th anniversary of Parliament's triumph over the monarchy. 'Of course, this was not a revolution but a change carried out calmly without a bloodbath', she added. She said, 'the rights of man were part of the Jewish-Christian tradition which proclaimed the importance of human beings and individual rights no government could take away. After that, we have the Magna Carta in 1215, the Bill of Rights in the 17th century and our calm revolution of 1688.' (*Guardian*, 13 July 1989.)

A call to abolish the Crown prerogative, while retaining the Queen as titular head of a new British Republic, was made last night by Mr

Tony Benn, the Labour MP for Chesterfield. During a debate at the Lyttelton Theatre in London on the role of republicanism – staged as part of the French Revolution bicentenary – he argued that Britain is not a democracy but a constitutional monarchy with subjects not citizens. He said that since 1979 the government had increasingly abused the use of Crown prerogative powers – including those to make war, sign treaties, agree to EC legislation, appoint ministers, peers, bishops, judges and the chairs of BBC and IBA. He said that neither the Queen nor the royal family was responsible for this, although 'the institution of the monarchy . . . gives legitimacy to these blatant denials of our liberties'. 'It would be perfectly possible to continue to recognise the Queen as the titular head of . . . a new British Republic or Commonwealth, so long as the present Crown Prerogatives, now exercised by the Prime Minister of the day, were made subject to the approval of the House of Commons, which we elect.' (*Guardian*, 13 July 1989.)

The legacy of rival radical and apologist Whigs who opposed one another during the 1680s is still with us, as is the use of history for the bolstering of a present political point of view. That this is so has been made possible by those seventeenth-century men against the State as it was then constituted.

CHAPTER SEVEN

MARX

K arl Marx was born in 1818 in the city of Trier in the Prussian Rhineland. His parents were Jewish but his father was forced to convert to Christianity in order to retain his legal post in the Prussian Civil Service. Trier today is a beautiful little city and the Marx family house has been refurbished to serve as a research centre for the study of Marx, Engels and the socialist movement. Next door lived the Baron von Westphalen whose daughter, Jenny, Marx was to marry.

Marx was a gifted student who studied at the universities of Bonn and Berlin. He combined legal studies with the study of philosophy and languages: English and Italian. In the hope of a university career he received his doctorate from the University of Jena but he became exercised by the radical upheavals in Germany at that time and turned instead to radical journalism. Writing first for the newspaper the *Rheinische Zeitung*, which was backed by liberal industrialists, Marx later went on to Paris where he met Friedrich Engels and led the League of Communists who published the famous *Communist Manifesto* in 1848. His increasing radicalism caused him to be evicted from Germany, France and Belgium and he arrived in London in 1849. He remained in England for the rest of his life and died in London in 1883.

During the years he spent in London he produced theories of capitalism in particular and a theory of the whole of human history in general. And he was a supervisory captain of nascent proletarian movements in Europe and around the world. Marx read and wrote in the splendid domed reading room of the British Library, where he acquired his massive learning in the history of economic thought. In the fields of philosophy, history and economics Marx was certainly one of the most accomplished men of his time. His death certificate noted only that he died at the age of 64, that his occupation was 'author' and that the cause of his death was 'laryngitis'. There must be some secret irony here because it has been Marx's voice which has dominated so much of twentieth-century history.

In the light of recent events in Eastern Europe it might be asked whether Marx has anything to tell us about alternative societies to those in the West. It might also be asked whether those who criticise him really know what, in fact, he said. But in one very important sense Marx is not acceptable or, rather 'respectable' for a middle-class capitalist culture whether or not Marxist experiments in the East have failed. And this is because of what he says about the inadequacies of our lives. Indeed, most of us do not care to have this made public. We assume it to be a private problem if we do not care for our jobs and see 'life' as something that begins with the first drink of the evening. But it was Marx's belief that precisely this division between our private and public lives was a symptom of a more general malaise. For some it would prove intolerable. It was his analysis of the way we live in a technological, capitalist society, and his understanding of capitalism from the standpoint of the individual, that have made his works so influential in the twentieth century. Along with the writings of Sigmund Freud on human psychology Marx's thought has dominated this century's social, political and historical movements. In his questioning and analysis of human nature, in part observed in the actual, historical conditions in which men had lived their lives, Marx placed himself in the line not only of great philosophers but also of sympathetic and distressed, ordinary people living in the social world as we know it. He asked readers to consider what human life is about.

There is much in Marx's writings that can appeal to those not interested in adhering to any *-ism*. Like every philosopher and analyst of society and politics, Marx had a model of man which depicts his capacities and his failings, and this model has its attractions for non-Marxists. Its attraction lies in the optimistic scope he gave to all human personality. He believed that the scope for human potential is recognised best perhaps by those who suffer most, and also by those who observe humanity degraded and are shocked and saddened by this. Part of Marx's optimism insisted that systems that regulate survival have not been static throughout history. Rather, they have evolved. In certain systems, the 'game's' rules themselves degrade *all* the players, deluding some and oppressing others, fulfilling *none* as multivalent individual human beings should be fulfilled.

That modern Western society consists of isolated and often lonely competitive survivors and losers, that the world is not caring, that everything has a price including friendship and love, that young people are 'alienated', and that work for very many people is boring if not hated, an unfulfilling necessity even if it pays well (which is *some* but insufficient compensation), are all Marxian perspectives that many hold without being Marxists. What is also attractive to some is that Marx does not attribute to man a natural evil, an original sin that is the source of the unfulfilling aspects of lived social life. Rather, he describes on the one hand, a relationship between social conditions and the rules that govern them; and on the other hand, individuals needing to live life, given the conditions they find themselves in. A catch-22 situation seems to have been established which Marx believed could only be broken, as it had been broken in the past, by the gradual consciousness, largely on the part of the most oppressed who live the most intolerable lives, of the fact that what they have been living is not what living a human life should be.

There are three subjects that we should consider if we are to understand Marx as a thinker against the middle-class State: these are his model of man, his analysis of the capitalist, bourgeois (middle-class) State and its eventual 'withering away', and, lastly, his theory of alienation as the capitalist version of human nature. Marx, like Freud, sought a means to overcome man's alienation through man's final reconciliation with the world, himself and others. But for Marx, unlike Freud, such a reconciliation would come about through a revolution in the external material world by which men regulated their survival and fulfilment. A revolution in the economic sphere of life would give rise to changes in the political. For Marx, politics is determined by the nature of the economic and not the other way round.

In constructing his model of man, Marx tried to set out the requirements that had to be fulfilled in order to make man 'human'. He presupposed a norm of human capacities which is fixed for the human species and yet these capacities are differently manifested in a variety of ways, depending on the historical conditions in which a particular individual finds himself living and producing. For Marx, every individual is a social being who derives his creative forces from his personal, individual, subjective existence in his world. The human spirit does not exist in a single form. Nor does it have national boundaries. Freedom is a part of man's spiritual life, a freedom of diversity of personal talents that is an essential human value with its own justification. Fulfilment consists in a freeing of *all* men from the conditions that hamper their growth as multifaceted individuals.

Marx did not return to the utopian belief that there are innate rules of cooperation which, of their own accord, would prevail in human society. Humans, by nature, are neither cooperative nor uncooperative. Rather, circumstances generate bad or good behaviour. He did not believe in original sin or its secular equivalent which says there is some fatal flaw in men which prevents them from enjoying and preserving peace and harmony so that were they presented with such blessings they would subvert them. Rather, he argued that man must make an effort consciously to absorb society back into himself. He must freely recognise that each individual is himself a bearer of community. This is how each individual rediscovers himself as a creative individual instead of seeing himself as an administered 'thing' in the regulation of society.

When Marx speaks of human *praxis*, he is referring to that universal creative, self-expressive activity of human individuals, and this is more than the simple adaptation of men to their natural environment. Animals simply adapt to their environments. But men, through their labour, their work, their effort, their *praxis*, constantly create themselves and their world. This means no person remains the same even in his own lifetime. Individual men, and the human species in general, have histories which are made by the purposeful human impulse to change the world through working on it so that the world might serve human ends that encompass more than mere material gratification and survival. Indeed, human life *is* active labour over and above the labour that is necessary for survival. What man's history demonstrates, to Marx, is that men have, with increasing success, sought a particularly human freedom where the labour that has been determined by necessity and by hostile nature or by mundane conditions, has decreased. Such necessary labour may, with increasing technological advances, virtually disappear.

The image of what is left is not that of a perpetual holiday in the sun. What is left is a creative, artistic, individual human life. In this sense Marx was an heir of the eighteenth-century Enlightenment and its successor, romanticism. So are we all. Marx was concerned, then, with the enrichment of the human being and he saw this as possible if, and only if, the State is no longer coercive. The State, in so far as it exists at all, remains simply an organiser of human potentials. He asks the reader to

> assume man to be man and his relationship to the world to be a human one: then you can exchange love only for love [and not for money or status], trust for trust etc. If you want to enjoy art, you must be an artistically cultivated person [and not simply rich enough to afford a box at the opera]; if you want to exercise influence over people you must be a person with a stimulating and encouraging effect on other people [and not one with money to buy votes or status]. Everyone of your relations to man and to nature must be a specific expression corresponding to the object of your will, of your real individual life. (*1844 Manuscripts.*)

In his early works, Marx took up many of the themes of the radical liberals and socialists of the time. He is not particularly unique in his vision. But it is a vision that none the less underlies his uniquely rigorous analysis of capitalism. It must be stressed that he believed there was something common to all men at all times. This was that every man as man possesses certain powers and has certain needs, some of which are natural and shared by other living beings, while others are specific to the human species. Once we consider man inside history, however, we see that these powers and needs are historically determined. Marx believed that throughout history men have been more or less conscious that they want the things they need. Man is a corporeal, living, real, sensuous, objective being and not simply a disembodied mind that affirms to itself that it exists simply because it thinks. Not only does man think but he also knows himself to have tendencies, impulses and abilities that seek fulfilment in objects that are outside his own body, such as eating, sex, labour, social companionship and variety in activity. Man needs the objects in the material world to express his own powers because as a natural being he is placed in the natural environment and suffers there, is limited and conditioned by his natural needs in an environment which is of itself inadequate to supply his needs or give him scope to exercise his powers.

Earlier thinkers saw the inadequacies of the natural world, which often was hostile as well, to be a given fact of man's tragic condition.

They too reorganised human impulses and tendencies, so dependent on the material world because of man's bodily requirements, and declared these to be the tragic outcome of the Fall. Their solution to this tragedy was an asceticism, a denial of bodily needs and a transcendence of them. But Marx argued that man's needs could be satisfied through labour. By this he meant not merely expending energy to survive but also to manage a naturally indifferent and often hostile material environment in order to serve man's creative purposes. Man alone, he believed, was uniquely possessed of a self-consciousness which enables him to see himself as an individual who is active, although not always successfully, in pursuing his own ends. He confirms himself by knowing this about himself and through mutual recognition he extends this to and has it extended by others. In being conscious of his past, that is, the record of his successes and failures in attaining his aims, and in basing possibilities which constitute his future on that past record, man knows himself as an individual with distinguishing powers and needs.

Something of great importance follows from a recognition that man is an historically situated, concrete individual. When such a person perceives something he orientates himself to it so that *how* he sees it and understands its purpose is related to the patterns, the assigned places and the values of the culture of which he is a part. Such a person perceives something and *appropriates* it. This means he makes an object meaningful to *him* as *his* object. Marx said that in our perception of the world we are limited to how it subjectively appears to us, given the cultural patterns we have absorbed in order to evaluate and understand anything we perceive. But the world is more than it appears. And men are more than they appear. A weaver or a coal miner, thus categorised by a particular society, is more than a weaver or coal miner. Here we arrive at Marx's analysis of the capitalist State. The question for capitalism that arises out of Marx's analysis of human needs and powers and their determination by cultural patterns is: Have we got room in our present society for evaluating people *seriously* in terms other than what they are economically worth?

In a capitalist society men perceive and then appropriate what they perceive. In other words, they give meaning to what they perceive, in a one-dimensional way. This does not lead to the enrichment of men's other powers. Capitalist appropriation is, for

Marx, an oversimplified, one-sided gratification expressed only in the sense of privately possessing or having. In capitalism, where men as individuals only relate to other individuals in the 'free' money market, man's human needs are eliminated from public consideration. The only true need here is money. Private ownership, with all it entails in the way of greed, status, the exclusion of others from what is one's own, with rights of use and abuse, is the only publicly recognised expression of human powers. The desire to own privately and exclusively is not, for Marx, a characteristic of human nature. But it is a characteristic of a certain kind of historically conditioned human nature. And according to Marx, the desire to own everything with which one comes into contact is the peculiar product of capitalism. In the end this means that the multiple, near-infinite ways in which men may relate to the world they use and create, and to other human beings, are reduced to a single relation of an individual to 'things' which themselves are considered only in terms of their exchange value – how much they can be sold for. The capitalist world is filled with nothing but commodities which are produced for a market and take on independent form. Social relations in the commercial process appear to all participants as relations among things over which they have no control since the exchange value is held to be in the thing and not as the embodiment or symbol of labour effort. Individual men, no matter what they do in preparing commodities for the money market, are effectively written out of the political and economic life of a capitalist society. This is because what is being considered in the market are seemingly autonomous things with variable prices. Exchange is regulated by independent factors divorced from the will of the creator.

The question that Marx was seeking to answer is: why does everything that man produces have a price? Indeed, why is value determined by that price? He says that it is peculiar to capitalism that objects have value *because* they represent money; this obsession with money is at the heart of Marx's labour theory of value.

What is capitalism? Marx defined it as comprising a free wage labourer who sells his labour power for an allotted time to someone who owns the instruments of production. He believed that this is a system of organisation of life that develops at a specific moment in history. Therefore one can both trace the beginnings of capitalism and foresee its end. Labour power is seen in capitalism as a commodity. Marx saw this as degradingly simple.

Man as a labourer is a commodity who functions as a thing among other things so that his individual, personal qualities and abilities are bought and sold like other things. His brains, muscles, energy, personality, his creative powers all get reduced to a single category: exchange value. His personality as a human individual is *reified*, turned into a thing, and this for Marx, is the measure of capitalist degradation because it happens to all people in the labour market.

The consequence of this reification is that the productive process in which a wage labourer is involved means nothing to him as such except as a means of staying alive. The wage labourer does not care about the company or its products. He works only to exist, and work – which is a natural aspect of human living – becomes something negative. This what Marx calls *alienated labour*.

Of course in working, the worker creates value but has no way of realising that value for himself or enriching his life by appropriating what he produces as something which is useful to him. In fact, only when he is not at work does he realise himself; only then, when he is released from the labour process does he belong to himself. His individual, personal life, that private realm, is external to what he actually does in the public world in order to survive. Effectively this means there is no community here. Rather, what we have are atomistic, competitive, wage labourers who compete with others in the same position for a contract to sell their labour power.

In increasingly advanced, technological, capitalist societies wage labourers sell their labour power for a fixed time in the same way as one might hire out a machine. Such men are free, legally free to dispose of their labour power and time to whomever they like. They are also free from the ownership of the means to production – they do not own the machines they work on, so that they must sell their labour power and time because this is all they have that can be recognised as exchangeable in the market. And with increasing sophistication of production methods and machines, there is an increasing division of labour. The labourer becomes increasingly subject to the machine.

Marx saw the division of labour as the fragmentation of multi-faceted men where for most of the day the individual is shackled to part activities. He produces parts of things which do not concern him. His work is degraded to an activity that is necessary to him only as a means of satisfying elementary needs through his wage packet. And as capitalism becomes more advanced and technically more sophisticated, Marx believed it prefers, if it does not already create, stupid, mechanised, one-dimensional workers with no human skills that are valued other than the ability to perform the task imposed on them.

What are the consequences of the institution of exchange and the division of labour? Marx said they contribute to the atomistic, 'individualistic' character of society in which there appear to exist independent spheres of activity. Each sphere of activity has its own norms. Each sphere applies to the individual different and *opposing* yardsticks: on the one hand, there is the sphere of moral dos and don'ts; on the other there is the 'neutral' sphere of the economy. The division of labour separates men as part workers in a production system which pays them for performing an unvarying and narrow task. But then it reunites them, but only through the exchange system where they enter the market to sell their labour in return for wages. Money reunites them.

Many political economists of Marx's generation and before, especially in the eighteenth century, saw this division of labour and the reuniting in the exchange system as both natural and eternal. But Marx saw it as alienating, unnatural and peculiar to a certain phase in men's history. Only in capitalism does the human and social act in which men's products reciprocally complement one another become alienated to a far greater degree than at any other period in history. In capitalism the human and social act of labour takes on the appearance of a material thing, money, which is external to man. Through this alien mediation, through money, which unites man with man, man regards his relationship to others as determined by a power that is independent of himself and them. Objects now have value only because they represent money.

There is a paradox here and Marx recognised it wholeheartedly. The increasing division of labour, of specialist skills, has increased labour's productivity. It has enabled men to combat scarcity because it is evident that science and technology have increased men's control of nature. But because of capitalism's institutions of exchange, there has been a failure to pass on these benefits to the individual whose multifaceted development is denied. His development is also stunted because such a specialist has become nothing more than a tool with a voice in the production of commodities. Today we unashamedly refer to specialist wage earners in the productive process as 'operatives'.

The great eighteenth-century economic theorist, Adam Smith, himself recognised that this division of labour had led to a situation in which *in principle* 'a porter differs less from a philosopher than a mastiff from a greyhound: but it is the division of labour that has set a gulf between them'. Marx agreed. But where Marx differed was that he was not persuaded by Smith's doctrine of 'the invisible hand'. According to Adam Smith, when everyone engages in self-seeking activity, the result is better for all, than when everyone tries directly to do good. Marx did agree, however, that this division of labour led directly to the formation of the liberal State. It also led to the rise of ideology, the sanctification of private property and the division of society into social classes.

Marx observed the historical development of the division of labour as it responded increasingly to technological progress. Increasingly there was an isolation of each stage of production which led to an invariable function of the labourer. Those who instal brakes in cars do only this. This ties down individuals to a particular calling and even includes a class of unskilled labourers. It was the early social division of labour in the sixteenth century which led to a further division of labour in manufacturing and this in turn saw the emergence of the modern eighteenth- and nineteenth-century State, whose laws justified what Marx saw as 'civilised exploitation'. The worker became an appendage of the machine.

But had not the French Revolution insisted on the equality and liberty of all Frenchmen as citizens? Did ideas and ideals count for nothing? Marx did indeed reflect on the French Revolution but insisted that because it was a political rather than an economic revolution, it merely bolstered the bourgeois State. It did indeed rid itself of an aristocracy. It replaced this aristocracy with men with middle-class values, concerned with the security of private property. And it ensured the capitalist exchange system – ending feudalism and bringing in the next historical mode of organising social economics – capitalism.

In analysing the French Constitution of 1791–5, after the French Revolution, Marx insisted that 'none of the so-called rights of man goes beyond egoistic man, man as he is in civil society, namely withdrawn behind the private interests and whims and separated from the community. . . . The only bond that holds them together is natural necessity, need and private interests, the maintenance of their property and egoistic persons.' The exchange system which gave rise to middle-class ideas about liberty, equality and fraternity, without realising such ideals at the economic base of society, was only a surface phenomenon to Marx. 'In the depths entirely different processes go on, in which this apparent individual equality and liberty disappear.' You cannot alter politics without first altering the economic structure of society on which politics is sustained.

Marx insisted that at the heart of democratic liberalism, based as it is on exchange and the division of labour, is radical alienation. What does alienation mean? Marx noted that eighteenth- and nineteenth-century capitalist political economists described the situation well. However, they assumed without proof that man is everywhere nothing but a self-interested egoist. Therefore they accepted the fact and necessity of private property as the natural consequence of a competitive war among the greedy. But Marx said that greed is not a necessary feature of human psychology. The man who proclaims 'greed is good' is an alienated man; he is a man who has become alienated, competitive and private *because* he lives in an exchange-based, money economy. This is rightly reflected in the political economists' conception of civil society 'in which every individual is a totality of needs and only exists for the other person as the other exists for him, insofar as each becomes a means for the other' (*Economic and Philosophical Manuscripts*). This type of psychology emerges, said Marx, from certain types of societies which arrange their economics as do capitalists, with an exchange system and a division of labour.

For Marx, odd as it may sound, the root of all evil is money! The division of labour is a form of alienation. And private property is a secondary consequence of the division of labour which produces alienated labour. Man is now subjected to his own works which, as products, become independent things expressed in money. The supreme form of what Marx colourfully calls 'commodity fetishism' is money taken as a standard of value and means of exchange. What this means is that exchange value has come to dominate use value. Man produces products for money rather than for their use to him.

The division of labour had led to alienated labour which itself was caused by increasing technological progress. But technological progress advanced *without* a progressive conquest of individual freedom. Instead, increasing technological progress has increasingly degraded the individual into a thing, a tool of production of things, and this historical, scientific development had, Marx believed, reached its nadir in capitalism and its product the liberal State. Marx was not against technological advance. Indeed, he saw it as a necessity for man's eventual freedom. But it must be an advance that benefits the *producer*. In the liberal state technological advance benefits the owner who is separated from the producer.

There is in Marx's writings a concept of the State as truly representing the whole community where there is no difference between rulers and ruled. Hence, he is not against the State but against the *capitalist* State. When the State represents the whole community and not merely one section of the community, then the State has no value in and of itself. The true State is not in origin or in value independent of the empirical living individuals comprising it. It is not some bureaucracy over and above individuals, a public entity divorced from private men. It is not some universal substance over and above concrete individuals. This is what Marx means when he says that 'man *is* the world of man, the state, society'. And the laws of this true state correspond to human nature.

But the laws of the State as we know it are maintained by police methods and are binding in only an external sense. As Gerry Cohen, Professor of Social and Political Theory at Oxford University, explains, the State is an institution that serves several functions for Marx. Firstly, it has an organising and coordinating role to play in society. But it need not do this through coercive repression. A central authority need only declare that everyone drive on the same side of the road, for instance, so that all but the insane will fall in with this. That there may be a penalty for driving on the wrong side of the road is only a secondary consideration. But secondly, the State, as historically conceived, also wields coercive power and this, in the liberal State, is perhaps its most important function. The application of its coercive power is to be seen in the protecting of the property structure and this means the State is an instrument which protects existing class divisions where one class dominates another. Marx sees this kind of state as an agent of sectional groups in society. It creates a fictitious community out of atomistic, antagonistic, competitive private owners and it sees itself as having value in itself. Its value is as a supposedly impartial arbiter that mediates between the conflict of individual egos with particular interests. But, according to Marx, this State is a tool of certain particular interests. Furthermore, the bureaucracy, the civil servants who run the State, believe that their own interests are everyone's interests. This, said Marx, is an illusion. Instead, the origins of the State's authority and monopoly of force are economic. It originates in one group of society taking possession of the means of production while declaring that its monopoly of coercion is exercised in the name of the whole society. As Marx describes it, the bureaucracy of the liberal, capitalist State is characterised by secrecy, internal hierarchies, an adulation of authority and by rigid traditions.

Of course, Marx was analysing the nineteenth-century State. Does his analysis still hold? Marx pointed to a conflict that was meant to be central to the State's existence: that between the citizen and the private person. The citizen is given abstract, fictional attributes by the law of the State. In his public, collective life the citizen has rights and duties. But then there is also the private person who lives a concrete existence. Marx saw an antagonism between the individual and the collective life. He believed this antagonism was glossed over by the State which provided the egoistic, self-seeking character of private life with a legal framework. For Marx, this is a sign of true self-alienation because a truly integrated social being overcomes his own division between his private interests and those of the community of which he is a part. He argued that the individual must recognise his own forces as social forces. He should organise these himself and not be organised. And he must no longer separate social forces from himself and call them political forces. People who see the State as threatening their private spheres are radically alienated from what it means to be human and live a human life, because such a human life *is* a social life shared with multifaceted others. There is for Marx, a collective, generic character of human life and this is real life with society taking on a collective character. This means that private life coincides with public life rather than being antagonistic to it. This is what Marx meant for man to be truly reconciled to the world, himself, and others. The person who sees himself as alone and in competition with other loners is not living a human life. But it is not enough to change the political institutions of the state. Human emancipation is not secured through political means at all. It is secured through economic change.

The abolition of private property and class from the requirements to vote did not mean that private property, station in life and the differences of birth no longer had consequences for the kinds of life men led. To have universal suffrage changes nothing. Contrary to eighteenth-century Enlightenment reformers, Marx did not see social harmony resulting from legislative reform. He thought such legislative reform was meant only to reconcile the egoism of the individual with the collective interest. Instead, dealienation comes about through a conscious recognition of why man is alienated from his lot on earth. Man, he said, must envisage a dealienated world in which he affirms himself in a world *he* has created. Labour itself is not alienating. It can and should be creative and fulfilling. Work is an affirmation, not a denial of, humanity. But the division of labour is not creative. Technological progress must be used in a new way to ensure that human activity is freed from the constraints of physical need and hunger. Man should use technology to develop his own freedom instead of being enslaved to the material forces he does not control. And the way he comes to control material forces is through eradicating the breach between those who own the technological instruments, the machine, the plant, the capital from those who use it to create products. Men created the technology. They must use it and not be used by it. How can this come about?

Marx took a look at the span of human history. He found that the motive force for social progress throughout history had always been conflict. No humanitarian sentiment had ever changed things. And the world had never been changed by ideas alone. It had been changed by action. He said that the aims of earlier struggles for liberation had begun in a reform of men's consciousness, by which he meant people's awareness of the nature of their lives, of how reality is for *them*. He insisted that there was a difference between the utopian socialism of his contemporaries and his own scientific socialism because the scientific version converts the unconscious historical tendencies of millenarians and utopians into conscious tendencies. He had no interest in regaining some fictional lost paradise. Rather, he said that a scientific examination of history indicated that social progress came through conflict which itself was a consequence of men coming to understand consciously their own natures and behaviours within their historical contexts. For Marx, men are practical beings whose thoughts are the conscious aspect of how their private lives are governed by practical needs.

Consciousness, the mental aspect of human living, is a social process that is realised in speech and communication which spells out how real living is for men, at a particular historical moment.

Marx thought he saw a particular consciousness emerging in nineteenth-century capitalist society, a consciousness that was peculiar to capitalism itself. It defined what he insisted was a *false* dichotomy between the private and public roles of the individual. That the dichotomy was false was increasingly being realised. But no mere consciousness of the nature of people's lives had ever changed a thing. What was needed was not just another philosophy of life. And so he said 'the weapon of criticism has never substituted for criticism by weapons'. Revolution had always been and would now be the inevitable consequence of men coming to understand consciously their own nature and behaviour in a State that was not an expression of the whole of society. What needed to be destroyed was the existing state institutions and the bureaucratic class with its own interests.

For Marx, the State itself is not abolished by revolution. It will simply wither away as the instrument of one class when the political superstructure, which cannot be reformed, is violently removed. Professor Cohen reminds us that the State is not the primary oppressor. It is implicated in the oppression because Marx saw the capitalist state as the instrument of one class to oppress another. And he speculated that in many countries, namely Britain, The Netherlands and America, it would be possible to overcome capitalism and its instrumental State through peaceful, parliamentary means. In other states, violence would be necessary, not least because there would be a counter-movement on the part of the privileged whose interests were maintained by conserving the *status quo* in their favour. Most optimistically Marx believed that the agents of this revolution would be those who suffered most – the proletarian wage labourers.

As a social class the proletariat was symbolic of the capitalist system's degradation of humanity. Marx believed that their interests coincide with the interests of all individuals since their claims most starkly represent the universal needs of human beings. Their suffering is human suffering without the masks employed by middle-class culture. Hence it is their task to liberate themselves and everyone else from the division of labour and the exchange system: their liberation made for the liberation of all others. In the nineteenth-century working class Marx saw mankind stripped to its barest and most essential needs. He saw what Dickens saw and described in books like *Hard Times*. But he also said that the bourgeoisie was a product of an alienating society as well. It was not, however, in such a state of human degradation as the working class, although the dehumanisation of the middle-class capitalist personality was likewise transformed into an instrument for increasing capital. And this meant that the motives of capitalists, their good will, and even their charity, could not play any part in the exchange system which was all that mattered because this system considers only the circulation of money as capital and as an end in itself. But where the middle-class entrepreneur was compensated for his anonymity by money and power, the working class was effectively written out of human history and lumped together with the non-human assets of capital and machines.

With the projected revolution against the bureaucratic political superstructure of the liberal state, Marx believed, comes the destruction of the division of labour and in its wake, the end of private property. Their abolition is not the replacement of one type of politics for another, however, whatever may have occurred during this century in Eastern European Marxist experiments. Rather, the abolition of politics is the abolition of that public realm which abstracts man from his concrete existence and treats him as a thing. This means that for Marx there was to be no extinction of individuality nor a general levelling for the sake of some abstract universal good. Instead, the final phase of what was to be a two-stage revolution would be the establishment of communism. Here there would be no classes, no private property, no politics and no coercive state. Communism was meant to represent the full emancipation of the individual by destroying the estranged bureaucratic political world that was presided over by a self-interested bureaucracy that had previously 'managed the affairs of the middle class' and effectively had hived itself off as an élite. Marxist communism was not meant to deprive men of their individuality nor to reduce all to mediocrity. Rather it was meant to enable the flourishing of the individual as such who saw his own powers as social forces and took responsibility for his own life in community.

Marx believed that this kind of personal responsibility for the development of personal aptitudes in all their fullness and variety could only come about, and would only come about, in a community in which the sources of antagonism among individuals were done away with. Interpersonal problems at the psychological level would not be eradicated, as Professor Cohen emphasises. But the kind of antagonism that sprang from the historically specific, and not eternally natural, mutual isolation that *had* to arise in a society that divorced political and civic life from private life would end.

The division into the private and public had had to arise in the capitalist liberal state whose laws instituted private property as the only means by which individuals could assert themselves publicly and only through an opposition to others. When this system ended, and Marx believed it already harboured the seeds of its own destruction within itself, it would be replaced by cooperation among free workers who possessed in common the world's resources as well as the means of production, produced themselves by their own labour.

Marx's vision of communism *is* the dealienated State. And the reason Marx could imagine this communist scenario was because nineteenth-century capitalism had created the preconditions for the new society with its ever-progressive advances in technology. The new society would take up the technological achievements and evolve new forms of cooperation so that the men who created the technology would use it instead of being used by it. By the nineteenth century, capitalism was already developing cooperative factories and, for its own ends, transferring workers from one task to another, thereby undermining the original division of labour. The working class was inadvertently being made more versatile.

Communism has, then, as its preconditions, very advanced capitalist technology and a world market. It was not meant to be a utopian return to some idyllic and mythical craft culture. Even more advanced development was forecast for the communist system of the future where its beneficiaries were meant to be its creators. With the increase in technology what had previously been man's necessary work for survival would decrease, leaving more time for creative work. The products of 'creative labour' were to be the arts and sciences which gradually, even totally, would replace the drudgery of alienated and repugnant labour.

Based on an analysis of capitalism from the standpoint of the individual, Marx projected from within capitalism itself an aim of human emancipation which would emerge from the abolition of alienation through the destruction of the division of labour. It would not be enough to make the standard of living of wage labourers the same as that of the middle class because this would not abolish the fundamentally alienated society. Hence it was not simply a question of redistributing the same income produced in the same old way.

Socialism's aim, as Marx saw it, was to substitute production governed by social needs, by use value, for the capitalist concern with production to maximise exchange value.

Because Marx believed that labour (human effort) at all levels of lived life was the only source of value, he saw a future society in which all labour accrues to society in the collective satisfaction of integrated, individual men. But beyond the basic principle of a society that produced use values rather than exchange values, Marx did not provide a detailed description of the future. That would be left to his future adherents and revisionists. But in so far as Marx was a man against the liberal State (that representative of social alienation to its highest degree), Marx, and Engels his collaborator, insisted that such a State 'will disappear with the disappearance of the class divisions and go into the museum of antiquities by the side of the spinning wheel and the bronze axe' (Engels, *Origin of the Family*).

Marx was concerned with most people most of the time rather than with extraordinary and unusual individuals. In a dealienated society where the State is not distinct from the administration of production, where it is merely the organiser and not a distinct political entity, everyone would be extraordinary and individual if only in the sense that each would be living and not merely surviving. This tremendous optimism has its roots in Marx's understanding of consciousness. From the very beginning consciousness is a social product and it remains so as long as men exist at all. The individual cannot escape his mutual dependence on society even when he acts on his own, and even when he feels himself to be most individual. The tragedy of the capitalist social individual, according to Marx, is that he is compelled to be a competitive, isolated unit rather than a cooperative human being. But a person integrated humanly into a group leaves behind the conflict between man and society. He substitutes in his mind the realisation that he is human, replacing that separate, independent, aggressive individual he took himself to be within the liberal State. Competition and class hostility render cooperation almost impossible. This is not a statement about human nature but about the conditions in which it can find itself.

One of the claims made for capitalism is that it produces winners as well as losers and even the latter are inadvertently helped by the winners. Marx said this was untrue. There are no winners. This is because scarce resources impose certain constraints on people, but the greatest constraint is the fundamental attitude to labour and ownership of the means of production. What is left of the individual after all these divisions is man as the lowest common denominator, denuded, alienated, an abstract person, a statistic, a price tag. Having become an abstraction man is then classified by capitalism along with other abstractions: all are things and each has its price. The market is free and neutral.

Lastly, just as man makes the constitution where the State is to be subordinated to individual human needs, where it has no independent value, so too man makes religion. Marx insisted that religion was a natural outcome of man's dissatisfaction. He saw religion as a powerful opiate drug for people alienated from the world. During the nineteenth century opiates were freely available and widely used. But Marx did not advocate destroying religion. Nor did he believe it had been foisted on the people by a priestly caste. Instead he said that man must give up his illusions about social and political conditions so that religion was no longer needed. Religion will persist when society is repressive. Professor Cohen insists that there is no justification in Marx for the Soviet suppression of religious belief. If the society had been a fulfilling one religion would have withered away. Heaven needs to be projected as a wonderful place elsewhere but there would be no need for this super version of the good life when conditions here were fulfilling.

But, for Marx, it was not sufficient to split religion from the State and to disestablish the Church. Freeing the State from religion does not free mankind from its need for religion when conditions are unsatisfactory. And as we have seen, *political* revolution does not liberate people either from religion or from private property. Political revolutions and massive legislative changes merely give people the right to hold property and to profess their own religion. This does no more than confirm the dichotomy between the public and the private man. Religion is a symptom and not a cause of alienation. And in capitalism, Marx believed, men needed as much religion as they could get. Religion, like social class, nation and race, remains a prison from which each individual must escape in order to establish truly human relations. Collectively, these were all escapist fantasies to which we now in the twentieth century add vicarious living through film, pop and TV soap stars whose unreal lives give us the pleasure which cannot be derived from our own real lives.

Marx's model of man, his analysis of the bourgeois liberal State and his theory of capitalist alienation have been seen by some to offer a liberation theory for technological man. Marx's advocacy of violence in certain circumstances places him within the tradition followed by many other theories of man and society, except for pacifist ones. We have seen that very few do not advocate violence in some circumstances (just think of Locke and his friends engaged in their 'glorious revolution').

On the other hand, some have seen Marxism as yet another religion. They have pointed to both prophetic and messianic elements in his theory of a perpetual just war against politics until there is no longer a separate political realm. But still others like Professor Cohen have rejected this, saying that unlike Old Testament prophets Marx did not warn nor did he recall a straying community to its true commitments. Rather he was a forecaster, a predictor and had some of the passion of the prophet which he deployed to call men to arms. He was careful to say, in predicting the end of class antagonisms, insists Professor Cohen, that this would not necessarily also end interpersonal antagonisms. Nor did he predict perfect harmony among humans, as did millenarians. What he did say was that the economic domain, which has been such a source of sorrow and oppression, can cease to be so. And whatever interpersonal problems remained would not have a severe impact at the collective level.

Others have argued that Marx exaggerated the weight of 'the social' in human subjectivity. They believe this was to the detriment of an adequate account of the formation of personal identity. Not only did Marx pay insufficient attention to the power of sex and to its repression on human motivation; he did not examine closely enough the family, which is where people acquire most of their personal and class characteristics in childhood. Hence some have argued that having focused on capitalist factories, Marx omitted that factory for producing character, the family. As we shall see, Sigmund Freud would contribute to the analysis of the child as the seditious self against civilisation and not merely against the liberal State. But so long as people, their talents and their products can be measured in terms of money, Marx's theory of alienation will be seen by many as a useful explanation of why this is so. From the standpoint of the individual, the market is purely irresponsible. To some this is its virtue. To others this is its tragedy for man. But, as Marx insisted, different forms of human society that succeed one another in history, do succeed one another because they are successively appropriate at different times to the task of developing productive power. This must mean that like previous economic systems, capitalism would have its day. It would be succeeded by socialism. The continuity in historical development required these radical transformations.

Does this mean that Marx believed that the shift from capitalism to socialism would happen anyway in the course of history? It would happen, says Professor Cohen, if and only if humans agitated that it should happen, and according to Marx it was predictable that humans would so agitate.

Hence at given moments in history it is both historic and appropriate to be against the State. But as Professor Cohen explains, if you are a Marxist, you are committed to saying the following: that at certain moments in history, where you may not like the State or the system it supports – because you think people are exploited in it – none the less this system is the inevitable one to have for the time being. It may be heroic and admirable for certain people to stand up and oppose themselves to the State, but this would be futile. The time is not yet right. There is a proper time to reject the application of the State's coercive power which protects existing class divisions and the property structure. But when is the right time?

The preconditions for such revolutionary action must be very advanced technological economies. Professor Cohen tells us of the time when, in the 1870s, Russian revolutionaries were in a quandary that Marx had put them in, hating the oppressive relations of Czarist Russia and yet also realising that Russia was so backward economically that it was not yet ready to try socialism. They wrote to Marx. Marx learnt Russian to be able to answer them, and he replied that they *could* make a socialist revolution in such an economically backward country *but it would not succeed* unless there were revolutions in the more technologically advanced West. Such revolutions never happened.

Some have argued that you cannot use the failure of the Soviet experiment to impugn Marxism. It would be incredible to say that the Soviet experiment established the truth of Marxism. But the prematurity of that revolution in Marxist terms cannot falsify Marxist theory according to Professor Cohen. You do not have to have a world revolution to have realised Marxism but what *is* necessary is that the revolution should begin in countries that are relatively advanced in world economic terms. They take the rest of the world with them or they ignore the rest of the world. But Marxism cannot succeed in an economically backward part of the world.

In the end Marx probably made two large mistakes in his prognosis of capitalism. Each mistake was an extension into the future about things that were true in his own times but which ceased to be true for later times. Firstly, he seemed totally incapable of foreseeing just how much the capitalist State could humanise itself by implanting a welfare sector within itself. If you had depicted Sweden to Marx, he probably would have thought it an impossibility. Secondly, he was wrong to think that the anarchy of capitalist production, which led to business crises, would get worse and worse. He had no anticipation of any Keynesian possibility of a regulation and moderation of the business cycle.

Putting both mistakes together, you can infer, says Professor Cohen, that the longevity of capitalism would be much greater than Marx predicted. He did not foresee the strength within capitalism and its instruments of self-preservation.

As Professor Cohen points out, the experience of twentieth-century socialist countries has taught us two lessons. The notion that you can have a successful society *without* what Marx called bourgeois democracy, that is, liberal freedoms and a democratic order, is utter nonsense. This is because if nothing else people will feel so diminished that they will not work. It is becoming more and more clear that no socialist economic revolution can succeed in the absence of a democratic polity. We have also learned that nobody knows how to plan comprehensively and centrally for an economy. But some still say that the lesson that is *not* there to be learned, is that it is not possible to have an economy that is run on an egalitarian basis. None has yet been attempted. We now know that any feasible economy must have a strong market element but this does not mean it must be unrestrainedly free. Professor Cohen believes it is possible to design institutions in which to place the market so as to produce an egalitarian result.

It is true that the people believing in Marx's ideas built societies which brought about the contrary of what he believed. They brought about an effective tyranny of their people and also made their working class less powerful and less significant as players in governing the destiny of their societies.

Were their experiments a distortion of Marx or a necessary

consequence of implementing Marxist ideas? One answer provided by Professor Cohen is that Marx took for granted the correctness of democracy in resolving social affairs. But he did not specify the institutional nature of the socialist society to which he looked forward. This created a massive problem for his heirs. He spoke only of a free association of producers but he said he would refrain from producing recipes for the cookshops of the future. He thought the conditions that would prevail at the time would so dictate the details that it would be pointless to design them in advance. With hindsight, it would have been useful to have had more signposts which socialist architects could have used in order to stigmatise the Stalinisation of the Soviet Union. But Poland's Lech Walesa, non-Communist that he is, has apparently taken a lesson from Marx. He says that the political reforms of Poland are well on their way. He asks for economic help, 'do business with us and send managerial skills. Without these economic changes the political reforms will disintegrate.' Marx would have said the same: any attempt to make the political lead the economic will fail.

Has communism had its day? Will it not survive the twentieth century? How is it still possible to say one is a Marxist today?

Professor Cohen answers that a Marxist needs to believe three things: firstly, that capitalism is a form of society that is fundamentally unjust because it represses the powers of individual people. Secondly, that it is possible to have a society that is neither unjust nor oppressive, where resources are equally shared and people do have a setting to develop themselves; lastly, that this state of affairs cannot be achieved by peaceful negotiation. Something more militant is required because there remain strong class interests in the existing society against its transformation.

This does not mean that one must endorse particular ways that have been tried in Eastern Europe. And it does not mean that one must believe in comprehensive state planning. Indeed, some argue that we have not had what Marx would have called communism at all. The essentials for Marx's communism are that what you earn is not strongly conditioned by what you produce. Marx's communism provides people with what they need *as people* and separates their means of livelihood from their form of activity. Economic activities should reflect the will and bent of individuals, but how much remuneration you get should not depend on how productive you are. This spells out the classical definition of communism:

from each according to his contribution, to each according to his need.

And so it appears that people *did* attempt what Marx had in mind but they were too early, and so failed. The price of their failure has been to strengthen the State's authority rather than to undermine it. But we must recall that the primary arena for Marxism is not the State itself but the class system and a mode of economic production with its particular way of extracting profit. The State in liberal capitalism is the instrument of the owning class.

Marx was not concerned with whether or not there was an unfair distribution of happiness where the rich simply got more of it. Some did and some did not. Rather, he was concerned with the unfair distribution of the *means* for achieving happiness. This unfair distribution of the means to human fulfilment could be overcome, he believed, through the collective ownership of capital on the part of those who do the producing. Workers' cooperatives could be integrated into the market. And some see this as the future for northern Europe, a future that does not depend on the unit of collectivity being the nation state as a whole. Will the State then wither away leaving a system of self-governing cooperative enterprises of a future Europe?

CHAPTER EIGHT

FREUD

S igmund Freud was born in Moravia in 1856 but moved to Vienna when he was 3 years old. He lived there for most of his life, until he was 82. But with Hitler's invasion of Austria in 1938, he sought asylum in London and died there in 1939. Like Marx, he was Jewish, and like Marx he thought religion to be an illusion. He began his career as a student of anatomy and physiology of the nervous system. But when he went to study in Paris his interests turned to psychology.

Freud was the founder of the doctrine called psychoanalysis. Psychoanalysis began as a method of treating neurotic patients by investigating their minds. It then grew into a theory about the workings of the human mind in general. 'All over the world, probably at this very hour', as writer and broadcaster Michael Ignatieff so graphically puts it, 'there are people lying on couches, talking to a silent person who is just behind them out of their eyeline. They are following Freud's famous "talking cure". Freud believed that if you talked yourself right back to your infancy and to your earliest experiences with your mother and father, you could unlock the roots and origins of your adult conflicts.' Through his study of childhood sexual development and his examination of his patients' dreams, Freud uncovered the unconscious forces that influence all human thoughts and acts.

Freud was not a political theorist, so why is he being considered in a book about individuals and movements against the State? He had political views only as a consequence of having psychoanalytical views. But it was towards the end of his life that he turned his attention increasingly to the future of religion and the nature of religion and to the meaning of and future for civilisation. In a memorable exchange, he corresponded with Albert Einstein on the nature of war, and asked questions about whether the State is necessary, and whether the State repressed natural, human potentials. And he answered these questions.

Reading the case histories of some of Freud's early patients, Michael Ignatieff reminds us, they include hysterical women who came to him because they had developed horrible facial tics and could not understand why they had them. When they went through the talking cure they uncovered infantile traumas or some terrible story of cruelty by their husbands. They did not talk about the State. But Freud came to believe that the State's laws, for example the laws about marriage, institutionalised forms of cruelty at the social level and that these were having their effects on his patients at the individual level. Freud's patients talked about Mummy and Daddy but, Michael Ignatieff points out, behind Mummy and Daddy was the State.

Freud therefore plays an important part in any consideration of political theory because he showed how the State in its power and its laws and prohibitions 'gets into your skull, gets into your deepest, knotted fears' as Michael Ignatieff puts it. There is no other political theorist in the history of thinking about these subjects who looks at the law and its prohibitions as – to use the jargon – an 'intrapsychic experience'. He did not speak about this government or that government but rather about Civilisation itself, the apparatus of cultural convention. Cultural expectation and norms, informal rules, customs and habits of a society underlay the State's explicit prohibitions. Michael Ignatieff explains that, for Freud, it was the great carapace of civilisation which dictated all the ways in which we express ourselves. And civilisation – this vast structure of conventions and laws of which the State was a part – was always antithetical, always hostile to the infant inside us.

The 'father of psychoanalysis', as Freud was known, had spent many years of his life treating the mentally ill and disturbed only to say, in later years, that this had been a *detour* along the path of cultural analysis and criticism.

> My interest, after making a long detour through the natural sciences medicine and psychotherapy, returned to the cultural problems which had fascinated me long before, when I was a youth scarcely old enough for thinking. . . . I perceived ever more clearly that the

events of human history, the interactions between human nature, cultural development and the precipitate of primeval experiences (the most prominent of which is religion) are no more than a reflection of the dynamic conflicts between Ego, Id and Superego (which comprise the Unconscious) which psychoanalysis studies in the individual – are the very same processes repeated upon a wider stage.

The psychoanalytic study of the individual taught Freud that each of us is seditious. Michael Ignatieff explains that, 'within each of us is that little child who never plays by the rules: he smashes up the house with a kind of gleeful look on his face; he pees in the middle of the living-room. His infantile rebellion is perhaps curbed at the age of 18 months when he gets toilet-trained. But he never gets over what it costs to give up the child inside. And therefore the State and civilisation are always hostile to the unruly child inside us. We are always naturally seditious and the sedition comes from that absolutely unreconciled, furious little child who does not want to be toilet-trained, nor go to bed on time, or do what Mummy and Daddy say.' This is the straightforward way of saying that Freud developed a model of man and, like all other thinkers who had something to say about man in society, this model underlay his insights.

For Freud, human nature is static, a given, organic, closed system. It is driven by impulses of self-preservation and sexual gratification. Man is fundamentally antisocial and has to learn how to be social in order to survive. Freud challenges the whole tradition of political thinking from Aristotle onwards that says that man is by nature a political animal. Instead, following on from Charles Darwin's theory of evolution, Freud saw man as an unfinished product of nature who is given, biologically, certain instincts and impulses which are specific to human beings from their very beginning.

There is no doubt that the individual man of late-nineteenth-century culture is Freud's model for universal man. The passions and anxieties expressed as characteristic of man in nineteenth- and early twentieth-century society are taken to be eternal and biologically rooted. But Freud said that our human impulses or primary drives develop in specific social frameworks which serve to regulate the ways in which these impulses are manifested. At the core remains man as antisocial. And furthermore, from the standpoint of any ethical doctrine he is evil in the sense that he is driven by irrational and indeed aggressive forces in search of pleasure and satisfaction at the expense of the objective world. The objective world includes all other individuals who are similarly so inclined. Freud, then, presents us with the radically egocentric, individualist, pleasure-seeker and pain-avoider, the isolated sensualist who is dominated by his passions, the irrational, impulse-driven 'universe-unto-himself' that Thomas Hobbes had called 'natural man' in the mid-seventeenth century. St Augustine of Hippo, the great Christian theologian, in the fifth century similarly described the human child, showing him to be an expression of man's original sin and its antisocial nature. But whereas for Hobbes this isolated pleasure-seeker was effectively amoral and was only *prepared* to achieve his ends even if they sometimes required murder, violation and theft, Freud's model is even more threatening. Freud discovered that humans actively *wish* to kill their own kind, and instinctually see *no* barriers to sexual gratification with members of their own family or with members of their own gender. Men are cannibalistic, incestuous and aggressively murderous. Not only is the adult human never free from his childhood but his childhood was anything but innocent. Humans are simply biologically equipped with fixed desires which need satisfaction from others, be they things or people. Man is initially isolated and only interested in the satisfaction of his Ego (self-preservation) and his Id (sexual drives).

We begin with the child who is fundamentally antisocial and egocentric. But, from the very earliest years, the individual is always and necessarily in relation to others, having been born into a family in order to survive. Freud therefore provides what Marx would call a capitalist model of the individual. And like the eighteenth-century political economists of capitalism, Freud took this model to be universally applicable rather than specific to a socio-economic period in history. Freud describes each individual as working for himself, individualistically, and at his own risk. He is not primarily in cooperation with others, ever. Just as the market regulates relations between buying and selling, so too the individual, biologically equipped with fixed drives that need satisfaction from others, *uses* others as a *means* to his own ends. Socialisation in the family and in society is, then, the individual's prudential compromise with other individuals to achieve what he can *for himself*. Note that each individual's strivings and impulses are given *before* any contact with others. The individual must then learn how to enter an exchange system which at least partially satisfies his needs. This means that the child has been given instincts that are available for investment in social encounters. Society domesticates him through a direct satisfaction of only some of his biological drives. It checks others that are socially destructive by driving them into what may be considered culturally valuable strivings. It is this redirection of energies that is called *sublimation*.

If a society requires the suppression of impulses to a greater degree than it offers for redirection and sublimation, we end up with a neurotic individual. This is the ill-adjusted and suffering man.

Freud believed that man's instincts are never completely bound. Rather they are repressed, displaced or perverted. There is then a natural antagonism between man and civilisation, between the individual and *any* State. In every one of us there is the potentiality for criminality. This is not accidental nor is it an instance of degeneracy. Instead it is the product of a delicate balance of forces where biologically given impulses and social circumstances *could* produce 'sanity' or 'normality', but frequently do not. Is this the State's fault or the fault of the inadequately socialised individual? For Freud it was both.

Psychoanalysis had a role to play in all this. As the science of human irrationality, it attempted to understand unconscious strivings in order to replace the repression of antisocial urges with their negation through analysis. But why a *negation* of natural urges?

For Freud, civilisation has always been and will always be conditioned by a partial non-satisfaction of instinctual desires that leads to sublimation or reaction. Freud was no utopian – there was no society that could satisfy men's instinctual desires completely because such desires are fundamentally antisocial, against all social organisation. The alternative to Culture, the alternative to having fixed rules of behaviour, is total instinct satisfaction and this is barbarism. So Freud advised that men accept partial frustration and civilisation which comprises inhibited aims.

Freud insisted there was no possibility of man disobeying the laws of his nature. In the adult there will always continue to exist the primitive, infantile past side by side with the civilised, evolved and adapted 'mature' character. Tragically, man must work out his inevitable plight by recognising what his own nature is and then accepting social laws that govern that nature. This is not a recognition that is achieved once and for all. Past attitudes and impulses survive and, once formed in the child's mind, never perish. In suitable circumstances they can be brought to light and rationally understood. But it is a constant battle. For Freud, mental health and illness are continuous states of being.

Psychoanalysis assures that you do get 'toilet-trained'. Freud believed that the internalisation of rules was absolutely necessary as part of the maturation process. But he insisted that we do not grow up naturally. We have to be forced up the ladder. We do not want to grow up. Growing up is not a natural organic assumption of adulthood or adolescence. It is a process by which we are very unwillingly taught to adopt rules which in some part of ourselves we never fully accept.

From the standpoint of political theory, this is very important. As Michael Ignatieff points out, if the process of our passage from childhood to adulthood were a natural, organic unfolding process, then it would be very difficult to see why we need all these social rules and prohibitions. We would just unfold like flowers. Freud said we do not unfold like flowers. The internalisation of rules is a harsh and hard necessity. The three aspects of our personality, the Id, Ego and Superego, are warring all the time.

In Michael Ignatieff's words, the adult is divided internally between the three. The Id is a part of the Unconscious which is that explosive infant, to whom we have access in our dreams; the irrational, wild, aggressive, sexual character of dreams is that forgotten, unruly child. The Ego, that fragile adult who attempts to adjudicate between the claims of the Id and the Superego in order to preserve the self, tries to moderate the little voice saying, 'go for it, smash it' with the external world saying 'don't smash it, obey the rules'. The Superego's prohibitions are learnt from Mummy and Daddy in the first instance: 'Sit up straight, be polite, use a knife and fork' – the little anarchist is put in his place. But Freud prophesied that with the progress of Culture there would be an increase in the suppression of natural impulses. This would lead necessarily to the increasing frequency of neurotic disturbances, especially for an 'oversocialised' middle class.

Here, Michael Ignatieff says, runs the fault-line in Freud's theory. On the one hand, he was a revolutionary at the level of the bourgeois family. He observed the casualties of the late-nineteenth-century middle-class family in the form of young women whose families had made them ill through prohibitions against sexuality and against freedom in social life. Freud insisted that these women must become more free along with their men. He argued passionately against the kind of patriarchal domination in which he himself grew up. And yet he saw the State as the patriarchal family writ large, inspiring in the individual both fear and feelings of protection. The individual is hostile to it and yet cannot survive well without it. Parents, especially the Father, are replaced by the community. The family, and then the State and its politics, are forms of sexual sublimation. The individual's Unconscious, structured as Id, Ego and Superego, is a microcosm reflecting the macrocosmic struggle between the private and public, the irrationally impulsive, narcissistic and aggressive in conflict with the rational, repressive and coercive. The Id's blind, pleasure-seeking energy, and the Ego's self-preservative energy, are – and must be – gradually moderated internally by the Superego. It is the Superego, that priggish, moralising, internalisation of external coercion, which substitutes for the punitive Father and the State by encouraging feelings of guilt. In the end, whatever Freud thought about the repressive nature of the nineteenth-century bourgeois family, he knew that it could only be replaced by something more subtle: the individual would have to become his own gaoler. There would never be a seamless fit between the individual and society.

Although Freud criticised nineteenth-century society for its excessive concern to repress sexual expression, his essential message remained individualist. The State and any culture by its very definition *must* coerce men into rechannelling their natural aggression and chaotic sexual impulses. What Freud wanted was that men should be aware of this necessity. He wanted the individual to recognise the necessity of sublimation and repression and to come to rely on his own ingenuity in order to make the best of whatever situation he might find himself in. Therefore, Freud's theories were seen as a new ethic of rationality for cultured men which some say was modelled on what he wanted for himself. This was to be free from the despised infantile dependency and to cherish his own autonomy, relying on neither parent nor State directly. To his patients, he held out an ideal of self-realisation through psychoanalysis through which their irrational longings, their fantasies and dreams, might be rationalised and self-controlled.

If we must obey the State by being our own gaolers, and at the same time we recognise that we shall never be completely reconciled to this situation, is there a breaking-point for Freud? Michael Ignatieff thinks that Freud never determined when 'enough was enough'. He did not pursue the question of what happens when individuals look at the social rules and say 'I cannot bear this another moment'. That sense of boiling over, which we have seen to have been such a crucial point in the historical process, is never discussed. There is no theory of social revolution in Freud.

Instead he insisted that a man who is reconciled to civilisation and its necessity must educate himself to Reality. Some have argued that for Freud, the Reality Principle presupposes a middle-class theory of scarcity, where equal satisfaction is not possible. This turns his description of *homo sexualis* into a variation on the eighteenth-century economists' *homo economicus*. Therefore the child in us, bent on pursuing the Pleasure Principle, *must* be refocused to pursue the Reality Principle in a setting where we cannot afford to fantasise and where we have to play by the rules as they are rather than as we might wish them to be. Is this a high-minded theory of middle-class conformism?

Michael Ignatieff reminds us that Freud was a Jew in Austro-Hungarian society. He came to maturity at the end of the nineteenth century in an intensely anti-Semitic society in which Jews did not have an easily available public role to play. They were important as newspaper editors, doctors, lawyers, but no Jew could take it for granted that he would become a public figure. And hence, in his bones, Freud sensed that the private sphere was the real world. The public world was dangerous: it was filled with anti-Semites and street agitators. Freud lived through the whole horror of the rise of Nazism and he was chased from Vienna in 1938 by a public world gone mad. Put more analytically, Freud did not see man as a natural citizen. Rather man was essentially a private, family animal. If this was the crucial sphere of human life then only with a great deal of suspicion could one regard the State as the Father's substitute. And if the State, like the Father, was necessary, then the allegiance we call patriotism was a kind of sublimation, a displacement into the public sphere of all those primitive bondings within the family. But Freud was very wary of the extent of such possible sublimation.

Michael Ignatieff recounts that when, in 1938, the Gestapo marched into his consulting rooms, arrested his daughter and threatened him, Freud was in complete and utter despair. When the Gestapo returned his daughter, they made him sign a piece of paper to testify that they had not destroyed his house. Freud signed, wryly adding 'I can recommend the Gestapo to anyone, Sigmund Freud'.

What we have, then, is a man of enormous insight into the private realm of children and adults who lived through the collapse of public politics in central Europe in the 1920s and 1930s. He saw with his own eyes the Fascist State becoming a predator on its own citizens. And he interpreted this, argues Michael Ignatieff, as the running wild of private, family, tribal passions in the public sphere where it would become a source of real danger to individuals. He uncovered the source of nationalism in the irrational. But his experience and his theory did not lead him to suggest that civilisation and government were the source of the problem. Rather it was – and is – man as he is that leads to society as it is. Man's instincts are selfish and unregenerate for Freud no matter what the economic bases of social systems might be. The State will always be and *must* be antithetical to human nature.

Until 1920, Freud continued to refine his original theory around the necessity of a conflict between the Ego and the Id. He insisted that it was sexual desires of infantile provenance that remained there in repressed form in the adult, ready to terrorise him in unguarded moments. But during the 1920s he went further. He described a life-instinct in all of us, Eros, which comprised the self-preservative Ego along with the narcissistic libidinal sexual drives of the Id. In addition, however, there was an opposing force in the individual's character which was not sexual. Freud discovered the power of non-erotic aggression. The life-instinct, which unites individuals so that civilisation serves Eros, is always opposed by a death instinct, Thanatos, and this is a disintegrative force. The individual was now described as the battlefield between life and death instincts unto the final encounter when death would be victorious.

Freud had not originally believed that there was a separate, aggressive instinct in man in addition to his chaotic impulsive sexuality. But an increasingly pessimistic stance led him to see evidence for a more terrible aspect of men which, he believed, indicated a continuity with the destructive aggressiveness of animals. Personally suffering from cancer of the jaw and witnessing the cultural collapse in the aftermath of the First World War, Freud pinpointed the non-erotic urge, the death instinct, which was continuously engaged in an attempt to destroy all external authority.

He believed that this non-erotic aggression was usually turned inwards. But with increasing repression resulting from the progress of civilisation, he said there would be an increase in surplus aggressiveness that would be released on an ever-larger scale. Civilisation was showing itself to be leading to increasing destructiveness in the form of individual self-destructiveness and the destruction of others. The Superego, acting on the Ego and Id, could turn a suppressed aggressiveness to authority back on the individual in the form of guilt and conscience. But it could also be focused externally and tamed in the sense that man exercises his ingenuity to dominate nature. If untamed externally, Freud said it would destroy all civilisation.

He wrote to Albert Einstein: 'Conflicts between man and man are resolved in principle by the recourse to violence. It is the same in the animal kingdom from which man cannot claim exclusion.'

Although it has since been shown that this gratuitous violence is *not* characteristic of the animal kingdom, that indeed 'nature, red in tooth and claw' describes human beings rather than animals, and that the ritualistic nature of animal conflict often leads to the *diffusion* of situations that would lead to death, Freud became increasingly emphatic that psychoanalysis must intervene. It must rationalise neuroses and prevent psychosis. Man must be actively prevented from revolting against his Fate. Aggression was now the greatest impediment to civilisation. And what Marx had proposed would not solve the fundamental problem. In his famous essay, *Civilisation and its Discontents* (1930), Freud attempted to explain why.

Men are not gentle creatures who want to be loved and who at the most can defend themselves if they are attacked; they are, on the contrary, creatures among whose instinctual endowments is to be reckoned a powerful share of aggressiveness. As a result, their neighbour is for them not only a potential helper or sexual object but also someone who tempts them to satisfy their aggressiveness on him, to exploit his capacity for work without compensation, to use him sexually without his consent, to seize his possessions, to humiliate him, to cause him pain, to torture and to kill him. *Homo homini lupus*. Who in the face of all his experience of life and of history will have the courage to dispute this assertion?

When the mental counterforces which ordinarily inhibit aggression are out of action, it also manifests itself spontaneously and reveals man as a savage beast to whom consideration towards his own kind is something alien. It is this primary mutual hostility of human beings that threatens civilization with disintegration. Again, the interest of work in common would not hold it together; instinctual passions are stronger than reasonable interests. Civilization has to finally decide to set limits to man's aggressive instincts and to hold the manifestations of them in check by psychical reaction formations. Civilization hopes to prevent the crudest excesses of brutal violence by itself assuming the right to use violence against criminals, but the law is not able to lay hold of the more cautious and refined manifestations of human aggressiveness.

Hence strife and competition are indispensable to civilization. Civilization has not tried to eliminate these from human activity. We want opposition not enmity from civilization and civilization has frequently misused natural opposition making it an occasion for enmity.

According to the communists man is wholly good and well disposed to his neighbour. But private property corrupts his nature, giving the individual power and thereby the temptation to ill treat his neighbour. And the oppressed are excluded from possessions and rebel in hostility. I have no concern with any economic criticisms of the communist system. I cannot enquire into whether the abolition of private property is expedient or advantageous. But I am able to recognize that the psychological premisses on which the system is based are an untenable illusion. In abolishing private property we deprive the human love of aggression of one of its instruments, certainly a strong one, though certainly not the strongest; but we have in no way altered the differences in power and influence which are misused by aggressiveness nor have we altered anything of its nature. Aggressiveness was not created by property. It reigned almost without limit in primitive times when property was still very scanty and it already shows itself in the nursery almost before property has given up its primal, anal form. It forms the basis of every relation of affection and love among people (with the single exception, perhaps, of the mother's relation to her male child).

If we do away with private property, there still remains prerogative in the field of sexual relationships. If this were removed through complete freedom of sexual life, abolishing the family, the germ-cell of civilization, we cannot, it is true, easily foresee what new paths the development of civilization could take. But one thing we can expect, and that is that this indestructible feature of human nature will follow it there.

Community love depends on aggression towards nonmembers. When once the Apostle Paul had posited universal love between men as the foundation of his Christian community, extreme intolerance on the part of Christendom towards those who remained outside it became the inevitable consequence. And it is intelligible that the attempt to establish a new, communist civilization in Russia should find its psychological support in the persecution of the bourgeois. One only wonders, with concern, what the Soviets will do after they have wiped out their bourgeois.

Clearly then civilization imposes such great sacrifices both on man's sexuality and on his aggressiveness. We see why he is not happy in civilization, for civilized man has exchanged a portion of his possibilities of happiness for a portion of security. But a criticism of the inadequacies of our civilization should not be interpreted as our being enemies of civilization. We may expect gradually to carry through such alterations in our civilization as will better satisfy our needs and will escape our criticism. But perhaps we may also familiarize ourselves with the idea that there are difficulties attaching to the nature of civilization which will not yield to any attempts at reform.

The inclination to aggression is an original, self subsisting, instinctual disposition in man and it constitutes the greatest impediment to civilization. What means does civilization employ to inhibit aggressiveness and even get rid of it? Individual anxiety. The individual is motivated to submit to outside authorities because as a child he is helpless and dependent. The threat of a loss of love becomes defined as what is 'bad' by the individual. His individual aggressiveness is therefore introjected, internalised, sent back to his own ego. His superego, acting against his own ego, becomes his conscience, acting in a way it would have liked to have acted on extraneous individuals. Anxiety, first from outside authorities, then from superego, is the cause of instinctual renunciations. Conscience is the result of instinctual renunciation, or that instinctual renunciation (imposed on us from without) creates the conscience which then demands further instinctual renunciation.

The price of civilization is our lost happiness through a heightened sense of guilt. It is probable that the sense of guilt produced by civilization is not perceived as such, remaining largely unconscious and it appears instead as a sort of malaise, a dissatisfaction for which people seek other motivations. And just as the individual evolves a conscience, so too the community evolves a super ego in the form of its ethics.

Today we are led to make two reproaches against the superego of the individual. In the severity of its commands and prohibitions it troubles itself too little about the happiness of the ego, in that it takes insufficient account of the resistance against obeying them – of the instinctual strength of the ID and of the difficulties presented by the real external environment. Consequently we are very often obliged, for therapeutic purposes, to oppose the super ego and we endeavour to lower its demands. Exactly the same objection can be made against the ethical demands of the cultural super ego. It too does not trouble itself enough about the facts of the mental constitution of human beings . . . it assumes that a man's ego is psychologically capable of anything that is required of it, that his ego has unlimited mastery over his id. This is a mistake.

And in his earlier work, *The Future of an Illusion* (1927), Freud had already dismissed Marxism as too optimistic an illusion because civilisation itself must be recognised as requiring coercion. The scientific analysis of the human mind showed that economic revolutions would not solve the problem of what man is.

Human civilization . . . presents . . . two aspects to the observer. It includes on the one hand all the knowledge and capacity that men have acquired in order to control the forces of nature and extract its wealth for the satisfaction of human needs, and on the other hand, all the regulations necessary in order to adjust the relations of men to one another and especially the distribution of the available wealth. The two trends of civilization are not independent of each other: firstly because the mutual relations of men are profoundly influenced by the amount of instinctual satisfaction which the existing wealth makes possible; secondly, because an individual man can himself come to function as wealth in relation to another one, in so far as the other person makes use of his capacity for work, or chooses him as a sexual object; and thirdly, moreover, because every individual is virtually an enemy of civilization, though civilization is supposed to be an object of universal human interest.

. . . One thus gets an impression that civilization is something which was imposed on a resisting majority by a minority which understood how to obtain possessions of the means to power and coercion. It is of course natural to assume that these difficulties are not inherent in the nature of civilization itself but are determined by the imperfections of the cultural forms which have so far been developed. And in fact it is not difficult to indicate these defects. One would think that a reordering of human relations should be possible which could remove the sources of dissatisfaction with civilization by renouncing coercion and the suppression of the instincts, so that undisturbed by internal discord, men might devote themselves to the acquisition of wealth and its enjoyment. That would be the golden age, *but it is questionable if such a state of affairs can be realized*. It seems rather that every civilization must be built upon coercion and renunciation of instinct; it does not even seem certain that if coercion were to cease, the majority of human beings would be prepared to undertake to perform the work necessary for acquiring new wealth . . . there are present in all men destructive and therefore antisocial and anticultural trends and that in a great number of people these are strong enough to determine their behaviour in human society.

Therefore an understanding of psychology is decisive. . . . Turning to the restrictions on certain oppressed classes in society, it is to be expected that these underprivileged classes will envy the favoured ones their privileges and will do all they can to free themselves from their own surplus privation. Where this is not possible, a permanent measure of discontent will persist within the culture concerned and this can lead to dangerous revolts. If however, a culture has not got beyond a point at which satisfaction of one portion of its participants depends on the suppression of another, and perhaps larger portion, and this is the case in all present day cultures, it is understandable that the suppressed people should develop an intense hostility towards a culture whose existence they make possible by their work but in whose wealth they have too small a share. In such conditions an internalization of the cultural prohibitions among the suppressed people is not to be expected. On the contrary, they are not prepared to acknowledge the prohibitions; they are intent on destroying the culture itself, and possibly even on doing away with the postulates on which it is based. It goes without saying that a civilization which leaves so large a number of its participants unsatisfied and drives them into revolt neither has nor deserves the prospect of a lasting existence.

For Freud, then, it was the progress of mental science rather than economics that could effect transformations rather than revolution in civilisation.

It is often said that Freud, as one of the great architects of our present conception of man, could not have existed without Darwin. It is also doubtful if he could have existed without Marx. Although there is no evidence that Freud read Marx in any serious way, he did respond to the Russian revolution and its apparent consequences during the late 1920s and he responded to what he took to be the communist model of man. He disagreed with it thoroughly. But the two men had much in common.

Freud, like Marx, saw the problem of alienation and its consequences as a primary aim of a scientific analysis of society. In different ways both men, in having identified this problem, sought its elimination. For Marx, conflict was the motive force in historical progress. For Freud, conflict was the motive force that enabled the child to become an adult. Conflict would end in Marx's communist society while, for Freud, conflict could only be contained, and with increasing pessimism Freud doubted even this. Both men presented a secular analysis of man in society, treating religion as an escapist fantasy which could be rationally understood. For Marx, religion was a symptom of socially alienated man; for Freud, it was a remnant of infantile behaviour that must be overcome in adult life. And just as Marx has been seen by some as the prophet of a new world religion, so too it has been claimed that Freud, as the prophetic founder of psychoanalysis, saw himself as a new Moses founding a religion in which the analyst was the priestly intercessor between the patient and his private demons.

Freud, like Marx, also believed that all men are naturally against the State. And through the development of the science of psychoanalysis, Freud's aim was to reconcile man with the world, himself and others. Both men observed a split between the private man and the public realm, but for Marx this was a condition that was characteristic of a specific moment in history; it was especially intense in capitalism. For Freud, it was a consequence of the universally tragic nature of man. Both men argued for the necessity to give up fantasies and illusions so that rationality would prevail in man's understanding of his home in the world among others. But where Marx believed optimistically that reason could and would triumph, Freud, the pessimist, underlined its unlikely victory. Both men saw themselves as scientists rather than philosophers, Marx as a social scientist, Freud as a scientist of the human mind. Both men criticised society in general and their own in particular, but where Marx insisted that criticism must lead to the violent transformation of external relations among men, Freud preached a personal, internal psychological revolution. Neither had any hopes in politics: for Marx, this meant there were no hopes in altering men's social conditions through legislative reforms or humanitarian ideals. For Freud, this meant that man's salvation was not fought out on the public stage but rather within himself. Marx was the external social changer, Freud the internal psychological realigner. If for Marx the realm of economics was to be investigated to produce a truly human life for all men, then for Freud it was the realm of psychological economics that determined whether an individual could be satisfactorily integrated into the world or not.

Michael Ignatieff says that Freud is usually regarded by Marxists as a bourgeois individualist who is deeply reactionary, not believing in revolution or in the possibility of massive social transformation. He did not believe that human beings could create a political system on earth that would redeem human nature. The Marxian claim, on the contrary, is that human nature is not finite or given. Rather it is historical. If you develop a just social system then you can change the human material out of which those systems are built. To the Freudian claim that you will never get rid of that seditious infant, Marxists say: 'Give me justice, bread, fairness and you will change those selfish, unregenerate human instincts and make a new man.' Freud, Michael Ignatieff continues, disagreed as profoundly as he could with the view that human nature was not fixed or imprisoned in a past so that it could be remade.

In his inheritance, Freud was a nineteenth-century liberal believing in constitutions and in what Marx disparagingly called bourgeois liberties. Marx heroically broke with bourgeois liberalism – with legal equality which hid the fact that some are socially more equal than others. This break with the limits of bourgeois liberalism was a break with the idea that the best human beings can hope for is a society in which individuals are protected from the State by an entrenched constitution and civil rights and legal protections. His objection to this idea was simply that it left the whole social inequality generated by the market untouched. Unless you moved to a society that redistributed wealth from the beginning, and redealt the cards, you would have the grotesque result of people who are formally equal in a legal sense but who remain socially unequal in their real lives. Michael Ignatieff insists that Marx wanted a society in which that contradiction between the formal freedom that a liberal society promises and the real inequalities it delivers was abolished.

Communism tried to do this. But, as some see it, the problem was that Marx's heirs did not pay any respect to constitutional rights at all. Nor did they envisage for one moment that the State itself would become the enemy of the people. What Marx could not foresee is that a communist state could become a source of oppression to its own people. Hence Michael Ignatieff says that Marx was indifferent to that whole liberal structure of protections, rights and guarantees that our constitutions erect against the power of the State. And he believed that the State would be an executive organ whose coercive aspects would wither away as social justice arrived. Michael Ignatieff believes that all that we have discovered is that communist power created the greatest State engine for the oppression of human beings the world has seen since the Pharoahs. It did so because communist societies never put any faith in the idea of bourgeois constitutions and liberties and protections.

Freud turned his back on this kind of wholesale external rational planning. Instead he focused within. When he was asked what were the requisites of a happy life he answered: 'Love and work'. He did not speak of a happy constitutional monarchy along British lines or effective civil liberties and equality before the law for all. Rather the child, the prepolitical antisocial child, is father to the man.

Marx had been criticised for not having sufficiently investigated either the development of personal identity or that factory of human character production, the family. In having addressed himself precisely to these areas, Freud supplemented and refined a critical discourse on society and the individual so that what were once the original insights of Marx and Freud have entered our common knowledge no matter where we lie on the political spectrum. In one sense or another, everyone of us today is a Marxist and a Freudian, even when we believe that aspects of their analysis of society and the individual have been falsified. This is because both men's ideas, in agreement or in opposition to one another, have set the agenda of much of the debate concerning how twentieth-century men and women are reconciled to living in society.

But are we the children of these two men still? Michael Ignatieff reminds us of a wonderful metaphor in the writings of the nineteenth-century German philosopher Hegel. It concerns an Owl which takes flight at dusk. Hegel uses it to describe the state of affairs, historically, when a doctrine is finishing, its effects petering out and it is losing its impact. And the Owl of History flies on to other perches and other destinations. It is now a century since Marx and Freud, those two nineteenth-century patriarchs, lived and described the conditions of men in that world. Perhaps now the Owl of Minerva is departing those theories and history is moving on to something else. It is too early to tell on which perch the Owl will alight. But she never flies backwards.

Neither will these two men's insights be forgotten utterly. It is not surprising that Freud, in particular, has been interpreted as a radical as well as a conservative. Certainly he has been used by the politically radical and conservative to support their respective and opposing views. But he also offends ideological totalitarians of both left and right, and unsurprisingly has been given a home with the liberal, intellectual middle class. He has held out hope for that cultured, perhaps overly socialised group of believers in a scientific method to exorcise the irrational, to rationalise it and thereby allow such people to take control of life within, rather than in opposition to, the State.

But as Karl Krauss once observed, psychoanalysis itself may have become the illness for which it purported to be a cure.

CHAPTER NINE

WOMEN

A nyone who was at university during the 1960s and who took a course in the history of political thought, read the great texts from Plato to Marx (or, more colloquially, from Plato to NATO), and learned a distinctive language and a progressive story about the recognition of individual human rights. The starting point was the ancient classical texts of Plato and Aristotle which spoke about the rational, good life for man. Aristotle said that by nature man was a political animal. His goal was a peculiarly human kind of happiness that could be achieved through political participation, publicly deciding on the 'common good' with friends and equals beyond the sphere of domestic and family relationships.

Family life was the necessary precursor to this good life. But, in addition, Aristotle's vision seemed so liberating, not least because it demanded that you think of yourself as a responsible person, potentially in control of your life, or at least so far as that is possible, given the circumstances into which you were born. Aristotle also held out an ideal of the active, articulate, rational but loving and generous life of political beings engaged in something better than merely surviving. He defined man as desirous of living well beyond merely living. He seemed concerned to elaborate on the conditions which enable people to realise their moral personalities among like-minded, reflective, socially concerned friends.

And if, as a female student, you had come across that passage in Aristotle's *Politics* where he says that women have no place in the public realm of the political, no place in making decisions that affect the common good beyond the family, because Aristotle believed that women possessed reason but not in an 'authoritative' way, you simply thought of him as a silly little ancient Greek. And anyway,

Aristotle was even more offensive in his racist remarks about non-Greeks whom he called barbarians.

Turning to the texts of the mid- and late seventeenth-century you felt even more at home, with a language that sounded very modern. It assumed that individuals were born free and equal and that governments were instituted among men, deriving their just powers from the consent of the governed. You assumed that, by this time, where the Rights of Man were discussed, 'man' was the generic term for human being.

You found the eighteenth-century Jean-Jacques Rousseau sympathetic not least because he began his famous *Social Contract* with the words that strike a chord with most adolescents: 'Man is born free but is everywhere in chains...How did this change come about? I do not know. What can make this change legitimate? I believe I can resolve this question.' Since the text was in an English translation you were not particularly sensitive to the French which used the masculine noun *l'homme* for those who were born free. You read the asides in Rousseau's *Discourse on the Inequality of Men* where he notes that woman's role is to stay at home, tend the hut and the children and educate her men to virtuous citizenship, but never was she to enter that sphere herself. The temptation was to dismiss him as 'Silly little neurotic Rousseau', knowing how he was tossed from pillar to post, and how he argued with everyone, put his children in a home for orphans where they would surely die, and sought a home for himself in Geneva, France, for a time even in England.

But then during the 1970s feminist scholars began systematically to comb the classical texts of political theory. They alleged a persistent gender bias across the centuries. They assembled a gloomy catalogue of evidence for a continuing tradition of misogynist rhetoric, a rhetoric to which Virginia Woolf had already alluded in *A Room of One's Own* in the 1930s. Why, she asked, are all these men so angry, so dismissive of women, so careful to delineate just what female characteristics naturally exclude women from that sphere of life beyond husband and children? But few feminist scholars seemed to show that this catalogue seriously affected the over-all theories that the great texts were propounding. And so, without any convincing analysis of *why* there were such descriptions of women as incapable of political engagement, you simply read beyond these passages in order to get at the *pure theory* which appeared sexually neutral in terms of its message.

But the 1980s have seen a new development. We are now taken through passages in the standard theorists and shown how the arguments shift subtly from claims about individuals of unspecified sex, to claims which could be and were only made of male individuals. Today we are left in no doubt that the individuals described in liberal and socialist accounts of freedom and equality of individuals from the seventeenth century onwards are *male* individuals. From the seventeenth century onwards we have been proclaiming the Rights of Man but we have meant the rights of *men*.

Of course, if this has been the case in the major texts of political theory, we have known it to be true 'on the ground'. In Britain, women over 30 only got the vote in 1918. And this has led to a number of women arguing that the very idea and reality of the State is and has been a construction that is exclusively male and that it suits a masculine way of organising the world to their own advantage, or at least to the advantage of more powerful men. Some have tried to examine whether the so-called separate realm of the political is somehow in conflict with what it has always meant, throughout history, to be female. Others have insisted that the very language of rights and obligations, of contract and governance, is an implicitly gendered language. And some have even argued that what men define as fairness and justice is different from how women define these key terms in social life.

Women have begun to ask the questions that men seem to have been asking and answering for centuries, and some women are now providing their own answers. Two of the most prominent questions asked are: Is there a natural difference between men and women that actually matters beyond the respective, specialised role of men and women in sexual productivity? Is there a woman's realm that is somehow naturally different from the man's realm – is hers private and his public? The answers to these questions are varied. But most women seem to have come to the conclusion that the private or sexual sphere of human relations is just as *political* as the public realm and that neither area of human activity is necessarily the exclusive preserve of either sex. It means that what we are, and always have been, talking about in both 'spheres' is relationships of power and dependency. Such relationships are not natural but the consequences of the ways we have 'chosen' to arrange our economic and emotional lives.

For both men and women, the turning of the key in the lock to that place called home and family is not, sadly, equivalent to 'getting off the world' and entering a space of security, relaxation and trust, which has nothing to do with the public world. The State has always invaded the so-called private sphere and, indeed, has been active in preserving what it finds there. Many women today seem aware that the implicit if not explicit interference of the State, the political, the public realm, in the so-called private sphere, whether well intentioned or manipulative, has effectively left women holding the sharp end of the stick and largely to their disadvantage.

If we are to try to explain what current feminist positions mean and why some women believe that there has been a distinctively Western, liberal, capitalist concern to edit women out of a shared history, it is important to trace the origin and developments of our idea of the modern State. There have always been some women against the State. We can see why if we examine how the Western, liberal tradition seeks to explain the creation of *civil* society from an original, politically unorganised 'state of nature'.

Once it was accepted that individuals were born free and equal to each other, and this was made most clear during the seventeenth century, then none of the old arguments for civil subordination as a natural condition could be accepted. No longer could one argue that some men were born to rule and others to be ruled. As Carole Pateman has recently argued in *The Sexual Contract*:

> Arguments that rulers and masters exercised their power through God's will had to be rejected; might or force could no longer be translated into political right; appeals to custom and tradition were no longer sufficient; nor were the various arguments from nature, whether they looked to the generative power of the father, or to superior birth, strength, ability or rationality. All these familiar arguments became unacceptable because the doctrine of individual freedom and equality entailed that there was only one justification for subordination. A naturally free and equal individual must, necessarily *agree* to be ruled by another. The creation of civil mastery and civil subordination must be voluntary; such relationships can be brought into being in one way only, through agreement. There are a variety of forms of free agreement but . . . contract has become paradigmatic of voluntary agreement (pp. 39–40).

Contract theorists of the seventeenth and eighteenth centuries like Thomas Hobbes, John Locke and Jean-Jacques Rousseau argued that both sexes were naturally free and equal, and yet they also insisted that men's right over women has a natural basis. While relations of political subordination between *men* as heads of households must originate in a contract to which individual men consent if subordination to civil authority, and thereby the creation of the State, is to be legitimate, women are somehow 'born into' subjection. What did this mean?

When theorists described the 'natural' characteristics of individuals they wrote as though these were common to all humans. But they also held that natural capacities were sexually differentiated. The consequence of this two-pronged argument is that women, in the natural state before the formation of any political society, actually always agree to subordinate themselves to men; they agree to become servants through the marriage contract by which they voluntarily hand over their rights and forfeit the individual privilege of the franchise. Through men's conjugal mastery the wife is subsumed beneath her husband and is thereby excluded from becoming a civil individual herself and in her own right. And yet the marriage contract is the only one into which women can enter freely. Paradoxically, despite there being a contract made which presumes the existence of two free parties, the sphere of family and marriage is not to be considered part of the political sphere. What goes on in the family is not the State's concern. The separate realms of private and public are, in truth, not natural but established by conventions that assume that the 'natural' family is pre-political. Ironically, the State, a product of voluntary contract between equals, conserves the family as something outside the State. From this theory, and its positive enactment in law, we get what we today call the separate realms of the private and public, the former inhabited by children and women, the latter inhabited by a freely constituted fraternity of men.

At the heart of the scenario where individuals make contracts is the notion that individuals recognise each other as property owners by making mutual use of or exchanging their property. But what is exchanged in the marriage contract? Carole Pateman argues that obedience is exchanged for protection, and the peculiarity of this exchange is that one party to the contract, who provides protection, has the right to determine how the other party will act to fulfil her side of the exchange. What is the incentive that motivates a woman to enter this kind of exchange? We need only point to prevailing social inequality where the weak party agrees to protection because effectively she has no choice. There is an uncomfortable resemblance to a slave contract here. Suddenly that awful image of 'lying back and thinking of England, or the new fridge' comes to mind!

Small shifts in this argument were developed during the nineteenth century. If an individual who is weak or prevented from earning a wage that is adequate to keep him or her alive voluntarily agrees to enter a slave contract, seeing it as to his or her advantage, then by so doing, as J. S. Mill, the English philosopher and economist, pointed out, 'he abdicates his liberty; he foregoes any future use of it beyond that single act. He therefore defeats, in his own case, the very purpose which is the justification of allowing him to dispose of himself . . . The principle of freedom cannot require that he should be free *not* to be free. It is not freedom to be allowed to alienate his freedom.' But when J. S. Mill went on to apply his argument to the marriage contract and the subjection of women, he found that he was not widely supported.

If, according to J. S. Mill, no free individual can make a contract that denies his or her own freedom, and any contract that creates a relationship of subordination is invalid, then how had the sexual contract escaped consideration? Here theory gave place to reality. As capitalism grew in sophistication and the Industrial Revolution separated the workplace from the household, women were increasingly deprived of an economic basis for independence.

In seventeenth-century Britain, especially in Puritan households, wives were subordinate to their husbands but they were not necessarily economic dependants. The small independent farm or family business, where family members worked side by side, had a place for the wife as inferior partner. Married women were allowed to trade and were often engaged in a wide variety of occupations. But as crafts became more intensively capitalised the wives of wealthier tradesmen no longer worked in the business. They moved indoors and the external world of work became the realm of men. By the middle of the nineteenth century, as a consequence of an increasing separation of the workplace and home, the wife had become a full-time housewife among the 'respectable' middle class, or more accurately, she was an upper servant in the home directing lower servants. For the middle class, this situation of '*er indoors* was already clear in the eighteenth century where 'not to work' became the mark of such women's class superiority, precisely at a time when for their men, work – what his skills were worth in the capitalised market – was a criterion of dignity and value. In her book *Women, Resistance and Revolutions*, Sheila Rowbotham has noted that 'as bourgeois man justified himself through work, asserting his own industry and usefulness against the idea of aristocratic leisure, his woman's life was becoming increasingly useless. Bourgeois women did not make capitalism, they merely attached themselves to its makers and lived off their man's activity' (p. 29).

Over two centuries, then, women who had been initially engaged in family businesses, in brewing, medicine, surgery and midwifery, were either excluded from such professions or their crafts were downgraded.

The distinguished lawyer Sir William Blackstone (1723–80) could therefore speak about the consequences of the marriage contract in the eighteenth century in the following terms: 'By marriage, the husband and wife are one person in law; that is, the very being or legal existence of the woman is suspended during the marriage or at least is incorporated into that of the husband under whose wing, protection and cover, she performs everything and is therefore called . . . a feme-covert . . . her husband (being called) her baron or lord.'

Behind the eighteenth-century State's legal definition of the civil person (a definition that accurately mirrored economic realities of independence and dependence) another argument was kept alive. It seemed to explain why economic and legal relations had developed as they had done. This was the argument based on the idea that the physical differences between men's and women's bodies led to a moral differentiation. Aristotle's analysis of female capacities and incapacities, measured against those of males, was repeated and elaborated upon by Jean-Jacques Rousseau. He said that women, unlike men, could not control their unlimited desires by themselves. Hence they could not develop the morality that is required in civil society. Men, according to Rousseau, control their passions through their reason, while women lack the capacity to sublimate their passions and so are a perpetual source of disorder. This is the reason why they have always been, and must continue to be, subjected to the judgements and the rule of men.

Furthermore, the analysis goes, women's attachments remain particularised. Unlike men they have no capacity to universalise their sentiments away from the little world of family. They cannot develop a sense of fraternity among people who are not related to them. Therefore women's and men's bodies do not have the same political meaning. Indeed, women's bodies have no political meaning at all. Women represent what is natural and prior to the political. The original contract which creates the political order presupposes that passion and partiality can be constrained by reason, and reason is a characteristic of males alone. The State is undoubtedly created by men and for men. In Lord Chesterfield's words, women are merely 'children of a larger growth'!

The legacy of this sexual analysis of personality lives on in the plausible story of a well-known Oxford don of an earlier generation who carefully asked his young men students what they *thought* about a particular issue and his young women what they *felt* about it.

What this means is that the development of political theory and its judicial reflection in Western, liberal, capitalist societies from the seventeenth century onwards tells a story of how men created the modern State from the original contract. This tells us that the legitimate State is an artificial body, the body politic of civil society, 'the artificial *man* we call the commonwealth', as Thomas Hobbes said. The State is a creation of reason and agreement. Of course, the original contract to create the body politic is *not* to be understood as a real, historical event. The State should be understood *as if* it had its origins in an original contract agreed to by free and equal individual men. So that when we speak of the origins of the modern State today, we mean this Western model based on a fictional contract theory. The place such contract theory gives to the marriage contract is culturally and historically specific. As Carole Pateman points out,

> exogamous marriage may or may not be a universal feature of human social life, but its social meaning does not remain unchanged across history or across cultures. In particular, marriage and the kinship alliances established through the 'exchange of women' occupy a different place in the traditional societies [from which anthropologists and ethnographers draw their data, from the place it occupies in the modern State]. Traditional societies are structured by kinship relations, but the move from the state of nature . . . to *civil* society is a move into a social order in which 'kinship' is sloughed off into its own separate, private sphere and reconstituted as the modern family. The story of the original contract tells of the genesis of a

society that is structured into two spheres – although we are usually told only half the story and so we only hear about the origin of the public 'universal' sphere, that of the State (p. 112).

This, then, is history, *his* story. But what, then, is *her* story? In *Persuasion*, Jane Austin famously acknowledged that the pen has always been in men's hands. But women's voices can be heard from the past. None the less, some think that 'herstory' cannot be told because when women spoke in the past their language and ideas were formed by patriarchy; they simply mouthed the 'truths' men told them were true. But Professor Janet Todd, Professor of English at the University of East Anglia, believes that if one is prepared to listen to what women have actually been saying, rather than what one would wish them to say, then one can slowly build up a 'herstory', even if it is not the story one might want to hear because it is so filled with collusions and adaptations.

Actually, there is no *beginning* of feminism as a beginning of women's defiance but there are historical moments when women resisted the social conditions in which they found themselves. Professor Todd believes that modern feminism can be traced back to the seventeenth and eighteenth centuries in England, especially to the dissenting religious movements on the one hand and then as a consequence of the Enlightenment on the other.

From the seventeenth century onwards numerous efforts were made to achieve religious and civic toleration for Protestant nonconformist churches that did not adhere to the Church of England. And it was significant that the Quakers and Shakers (for example, Mother Ann Lee of Manchester) in the seventeenth century allowed women to speak and preach in ways that no other sects did. If every individual should aspire to a direct communion with God, and God dwelt in every human being, then according to Puritans, women and men were to be considered equal in their spiritual search. Within self-governing Puritan communities, women found a limited equality and some scope for self-expression in a religious grouping that proclaimed the priesthood of *all* believers. The Quaker George Fox believed that male domination belonged to sin. In the new life men and women would be equals. Individuals were independent owners of their own persons and capacities. Hence they also possessed a right of resistance to any violation of the same.

Thereafter in the eighteenth century women like Mary

Wollstonecraft and her friend Mary Hayes argued against the Established Church, suggesting that women might speak out more openly on religious topics as they could in those sects outside the Church of England. But Wollstonecraft was also influenced by the general cultural and political movement of the time across Europe, known as the Enlightenment, a movement that emphasised the seminal role of reason in explaining man to himself and in supporting those efforts that would produce a more rational State. In her *Vindication of the Rights of Woman* (1792) Wollstonecraft saw immediately that the Rights of Man did not include women, and she set about adapting them for women. Women, she said, should have access to institutions dominated by men and especially access to education. Professor Todd reminds us that she suggested that they might even have access to government. Intellectually, women and men were to be considered equal and, for the purposes of the State and its institutions, women should be considered identical with men. She was claiming for women, as one half of the human race, 'the virtues of humanity'.

Wollstonecraft was immensely sensitive to the problem of language itself. When she started writing, Professor Todd says, she originally wrote 'The Rights of Men' and then became aware that women were not included in that generic word 'men' or 'man'. She then proceeded to write 'The Rights of Woman' and she had a great deal of trouble with pronouns. She found that she had to keep talking about 'the Being and its Life' to avoid the gendered pronoun his or her. And she wrote the *Vindication* in six weeks, believing, as did other radicals, that human character was formed from environment. Hence the necessity of changing women's environment so that no woman need show an 'outward obedience and a scrupulous attention to a puerile kind of propriety' in order to be a momentary source of pleasure for men. As might be expected of a woman of her class, Wollstonecraft suggested an orderly, methodical education that would equip middle-class women to take an active part in industrial capitalism.

Wollstonecraft was, however, a relatively lone voice in the eighteenth century. And it is sad to consider that the response to her feminist writings was far less than the degree to which her own personal and unhappy life – she had an illegitimate child – was held up to scrutiny: 'her whoredoms were known enough'! The contempt for any kind of apparently feminist statement took the form of either sexual abuse or the belittling of women into 'the fair sex' who should be hurried back to the boudoir as quickly as possible.

Other women who argued for women's rights wanted to change the State in order to make it more suitable for women to enter it. Most, however, decided that patriarchy was too powerful to fight with any success. Instead, they adopted the tactic of trying to influence the public sphere by emphasising the uniquely bene- volent, perhaps even irrational and certainly non-dominant aspects of so-called female nature which gave them a specially moral rather than logical role to play in influencing the State, without being politically active within it. This developed into a notion that women were actually morally superior to men precisely at a time when an increasing emphasis was placed on an exclusively domestic role for women. If the soul and the mind *were* gendered then some women came to believe they had a unique, moral role to play in society. But was their moral voice only to be heard in the kitchen or the boudoir? The rigid divide between the roles of men and women, formulated during the eighteenth century, was to be restated during the Vic- torian period.

One of the ways in which middle-class women expressed the notion of exaggerated separate spheres for men and women was to write novels that were concerned with communities of women who cared for the poor and the ill and which provided a framework for themselves. Often these fantasies took the form of colleges or insti- tutions that were projected outside male institutions in which women could develop intellectually apart from men. Usually these communities of women had a sort of flamboyant chastity about them where men had no role to play at all. By the mid-eighteenth century such fantasies were even more defensive. They depicted refuges for women who had had a bad time in the world. And they stressed the caring, benevolent aspects of women. When, in some of these stories, a man entered as an observer, he was shown to be so amazed and impressed by the way the women were behaving and acting, the way they governed their small world, that he would go off with the intent of trying to convey a bit of this to the masculine world and to set up an equivalent community.

If a number of early feminists were influenced by the French Revolution and the Enlightenment, they rapidly realised that the cry for liberty, equality and fraternity (not sorority) had little to do with them. The notion of justice for women was almost non-existent in this period, because women's relationship to the law was a very tenuous thing. As Wollstonecraft said, 'it is justice not charity that is wanting in the world'. Professor Todd reminds us that all of this comes back to the problem of marriage. If, as Sir William Blackstone said in his *Commentaries on the Laws of England*, woman was subsumed into the man upon marriage, then woman after marriage had no existence before the law. She was civilly dead. She could not pursue her own case if she were married. And numerous women writers who might not even be considered early feminists at all, like Mary Astell, wrote about the injustices of marriage. She also asked in her *A Serious Proposal to the Ladies* (1694): 'how can you be content to be in the world like Tulips in a garden, to make a fine show and be good for nothing?' She too gathered round her a group of privileged women in support of a female academy. Lady Mary Wortley Montague expressed the misery of being an intellectual woman when culture dictated that she be a domestic being with few intellectual pursuits. Separatist communities were, therefore, frequent fantasies for the liberation of the female, especially in England where the Catholic convent was no option for Protestant women.

Professor Todd says that among those women writers who were not feminists, one sees a great deal of effort going into supporting the idea of 'the moral woman' and on making women put up with the status quo. The majority of women writers had taken up this position. And Professor Todd believes that in some ways this more conservative writing suggests an even bleaker picture of patriarchy than the one presented by more radical, feminist works. They very rarely say that women will joyfully go into marriage and put up with their subordination. What they do say is that it is a bleak world, that it is difficult and miserable, but a woman must enter it. There are extraordinary metaphors for this need for women to subordinate themselves. People like Jane West and Hannah More, writing at the same time as Mary Wollstonecraft but absolutely supporting the patriarchal status quo, none the less describe the entry of women into the marriage contract as a sort of entry into hell. The alternatives were the wretched life of the spinster or the social disgrace of sexual indiscretion and prostitution.

The poet, Percy Bysshe Shelley, Mary Wollstonecraft's son-in-law, took up this thread when, in *Queen Mab*, he wrote, 'Can man be free if woman be a slave?' He went further and argued that relationships should be freely contracted and freely dissolved.

'Love withers under constraint'. The institution of the marriage bond is an intolerable oppression. And because the personal and the public are always linked, 'not even the intercourse of the sexes is exempt from the despotism of positive institution'.

But the marriage contract was only one issue in a broad canvas of complaint at the beginning of the nineteenth century. As Sarah Perrigo, who lectures in Politics at Bradford University, tells us, the early feminist movement in the nineteenth century picked up on the discourse of rights, a discourse that was prominent among all groups in society that were excluded from citizenship. The right to vote and the right to participate in public society was demanded by all those excluded, some men and all women. As the public sphere expanded and larger numbers of men were given the rights of citizenship, first granted to middle-class men, those still excluded argued for further extensions of civil and political rights.

The right to vote was talked about quite early on in the 1850s and 1860s among a small group of middle-class intellectual women who usually came from liberal, intellectual backgrounds with families who supported liberal ideals and equal citizenship for all. But if the mid-century feminists demanded the vote, they also realised that the vote was probably going to be quite a long struggle and that there were other rights that women required that would enable them to prove themselves worthy of citizenship. The rights to education were uppermost. Public education was expanding for middle-class boys through public schools. But girls were excluded from this general educational expansion, being educated at home, if at all, and to be no more than wives and mothers. Earning a living, earning wages, was seen as something highly undesirable for middle-class, respectable Victorian women. The middle-class feminists were concerned to see themselves as highly respectable in their demands for something that was completely rational. Sarah Perrigo notes how they went out of their way not to offend and tried to court liberal opinion. When middle-class men got the vote in 1832 (and by 1864 those men called the Aristocracy of Labour also got the vote) they argued that it was only logical that women should no longer be excluded.

The logic of this argument did not impress many men. And the feminists soon discovered an immense opposition to all of their demands. Education was not to be opened to them, and the opposition of the universities to admitting women to courses, particularly in subjects like medicine, was enormous. Only 150 years ago, Perrigo reminds us, those early pioneers for women who were studying medicine in Edinburgh were stoned by students and their professors as they went to their classes. Indeed women had to wait well into this century before they were recognised as eligible for a university degree from Oxford and Cambridge, although they had studied at one of the women's colleges. Middle-class women wanted the same rights as men of the same social class. But some of them wanted to go further, to use the vote to transform politics altogether and to transform the State, to feminise the public world and to create an ethical polity. Some saw themselves as part of an androgynous society where at least in the public world men and women would have equal rights. Hence some argued that the private and public spheres, the civilly dead and civilly alive spheres, had been created by social conditioning and by a lack of women's education – all in the interests of men. For those who did not believe that men and women were the same, the argument was put forward that women's moral superiority must be used to moralise the public sphere, to curb evils like alcohol abuse, violence, prostitution and general sexual excesses that were seen as the product of what they called unbridled masculinity.

Behind this argument was a more general moral condemnation of industrialised capitalism. From the first quarter of the nineteenth century small groups of radical men and women called into question the general political corruption and the economic basis of a society of mills, factories, industry, competition and money-making in Britain. From this moral criticism of social evils emerged a number of movements that focused on the ways in which industrial capitalism denied the possibility of truly human relations. A new kind of freedom in work, government and love was demanded and attempts were made to set up cooperative societies, sympathetic to the needs of women, which would be serious alternatives to the prevailing competitive society. In the 1820s, Robert Owen established factories that were collectively owned and where domestic drudgery – cooking, washing, the heating of rooms – was distributed equally among workers.

Once again the institution of marriage was attacked. William Thompson noted that 'each man yokes a woman to his establishment and calls it a contract'. 'Home', he said, 'is the eternal prisonhouse of the wife. The husband paints it as the abode of calm bliss, but takes care to find outside of doors, for his own use, a species of bliss not quite so calm, but of more varied and stimulating description.' He urged men and women to struggle for an alternative society, one where men would be secure in their jobs and not fear the economic competition of women. Such a society would be one of cooperators. It would be socialist, which did not mean a return to some idyllic, rural bliss, but would ensure that workers owned the means of production and shared in the profits of production.

This makes it clear that the voice of middle-class feminists was to some degree in conflict with a feminism that was included in working-class socialist experiments. The former sought acceptance from the middle-class world, while the latter sought an alternative world completely.

If working-class women did not become involved in what might be termed feminist politics until the end of the nineteenth century, there was a movement early on in the nineteenth century that was part and parcel of utopian socialism. It was concerned with the restructuring of society and included equality for women. Feminism was integral to their socialist vision, a vision which sought to end the development of capitalism and to transform it into a socialist society. To the name of Owen we can add those of Fourier and Saint Simon in France. They criticised all aspects of what they saw as domination, hierarchy and subordination that were integral to industrial capitalism. And for them the family was a crucial *locus* for the development of authoritarianism, submission and tyranny. If the new human being was to be created then the family had to be transformed in socialism. They looked to the issues of monogamy and marriage and advocated destroying monogamy so that women were not owned by men. Fourier argued that the change in any historical epoch can always be determined by the progress of women towards freedom. In the relation of women to men, of the weak to the strong, one sees the victory of human nature over brutality. 'The degree of emancipation of women is the natural measure of general emancipation'. Since, for Fourier, there was always a connection between economics and sexual oppression, he argued for the setting-up of cooperative communities where both sexes were equal and the women economically independent of men. Children were to be brought up cooperatively and women were to be educated not only to domesticity but to political participation.

The organisation of work was to be determined by individual preferences and talent; individuals were to contribute to the collective society by doing what they enjoyed doing, such enjoyment being determined by Fourier's elaborate analysis of character types. Utopian socialists coupled the demand for the emancipation of the wage earner with the demand for women's emancipation.

But they did not have the methodical economic analysis of society that would later be provided by Marx. Their experiments, where tried, were successful for a relatively brief period. But their wisdom disappeared in the 1840s and 1850s in Britain with the development of the Labour Movement which sought to be integrated into industrial society rather than to fight against it.

The textile industry in the north of England became a centre for the development of socialism and women played an unusually strong role here. Sarah Perrigo says that textiles was the one area where married women worked and became involved in a whole series of reforms concerning working women. Lancashire women continued to work after marriage and they were practically the only group of women in the country who did so, full time. Elsewhere working women were not visible, doing the slop work, the outwork, charring and cleaning, to earn money but they did not appear in the statistics. And the Mill Girls were the only significant number of women who were organised in trades unions. They were closely integrated into the development of the Labour Movement: the weavers' union comprised two women to every man. In Lancashire and Yorkshire a form of ethical socialism developed which debated the same issues that middle-class feminists were raising. By the 1890s socialists and feminists combined to look for much more than just votes for women.

By 1901 when the Labour Party was set up and the textile unions were affiliated to the Labour Representation Committee, trades unions were expected to pay a fee to the Labour fund. The textile women recognised the irony of having to donate money every week to a fund that would get Labour *men* into Parliament. Many women therefore supported the suffrage movement, and the National Union of Women Suffrage Societies had one of its major headquarters in Manchester. The women in mill towns would meet and hear women coming from Manchester to speak about female suffrage.

Sarah Perrigo reminds us that in addition to the vote, these women also had to deal with a general hostility from trades unions themselves towards working married women. The unions had adopted the middle-class ideal of women being at home, doing domestic tasks and not being forced into competition with men. The trade union movement, outside of textiles, had organised to exclude women along with unskilled male workers. From this opposition came the demands to the same rights to organise and protect themselves at work as their men.

Many women who were active in socialism accepted the Marxist analysis of society which insisted that the liberation of women was dependent on the emancipation of working-class men. Working women were not women so much as proletarians. Working-class families had been broken up by the capitalist factory system and the move into industrialised towns. Marxist sociology concentrated on work relations rather than on family relations. The working-class family was seen as the cellular form of civilised society so that only with the change in society would the family be altered and the relation of men and women changed. Engels, Marx's collaborator, wrote in *The Origin of the Family* that

> the first class opposition that occurs in history coincides with the development of antagonism between man and woman in monogamous marriage, and the first class oppression coincides with that of the female sex by the male. Monogamous marriage was a great historical step forward; nevertheless, together with slavery and private wealth it opens the period that has lasted until today in which every step forward is also relatively a step backwards, in which property and development for some is won through the misery and frustration of others. It is the cellular form of civilised society in which the nature of the oppositions and contradictions fully acting in that society can be already studied.

Engels argued that middle-class women were oppressed in a particular way because they had been transformed, through marriage, into the private property of their husbands. But he insisted that proletarian women had no need of the middle-class feminist movement because their interest was a class interest. The working-class family, not being structured around private property, meant that working men and women were united in their interest as workers. Engels believed that capitalism would increasingly drag women into production and work and thereby proletarianise them, breaking up the family completely. Although he did refer to the brutality of proletarian men towards their wives, he thought this was a legacy of the bourgeois ideology about male superiority and that it would disappear with the Revolution, where children and domestic work would be socialised. Women did not have different interests from men. Slavery had been eliminated. Thereafter, the elimination of private property and the elimination of economic dependence of women on men required a proletarian consciousness of the workers' situation.

There was no specific sense in which women as agents could change the relations of production. Not only was reproduction not seen as part of the material world or as a determining factor in history. Sheila Rowbotham has argued that Marxist sociology forgets 'that we see the world through relations in the family, describe it in a language first learned in the family and through eyes which grew accustomed to other human beings first in the family'.

But the situation that was described in which the working-class family survived pointed to the effective elimination of the working-class family at the same time that 'family' was being idealised in middle-class circles. For the mid-Victorian middle-class family, the household was seen as the final refuge for all those human qualities that were unable to survive in the outside world of free-market capitalism. The family was preserved as the abode of true human feeling where the woman was confined in order to enable her man to be himself and to bolster him in his forays into the world of work. In return, he protected her from the harsh world in exchange for his home being a haven of peace. This ideal is still with us. But who lives it?

Hence one of the reasons women were denied the vote by nineteenth-century conservatives and some liberals was that women did not and ought not to fight in defence of their country. The argument that rebutted this was that liberal, civilised society was not based on 'might makes right'. Contract theory from the seventeenth century onwards had insisted that government was not a consequence of might but rather was created by a voluntary agreement made by free and equal individuals.

If contract theory is the bedrock of our modern State and through *very* recent laws has consciously included women in that generic term *man*, then is the State still to be seen as a male construct and are there women who are still against the State?

In what Sarah Perrigo calls the second wave of the women's

movement, one of the major feminist claims has been that women as women actually operate in ways that are different from the ways in which men organise themselves. They do not set up bureaucracies and hierarchies. They are much more radically democratic. The feminist movement, in fact, in Sarah Perrigo's view, does not have an organised structure; it has no leaders, no stars and, by implication, no palace coup. It has much in common with libertarian socialist theory which speaks about the need to organise in radically democratic ways where everyone is equal and everyone is heard. And it is non-violent. It does not divide the world into the private and public spheres. The private sphere, so called, is just as penetrated with power relations as is the so-called public, and each sphere is a product not of nature but of convention. The personal is political. The feminists have therefore been very critical of the State and its part in conserving the middle-class family while it pretends that this family is outside the State and outside politics. The State's laws prop up the nuclear family and yet it refuses to intervene in the private sphere which conserves the relationships of subordination and domination between men and women. The police and legal institutions, Sarah Perrigo emphasises, seem most reluctant to involve themselves in 'domestic disputes' and women therefore remain vulnerable to men in the family. The family, as we know it, however, is not a biologically necessary and natural entity but rather an historical institution that has changed in enormous ways. Today's family of husband, wife and children probably only has a history of some 200 years, if that.

Furthermore, some feminists, both in the nineteenth century and today, have argued that violence and militarism, which are at the heart of the modern State, are essentially masculine characteristics. Others insist that there are no sexually differentiated social characteristics, and that men are not violent and women pacific by nature, but rather that these are socially constructed characteristics. But generally, feminists of all persuasions argue that the State is organised in ways that conserve male power and most specifically is interested in fortifying a particular image of family which ensures the subservience of women. Where Marxism challenged the liberal definition of what politics is and whose class interest it served, feminism widens this out and argues that there is nothing that is not political. No area of life is free from power domination and this is why so many people find feminism so uncomfortable. To suggest that something like love or personal relationships between men and women are political or that families are political, means that none of us has any refuge.

The wide spectrum of feminist challenges to the State ranges from the reformers to the more revolutionary desire either for complete social transformation or for complete separation. If we really had equal opportunity, Sarah Perrigo insists, then this would mean that 50 per cent of judges, 50 per cent of MPs, 50 per cent of all groups who have power and authority in our society would have to be women. Once you begin to think in these terms then the whole nature of the private/public relationship, the relationship of the family and reproduction to the public sphere of work would be totally transformed. Work would have to be organised around domestic responsibilities and the ways in which both men and women integrate their personal lives into the world of work. Child-care responsibilities would be responsibilities for parents and not simply for women. Public institutions would have to be reorganised around the family rather than the other way round. The serious question about the quality of life would be answered in terms of a radiation outwards from the place of loving relationships. The only reason it is easy for men to have that so-called higher life of public engagement and responsibility, so dear to the Greeks, is because women have provided the necessary preconditions. And the sad irony is that for most men who are not massively successful, life from nine to five is not a fulfilling realm of activity. Life begins after work if there is any energy left for it. And the family becomes the arena where vent is given to public frustrations precisely because most men have little power over the directions of their lives at work. Economically dependent women at home have even less over theirs.

This means that feminism spreads right across ideologies, be they of the capitalist State, the social democratic State or the communist State. In all States, women, as they increasingly enter the workforce, have found themselves working full time and then coming home to do the cooking, cleaning, shopping and taking care of the children. In the 1970s in America there was a great rush of enthusiasm for women who 'did it all'. Superwoman. But can anyone do it all? And who wants to do it all? Suddenly it was realised that in order for successful women to be both mothers and career women, they had to spend their salaries hiring other women to do the domestic work for which they themselves had neither taste nor time. What has been replicated on a much larger scale is the old aristocratic situation where children are cared for by nannies. The sexual division of labour in the home has not changed: women step in for other women. And ambitious professional men and women may not seriously know who their children *are*.

Perhaps Scandinavia has been most progressive in producing the kind of welfare legislation that provides paternity rights for men and deals more adequately with women's economic dependence on men. Some feminists have argued, however, that what Scandinavia has actually done is to remove women's economic dependence on individual men and place it on the State. Women are totally reliant on the State in order to be equal in the public sphere. But there has been an attempt to provide facilities that are not just for women but rather for parents who care for children. The State has been used to transform attitudes to private responsibilities on the part of both sexes. And women have transformed the State by putting women's issues on the agenda to show that they are general issues, not gender issues. At the same time those issues like transport, economics and defence, which at present are seen as issues that have nothing to do with gender, are shown to have a gender dimension in that they affect women differently from the ways they affect men.

If feminism says anything to the State of the 1990s it is that there is a need to democratise and decentralise the State. There is a need to depaternalise the State and to establish welfare services that are not simply passively consumed but are the result of the active participation of consumers – men and women – as citizens participating fully in society. Social services are there, or ought to be there, because they belong to the people who use them and are, or ought to be, controlled by the users. Rather than the State providing, there is a need for the collective society to provide. And that collective society is made up of both men and women, sometimes with very different needs. Mrs Thatcher may believe that there is no such thing as society, but for feminists, society is really all there is. And if society is really there, then the political universe as we have come to know it is in need of change. As Dr Joni Lovenduski, Director of the Centre for European Research at Loughborough University, points out, the political universe, the public administration and the organisations of politics, have been developed by men of a certain class for their convenience and they operate in ways that are comfortable for those men. She believes we are talking of a kind of politics that is class politics, gender politics and race politics, that has to do with privilege. There are some characteristics of this kind of politics that might be pointed to, such as a certain kind of assertive speech-making and the demagogic style of politics, that of course is not necessarily exclusively male. Women can learn to adopt these characteristics, as we have seen in recent political life. Further, you need to have a very loud and particular kind of deep voice which carries in particular chambers. Women tend not to have them; these chambers were not designed for them. And the laws and policies that have been made by political institutions have never favoured women, or even realised they were there. The State is not particularly sensitised to the fact that it has women clients. Its institutions do not contain very many women and some women say that if you go into them, then you will become a man. The only women who succeed in such institutions are, in fact, in drag. Joni Lovenduski says there is some evidence for this but there are also numerous instances, especially in Europe, of women going into such institutions in large enough numbers to have transformed them.

Today we might say that the formal obstacles to entry into these institutions have been removed. And Dr Lovenduski believes that it is significant that the new social movements of the 1960s, of which feminism was one, along with the civil rights movement, and the anti-Vietnam war movement, occurred in countries that were liberal democratic structures. All of these cognate movements have tended not to have individual leaders. They have tended to be interested in equality and collectivity. They have had egalitarian ideologies. Even when the ideology did not extend explicitly to women, women were involved in these movements. The early feminist groupings of the 1960s and 1970s were quite deliberately non-hierarchical. This created great problems for journalists, politicians and civil servants who were used to negotiating with a central responsible individual who could deliver the membership. The thing about the women's movement is that no one has been able to deliver the membership anyway. Dr Lovenduski believes that one of the most important things about the relationship between feminism and the State is that on the one hand you have this hierarchical organisation and you know where the top and bottom are, even if power is hidden. But in the women's movement, on the other hand, there is no hierarchy: there is a bit over here doing this and a bit over there doing that.

Feminism has been a movement of individuals who 'act locally and think globally'. It means that negotiating with the State can be extremely frustrating.

But this kind of diffused community politics does not necessarily mean that the community can operate without the State. This is because, Dr Lovenduski says, wherever women's movements have developed as movements, a liberal democratic political formation was a key factor. One of the most observable things about the women's movement of the 1970s and 1980s is that where there were no liberal democratic forms which afforded a greater or lesser degree of tolerance and support for such movements, they did not exist. It was remarkable that in the mid-1980s women's movements did not exist in Eastern Europe. Although there were occasional feminist voices to be heard in the Soviet Union there was no movement as such. And when Spain and Greece and Portugal democratised, one of the things that happened was the emergence of a woman's movement. It seems, then, that the woman's movement is a demonstration of *political* affluence in that a certain kind of State that allows plural forms effectively defines itself as a structure that contains contesting power groups. Without such pluralism you end up with revolution. And although feminism in the past has been a participant in revolutionary movements, it has never provided the leadership.

Only very recently have there been significant milestones in the United Kingdom, most of which are legislative. But behind the laws has grown a general recognition on the part of women of all political persuasions or none, that women can talk to other women and that often a woman's best friends are women. 'Sisterhood' may sound odd in a way that brotherhood does not, but it tangibly exists. Then, of course, there was the Equal Pay Act passed in 1970, as a result of a long feminist struggle. Joni Lovenduski notes that the final motivation for that Bill being passed was probably Britain's desire to become a member of the European Community and the Treaty of Rome insisted that members have an 'equal pay act'. Firms were given five years to implement it. Then, in 1975, the Sex Discrimination Act was passed which set up the Equal Opportunities Commission in Manchester. Throughout the 1970s there was a very diverse and active movement with a large number of priorities and it explored a large number of feminist issues. The movement met annually in conferences until 1978. It seemed to be a rising force, quite capable of proceeding from strength to strength. In 1979 Margaret Thatcher was elected and in some senses the sky fell in, says Dr Lovenduski. If Margaret Thatcher's election and that particular style of Conservative 'weakest against the wall' politics taught British feminism anything at all, it taught it to engage in politics to protect gains. And early in the 1980s an enormous number of British women moved into the Labour party and began to become engaged in politics. Their experience of the political universe has given women confidence.

Particularly in Scandinavian politics where large numbers of women have entered the political system, the political system has itself begun to be transformed. Dr Lovenduski thinks it seems to happen where the numbers of women involved reach 25 per cent. Where women only come in one by one they tend to get socialised into the process as it is. But with large numbers of women coming in at the same time, the institutions themselves get transformed and there is a transforming effect on the way institutions relate to their clientele. Joni Lovenduski thinks there is every likelihood in the 1990s that we will see significant numbers of women coming into national and political life in Britain. They are in the channels and in the pipelines.

In conclusion, Dr Lovenduski believes that what some women want is a more woman-friendly society where what constitutes a woman-friendly polity is women-centred institutions that are populated by women. Would men enjoy this State? They would have to get used to not being the only ones there but it would mean that men and women had more choices. The so-called distinction between the private and the public has not only already been eroded but was always a bit of a nonsense anyway. If it is argued that because of the past and present division of labour in which women have had to take the responsibility for caring, for social life and for relationships, they have developed certain skills that are certainly more valued by women if not by men, and women moving into public life take these skills with them. But in the longer term, if fewer and fewer women are responsible for the private life, it may be asked whether caring as a value in society will erode altogether. But then there are men who are carers and they have not been given their chance. If it is not in the chromosomes but comes from experience, then that kind of independence that liberates and dignifies the individual ought to be integrated into a better quality of life for both men and women. There will still be a need for responsible, coherent institutions to sort out the infrastructure, and crisis management and administration will still be required in a large community. But they can be radically transformed and, as Dr Lovenduski sums it up, we would instantly see that they were different because there would be more women ensuring that they were.

CHAPTER TEN

TERRORISTS

T he present generation in liberal democracies, especially in the West, has been much exercised by the phenomenon of terrorism. But a coherent definition of terrorism seems elusive. If we ask whether terrorism is crime or whether it is a form of miniature warfare, we are already in difficulties. According to Professor Richard Rubenstein of George Mason University, 'terrorism' is a word that indicates we have already judged the situation, given it a bad name and invoked a political swearword. He suggests this is because we use 'terrorism' to name that violence of those with whom we disagree very much. To understand the phenomenon, he says, we must begin by examining more neutrally the politically motivated use of violence by small groups who are attempting through violence to become large groups and thereby claim to be mass representatives.

If we define terrorism as crime it tells us nothing, Professor Rubenstein insists, because of course, it *is* crime in that it uses illegitimate means to achieve its ends, but this is precisely because the State's legitimacy is what is in question. And if we try to define terrorism as a particular *style* of violence, say kidnapping, hi-jacking or assassination, then we are faced with the problem that states also kidnap and assassinate. It cannot be that terrorists are simply enemies and those who use precisely the same tactics are friends or freedom fighters. To call someone a terrorist rather than a freedom fighter implies that the terrorist is isolated, without legitimacy and that he has no connection with the masses. But is this true?

Because of what liberal democracies *are*, because there is a tolerance of competing values in liberal democracies, the question of who are our friends and who our enemies becomes increasingly complicated to answer. Professor Rubenstein concludes that per-haps it is best to say that what we are looking at is small-group violence with a political motive. We are looking at a set of tactics for low-intensity warfare that is used by small groups, where such campaigns get played out at the level of mass psychology, at the level of the public perception of violence as this is expressed in the media. Has the twentieth century seen an escalation of the poli-tically motivated use of violence by small groups so that guerrilla warfare or terrorism is on the agenda as it never was in the past?

If we accept with Professor Charles Townshend, Professor of History at Keele University, that there is a continuum of political violence ranging from various strategies of sporadic violence through to full-blown warfare, then 'terrorism', like war, is political violence rather than crime. But it is criminalised by states because small-group violence uses illegitimate means to attain their ends instead of using the State's legitimate means. Violence against a supposedly legitimate government breaks either written or unwrit-ten rules about how politics should be done. States frequently respond to those who have broken the political rules by crimina-lising them. Some analysts like Professor Townshend see this as a kind of delusion on the part of governments. They argue that governments fail to see that what they are dealing with is not criminality but rather warfare. And what makes it further confusing for the general public is that ideologically or politically motivated violence appears to have as its immediate target what we think of as innocent people. This turns everyone into potential victims. And yet the real target of such violence is the locus of power, a particular government, from whom certain policies or actions are demanded. What seems to lie at the basis of our confusion over small-group insurgency violence is the degree to which individual citizens see themselves as fully responsible for government policies. To what extent are citizens in representative liberal democracies 'innocent' of their State's policies? If our elected governments act in our names, are we not implicated?

The specific motivations behind terrorist activities as we have come to know them from the late nineteenth century onwards have been linked to a variety of very specific social grievances. Unre-quited dissent is at the heart of modern terrorism as a tradition. But this tradition is said to begin in nineteenth-century Russia where certain anarchists specifically adopted terrorism because it seemed to be the only appropriate means of attacking the State in itself. In this book we have tried to understand various individuals and groups in our history who have been prepared, in some instances, to use violence against their states in order to reformulate political life or, indeed, to destroy the political as a separate realm of human action. Many such violent actors have been deemed freedom fighters. But during the nineteenth century the State took on a form and acquired a definition which we still recognise today. So that those against the 'modern' State are in some distinctive way against what we are and how we live. Hence the tradition of modern terrorism in nineteenth-century anarchism is separated from previous traditions of sedition and violence because the anarchist's target is the State as we define it now. And at the basis of anarchist thought is a hostility to the State itself.

Insisting that men are not naturally evil, nineteenth-century anarchists argued that men were perfectly capable of self-government. Centralised bureaucracies were not necessary for the maintenance of social order and the good life. Centralised bureaucracies were themselves the cause of unrequited dissent. Some argued that the State is no more than an excuse to maintain the myth that private property is natural and just. If property were seen instead as theft, then the State, whose purpose was to maintain it, was really in the business of excluding the vast majority of men from pursuing an independent life. The State ensured that the vast majority of men were slaves to wage labour. Who, then, needed the State? Here there seems to have been a clear perception that the State did not represent those governed so that its policies could not implicate the innocent who were, effectively, misgoverned. And some, but not all, anarchists were linked with violent attempts to overthrow government.

Charles Townshend explains that anarchists believed that by knocking out the lynchpins of the State system, and specifically senior ministers and ministers of police, they would somehow knock the guts out of the State. They would break the cycle of the pursuit of power which they believed to be at the root of why states exist in the first place. Anarchists believed that if they made the costs of that power too high, then if someone became a minister, he would run the risk of being killed. This would break the logic of the State itself. Anarchist terrorism of the late nineteenth and early twentieth centuries was based on this premise. And, says Professor Townshend, one has to say that it did not work.

But some analysts have taken the Russian example and seen a pattern that reappears in other situations which are ripe for terrorism. Professor Richard Rubenstein speaks of the Narodniks, a group of nineteenth-century Russian students and ex-students who represented the intelligentsia. They found themselves cut off not only from the State with which they were at odds for moral and political reasons, but also from the people they most wanted to lead: the peasantry and the working class. That situation which produces a severing of connections between a militant political grouping (and which very often represents the intelligentsia) and both the State and the potential mass followership, is ripe for terrorism. Rubenstein believes one can point to a series of social and economic events that set the stage for this cutting of connections. It was the Russian anarchist Prince Kropotkin who first noticed that terrorist activity tended to follow periods of rapid economic growth. The reason for this is that very rapid economic growth pulls classes apart in a society. It also breaks connections which had enabled the intellectuals to play an intermediary role – explaining the master's orders to the people and the people's needs to the State. When the intellectuals are cut loose, the preconditions for terrorism are met.

What we have, then, is the vindication of the theory that says that a rise in expectations followed by a very sharp drop-of, or a shocking reversal, as Professor Rubenstein puts it, sets the stage for many forms of political violence. Terrorism employs its tactics to achieve radical social changes that seemed promised but were then dashed. When an intelligentsia cannot play an intermediary role and when a rise in expectations is not sustained by the State itself, then the State comes to see its opponents as banded against law and order, against civilisation itself. In the view of governments there have been a thousand times as many anarchists in the world as there ever have been in reality.

To vindicate his analysis, Rubenstein looks at terrorism in the modern period, where he sees the great period of economic growth in the West and also in Latin America during the late 1950s and 1960s. Near the end of that period there was a mass organisation of political militants in both Western Europe, North America and Latin America. The subsequent period of economic stagnation, where jobs for young people that were both remunerative and politically meaningful were no longer available, led to a precipitation of young intellectuals into violent activity. It is interesting to notice that in the one country which managed to maintain or even increase its expenditure on social programmes, the United States, terrorism was really minimal. As Professor Rubenstein puts it,

> All we got over here was the Weathermen Underground – which was small potatoes compared with the IRA and the German Baader-Meinhof; and then we had the Black Panthers who were more the victims than the perpetrators of violence. But in Latin America and also in several Western European countries, there were hordes of young, well-educated people wanting jobs that would enable them not only to make a living but also to contribute to their societies. They found themselves without a possibility of that sort of employment and although it did not precipitate all of them into terrorist activity, it did encourage a certain percentage of them.

This means we are talking about the vision of a minority concerning a new society, where the possibilities of constructing a society far more just than the present society are aroused and then dashed. And we are talking about the capacity of a given political system to respond. It seems as though we are talking about the situation in progressive, liberal states rather than tyrannies.

And yet, there are those who would imagine that terrorism can only happen inside a state which is tyrannous in some way. If terrorism is an act against the State then somehow the State has to be either undemocratic or seriously oppressive and misbehaving. This is not true. History demonstrates, Professor Rubenstein reminds us, that where society is tyrannical and that tyranny an accepted fact of life, there will be little terrorism. In Nazi Germany there was little terrorism and in Stalinist Russia there was little terrorism. Equally, a democratic system that enables people to believe that their activities will make society significantly better is also a deterrent to terrorism. The problem seems to have arisen again and again in the middle ground, where there is either an inefficient tyrannical system or a more open democratic system which none the less offers people few if any opportunities to work for significant improvement. The lethal combination of political disappointment and the stranding of people with rising aspirations at the end of an economic boom, leads to terrorism on the part of some and membership of an extended support group that is not directly engaged in terrorist activities on the part of far more. When all that is available to people whose ideals have been sparked by rising economic and social improvements is 'politics as usual', extra-parliamentary activity is on the cards. And it embraces a range of expressions. It may be non-violent extra-parliamentary activity but, structurally speaking, non-violent activity, civil disobedience, is really terrorism without violence and can easily spill over into the impatience of violent action.

If there are times when people seem to be interested in political and social change, but they see the State as hostile on the one hand and the masses as asleep on the other, the question becomes, in Professor Rubenstein's analysis, 'how to wake up the sleeping masses?' Reading the literature of late-nineteenth-century Russian movements or the literature of the German Red Army Fraction or the literature of the Italian Red Brigades, the same question is posed: how do you wake up the masses, how do you change what at first looks like a factional group's perception to a mass movement?

One answer is dramatic non-violent activity which galvanises wealthy people. Professor Rubenstein draws on the example of Father Daniel Berrigan and his brother, also a Catholic priest, who poured blood on draft files to highlight the horrors of the Vietnam War to Americans. Another possibility is to attack the State and, in so doing, the State is provoked to counter-attack. The State is revealed to be more brutal than any of the sleeping masses ever thought. It is forced to step out from the forms of legitimacy, and once outside what the twentieth-century political theorist, Herbert Marcuse, called its 'veil of rationality' it engages in counter-violence as a form of revenge. To engage in an escalating series of acts and counter-acts based on revenge is precisely to play the terrorists' game. The State is as oppressive explicitly as its opponents said it always was implicitly. The calculation is that, once the State is seen for what it is, the public will be brought to such a pitch of excitement that a revolution will ensue. The theory goes, as Professor Rubenstein explains, that

> Since the State cannot surgically single out its enemy it comes down with a hard fist on all the inhabitants of the community. It increases surveillance; it adopts military tactics in peacetime.

Whether political terrorism is of the far right or far left, the theory that the State's counter-violence which involves ordinary people will then polarise the masses and precipitate out a large section of public opinion which favours the terrorist, is not usually true. It has been argued that there is not one instance in history in which terrorist activity has actually materially improved the political position of either the far left or far right through attracting mass support. Something else is needed.

If there is already in existence a mass movement, for example a nationalist movement, then by provoking the State to attack through the community, a mass movement can be galvanised into action. One of the secrets of the success of the IRA and the PLO and other nationalist movements is that a nationalist movement already in existence is provoked. When the fist comes down on Londonderry, it is not just the IRA Provos who suffer but rather everyone living in the community which has become a police state. Since nationalist sentiment was already there to begin with, the terrorists can take advantage of it. Mass movements, then, are not created by terrorist violence. But an already existent movement can be strengthened through terrorist violence.

Early anarchists used terror because they were against the very idea of the State. But today many examples of terrorism fall into two other categories. There is the fight against a government of another country: the classic national liberation struggle against a colonial power where the aim is to get the foreign occupiers out by whatever means. But there is also the internal struggle against the government of your own country. Those terrorist movements where the aim is simply to get rid of a foreign occupier (the least political) have been most successful. Even when the movement has paid lip service to socialism or capitalism or some religious philosophy, the real aim has been to make a territory ungovernable for colonial powers. The concern has been much less with the political nature of the State that will succeed the foreign occupation than with putting a native élite in place of a foreign élite so that business goes on as usual.

However, Professor Charles Townshend believes that if you scour the records of terrorist movements that have succeeded simply by using terrorism and nothing else, then there are very few examples that have succeeded even in driving the foreigners out. What usually seems to happen is that terrorism has been a component of a wider spectrum of the application of violence. And it is the breadth of the spectrum that is decisive. Terrorism has to demonstrate that it is not just the product of a small band of fanatics but rather that it does somehow represent and draw sustenance from a larger public feeling. If the terrorists can do this then they can succeed. The struggle is psychological. Looking at the ideas of the early terrorists who believed that by killing enough ministers of state they could destroy the State government itself, you find that the line of reasoning they followed was to show that the killing of ministers was 'educational'. The public would then see that the government is not invulnerable. It would show that resistance is possible and it would in the end bring the public up to such a pitch of excitement that there would be a revolution. Such initial sporadic violence puts pressure on governments that they are not normally used to dealing with. Governments respond by criminalising such activity. And the mystery of this kind of violence is that people persist with their self-declared war against the State even when they are getting nowhere with it, so far as anyone can tell. This is what makes Professor Townshend insist that the motivation behind terrorist acts must be political rather than criminal. If it is seen as a kind of warfare rather than crime, then we can begin to see why people should enlist in it even if the profits are not very great. There must be some emotional and intellectual political package which seems sufficiently important for people to go to some trouble and danger in order to bring it to pass. Terrorists who keep going, whether or not they achieve their ends, show signs of resilience because they are people with a cause, an ideology or a national message which at least strikes a chord with a number of people. One can never tell what proportion of people who agree with their ideas are prepared to enlist. And terrorist organisations have different methods of picking up recruits, some more strict than others.

As Professor Townshend explains, in conflicts between terrorist organisations and governments there is a struggle between two moralities, a conflict between two visions of the nature of the public sphere of government: how should government be organised, or should there be a government at all? Obviously, if you are on one side the view of the other will be the opposite to your own. What terrorists are engaged in is a struggle to test out the proportion of the people who accept their view rather than that of their opponents and if possible to enlarge that proportion to a majority. Therefore terrorist campaigns and guerrilla or insurgency campaigns are principally psychological struggles. They take place at the level of public perceptions of violence. If the public see such acts as crimes then the perpetrators of the acts will have failed. But if they see the acts as in some sense justifiable as acts of war, then terrorists have succeeded and the government has failed.

But we are still resistant to the idea of not simply dismissing terrorism as a kind of common criminality. We are still resistant to the notion that there may still be some kind of moral justification for terrorist acts if we do not support the terrorists' cause. We are not so resistant to favouring past forms of opposition to the State. We have kind words for men of violence in our past who fought and, we believe, secured, many of our present liberties. Why, then, are we resistant to those who use similar violent means today?

Professor Townshend asks that we compare what the old IRA did, which attacked Britain between 1919 and 1921 during the so-called Anglo-Irish War, to what the IRA does today. There is a vast difference. There was almost no placing of bombs in public places, for example. Today even when there is a warning that a bomb has been placed in a public space, there is still a very high chance of indiscriminate destruction being done. Such monstrous action was much more uncommon before the Second World War. As soon as you mention the War, it is borne in on us that the people who took the limits off the use of violence were the states that were involved in that war. An indiscriminate attack on civilians, which had happened in more limited ways in earlier warfare, became the method of making war for several of the states involved. From an analytical rather than a moral point of view, the British bombing of Germany was a campaign of terror. We have endless memoranda produced by the Royal Air Force before the war which are based precisely on this premise. The way to win the war was to break the morale of the civilian population, rather than to defeat the enemy army in the field. The First World War had shown what a terribly costly and time-consuming business field warfare was. There was a belief that once the bomber was invented, you could break through the whole log jam and crack the spirit of the enemy people. A new boundary had been crossed, a new moral dimension, and not just a new weapon, had been discovered. This was the application of violence to achieve a result that was primarily psychological. Of course, State terror is not a twentieth-century phenomenon. And perhaps earlier examples of State terror have been submerged in the mythology of the succeeding State. There is no doubt that State terrorism was used as an integral part of the French Revolution to mould the people into a coherent resistance.

But the Second World War was unlike wars that took place, say, in the eighteenth century which were more like chessboard wars. Then it was a matter of winning a theoretical victory and your opponent conceded a small piece of territory. But once the French Revolution came we begin to speak of ideological wars where one country is making war on the whole political system of another. As Professor Townshend explains: 'Now you may not want to take the country over in the simple physical sense, but it certainly wants to take it over in the ideological sense, and I think that's why, by common consent, war became more and more total in the twentieth century as it became more ideological. People thought they were fighting for national survival.'

Just as State war is of several different kinds, so too antiState war is of different kinds. There have been examples of people who used violence for essentially limited reformist purposes. But especially in the twentieth century, to be driven to the recourse of violence – which is not something somebody suddenly decides to do on the spur of the moment – there must be a sufficiently big reward. Current terrorists therefore aim for massive results, indeed, impossibly large results. These results cannot, they believe, be achieved through forming a political party. That their aims cannot be achieved within the present system or anything that is remotely like it leads them to attempt to foreshorten the historical process.

Some experts, who are perhaps closer to the centre of State decision-making, might find this analysis too accommodating. Dr Robert Kupperman, a senior adviser to the Centre for Strategic and International Studies (CSIS) in Washington DC, is involved in the field of national security studies and in talking about terrorist tactics and suitable responses with international agencies and other governments. When asked about the motivation and psychology of terrorists, he responds by saying that today's terrorists are more brutal than ever before. They are far more indiscriminate in their targets. They kill for the sake of killing. He refers to Abu Nidal 'who sent murderers in, fourteen and fifteen year-old, illiterate youngsters, with nothing but hand grenades and machine guns to kill civilian travellers in the airports of Rome and Vienna.' This he says is cynical, mass murder and is frightening. 'The same bastard killed people at prayer in a synagogue in Rome and in Turkey; destroyed, machine-gunned a two-year old child. There are no genteel rules of warfare or of combat.' And although there are immediate ideological situations that drive some terrorists, Dr Kupperman believes that after a while almost all terrorists turn nihilist and become contract murderers in a political circuit. Terror is a tactic and although there are sociological and political grievances that motivate groups, Dr Kupperman seems to want to point to an aspect of terrorist violence that has less to do with immediate grievances than with traditions of violence: the father-to-son hand-down of the Provisional IRA, the Basque Separatists ETA and the unending dispute between the Arab world and Israel. He does not want to dispute the case that those who resort to terrorist tactics have political grievances. But his interest is in seeing it as a tactic that, when combined with the media, has profound effects. Less interested in its causes than in its effects, Dr Kupperman sees terrorism as a way of causing the State to overreact, and the most successful target is a state that is democratic. Terrorism is unsuccessful in an absolutely entrenched totalitarian society.

How then, should governments – whoever they are – react to terror? Dr Kupperman answers: 'dispassionately'. The ideal broadcast following the hi-jacking of an airplane would be :'ladies and gentlemen, a plane has been hi-jacked. When the incident is over, we'll let you know what happened. You try to convince the media to cool it as much as possible. And you try very hard not to concede to the terrorists; you do not want to make the incident a *cause célèbre*.' The major issue is not to overreact. When asked if the American response to Libya had been an example of overreaction, Dr Kupperman answered: 'Yes. I think that Libya ended up being the messenger, and the ones we should have taken on (and I'm sorry we didn't') was Syria.' Worried about the spread of weaponry among smaller states, he believes that America should have bombed the Libyan chemical warfare facility eight months earlier when it had the chance to do it. 'And not ask for excuses or offer apologies to anyone'. Why certain people engage in terrorist tactics is of less consequence than that they do it. Someone who is willing to die for what he believes in, who literally drives a bomb into a crowd of the innocent, forfeits any nobility. And if certain terrorist organisations are indeed disaffected intellectuals, often the offspring of wealthy families, educated in Europe, who understand the tactics and politics involved, the men who go out and do the killing and bombing are not very bright. Dr Kupperman implies they are used by their intellectual leaders. This means that even if grievances were redressed to some degree, Dr Kupperman sees governments continuing to have to deal with a kind of terrorism that often goes on for its own sake: 'it is the cynical product of a nation.' And even if terrorism does not increase statistically, it will become technologically more sophisticated.

Democratic nations must, therefore, explain to their publics what their risks are. And they must try to make citizens understand why democratic states must be in the intelligence business and involved in covert operations. Furthermore, Dr Kupperman argues that the physical security of key places must be secured and with this come some restrictions, some losses of privacy and even some losses of freedom. Lastly, there must be an ability to manage crises in democratic states, what he calls a civil defence system in case of massive attacks. Here democratic states prepare by playing 'war games', an exercise in hypothetical attacks and responses in which both the US and Britain are already engaged. But along with what looks like a very small amount of conciliatory redressing of grievances by diplomatic means, Dr Kupperman wants to make it clear that he is not at all shy about massive military strikes against countries that sponsor terrorist destruction. At the heart of his analysis, beyond a discussion of certain groups' unrequited grievances, lies a belief that certain types of people, whatever their immediate cause, are 'virtually by birth and, professionally, in the business of terror'.

If terrorist groups rely so heavily on mass-media hype would governments be better protected by starving them of the 'oxygen of publicity'? Dr Kupperman says he cannot go as far as Mrs Thatcher because he believes nations given to democratic values must cover these events. Free societies owe their publics a free press. While he wants press restraint he does not want government curtailing of news. It is irresponsible for a nation that wishes to preserve and promulgate its democratic values to curtail a free press, which includes broadcasting interviews with spokesmen for terrorist activities. As Professor Townshend likewise points out, if such groups could be starved of the oxygen of publicity, because no one was interested in them in the first place, then states would have a point. But if they are starved by censorship and other forms of governmental repression then there is a very severe danger that this will rebound on the government. It will make the government look precisely like what its opponents have said of it. And more seriously, it will undermine the very value system which the government is in place to defend and from which it draws its own sustenance. People support the government to the extent that the government is representing their wider view of the national culture. To compromise important components of that wider view even in a temporary way is very dangerous.

This points to the seriousness of the liberal dilemma when faced with political violence. One of the great beliefs of liberalism in the field of political ideas is that there must be openness. Censorship deprives people of the opportunity to construct the best possible public philosophy. You have to allow that the right or wrong of a case cannot be decided by the government but rather it is decided in the public exchange of ideas. Terrorists with an ideological platform must be seen in a liberal democratic state as a group with a legitimate input into this exchange of ideas. Liberals will not tolerate lawlessness, murder and indiscriminate violence but where it is a question of saying that a certain group is absolutely worthless and indefensible, then you are denying the important public act of struggling against terrorism. Simply to brand them as criminals or insane, which is what most governments effectively do, is itself illiberal. The public is then cut off from testing the validity of their ideas.

But however good a cause, can it justify the means of the terrorist? Some terrorist acts plainly cannot be justified. Setting a bomb in a kindergarten cannot be accepted by anyone who is rationally participating in any political dialogue. If terrorist acts were all like this, then, Professor Townshend says, there would be much less of a problem consigning terrorism to the dustbin of politics and history. But most of the acts that have been carried out by organisations that have been labelled terrorist have not actually been incontrovertibly immoral in that way. Many have really been engagements with the armed, or semi-armed, forces of the State. And the public takes a very different view of this. To criminalise an entire organisation because some of its members have committed terrorist acts is, to Professor Townshend, an act of political blindness. Governments risk failing to understand what they are dealing with, and if they do this for long enough, then they will lose the struggle.

How best can states oppose terrorism without playing their game? If we can learn from history, a distinction needs to be drawn between military and political reasons for acting in certain ways. Professor Townshend believes that if we look at the 'clean version' of political violence, guerrilla warfare, it plainly is quite inappropriate for armies or governments to confront guerrillas using conventional big batta-lion methods. Guerrilla warfare requires that armies adopt a new set of tactics.

Unfortunately, in practice, it is a very short step from accepting that new tactics are required to adopting counter-terrorist tactics. In Palestine and other areas where the British were engaged in counter-insurgency campaigns, the forces of order, Professor Townshend asserts, did descend to the methods of their opponents because from a day-to-day perspective it seemed to be the only way of getting to grips with them. But from a political perspective it proved disastrous. From the perspective of a liberal democracy the cornerstone of any response to terrorism must be taking the law seriously. This does not mean that liberal states should produce anti-terrorist laws which are perfectly legal. Such laws themselves breach the spirit of existing legal traditions which comprise the fundamental values which the society is trying to defend in the first place. It is absolutely vital for liberal democracies to maintain an obligation to the sanctity of law on the part of the State and its servants, even at the price of ineffectiveness.

Professor Townshend insists that the law is and is seen to be the repository of public values. Good legal systems chime with the way the public looks at the world. He believes that in Britain, in parti-cular, there is a kind of self-righteousness that has developed over a long period of time. The legal system is supposed to be the best of all possible systems, not by any rationally apprehensible criterion, but because it was developed organically and has stood the test of time. If the legal system and the constitution are believed to represent the best balance between individual liberty and collective discipline then any opposition to this system by force is a heinous crime. But then of course the government itself cannot breach the legal tradi-tion by force. And governments cannot allow alteration in the manner in which security forces behave.

If the government permits the use of counter-terrorist methods, and Professor Townshend believes that unless a government prohi-bits them they will be used, it is almost inevitable that armies and police forces will attempt to use assassination and other extra-legal means. For Professor Townshend this is the way to lose rather than win against terrorism. The public perception of a police with extra-ordinary powers which may be deployed in an uncontrolled way is destructive of the very idea of a state's legitimacy. The State in its very essence is about the controlled deployment of force, the State is the monopoly of the legitimate use of force. Emergency powers lead to an increasing informality in the exercise of force and the use of if not secret then certainly very shadowy forces. At first there may be a fairly high public tolerance of the abnormal deployment of force to counter terrorism. But the problem soon arises when the forces that emerge in the murky area beneath the panoply of law become rather powerful and begin to do things which the public finds unacceptable. A gradual delegitimisation of the forces of law would be a victory for terrorism. The State would be driven to delegitimising itself.

Terrorists, says Professor Townshend, are bidders in a kind of political auction. They are bidding for public support. And it is the law that must fight terrorism and not the state as it steps outside Marcuse's 'veil of rationality'. The law also bids in a way for public support. It starts out with public support because we assume that the legal system of a constitutional country will command a very wide extent of public assent. The law must remain incorruptible to maintain its public credibility. The very idea of security forces being surgically successful in taking out members of terrorist organis-ations in a community, without arresting the wrong people or killing the innocent in the process, is an impossible one. In so far as many guerrilla organisations are just like any other military organis-ations, you can deal them swingeing blows. But if they exist, and have a penumbra of support around them, for reasons that are not simply a function of the personalities and the organisation of a particular group but rather depend on many people agreeing with their ideas, then the likelihood is that they will quickly reconstitute themselves. And Professor Townshend believes that there is very powerful historical evidence that this course of physical action will produce martyrs.

What must be elicited from history is that very few terrorist movements have succeeded. Unfortunately, this does not mean that they will disappear. But the real issue is how governments react to them. Governments carry an enormous amount of fire power, much more than any terrorist organisation that has ever existed. If a government changes its nature and becomes less liberal then indirectly the terrorist has been able to elicit a police state. As Professor Townshend argues, it is impossible for a liberal observer to applaud the use of political violence by any actor, be it the State or its opponents. Perhaps liberals must reject the view that there is a dominant strain of the irrational or insane in terrorist movements and at least attempt to understand why terrorism occurs. Surely if we say with Professor Townshend that it is impossible for any right-thinking person ever to use violence because it is self-evidently wrong, we know that this plainly is not true. We can see that many of the people who use violence are not pathological criminals but may, in fact, be idealists or even quite ordinary even well-intentioned people who are genuinely distressed by what they see as the great misdeeds of the states of the world. To deal with terrorism, then, one must try to understand the world properly, and to understand that violence is not used only by criminals. That is not to applaud the use of violence. Violence remains unacceptable. But there must be room for states to examine why perhaps well-meaning people have been driven to the use of violence and to acknowledge that for some 'the system' has failed; the system somehow has not accommodated them.

It may be impossible to change the system. In many cases the State can do nothing to accommodate them. But Professor Townshend points out that some kind of self-scrutiny must be the first response of states and their publics rather than what is perhaps the more frequent instinctive response to say that those who use violence must be connected with a cause that is wrong. In such an activity of self-scrutiny the legal system must command public assent to remain accessible, and it must be capable of producing changes.

But how, if you have two diametrically opposed views of what the State should be and whose state it should be, can the liberal tradition engage in a finding of solutions at all? Liberalism, unlike totalitarian regimes, does not provide an answer as to whose, among competing claims, might be the correct one. But what liberalism does provide is a legitimation of competing claims so that the vision behind some groups prepared to use terrorism can be and, some say, has been, brought into the legitimate forum. Until recently it has been thought that far-right terrorism against entire classes or ethnic groups, while a continuing threat in Europe, has somewhat declined with the rise to prominence of National Front parties. And those who supported the aims if not the means of the Baader-Meinhof terrorists in Germany of the 1970s have found a home in the Green party. Professor Rubenstein thinks there is a relationship between the decline of German terrorism and the rise of alternative political parties. As the Greens go up, the Red terrorists go down. It is a view supported by some former members of the Red Army Fraction (RAF).

This returns us to Professor Rubenstein's historical observation that terrorism is the violence of the intelligentsia. When one looks at nationalist terrorism, one sees that while the leadership generally comes from the intelligentsia there are numerous working-class people, farmers and so forth, in the masses of those who follow the movement. These are terrorist movements that have gathered larger mass support. At the heart of this support is an unrequited need for a recognition of their own existence. Professor Rubenstein is particularly interested in how terrorist activity attracts young people who use violence as a means to defend their own identity.

This sounds as though their action is more personal than political, that they are not so much rebelling against the State as rebelling against the circumstances of which the State is only a part. To Professor Rubenstein that distinction between personal and political activity is not very clear. There are times in which, in order to secure one's personal identity, one has to become a member of a group. And if the group is threatened, then the person is threatened. It is insufficient to discredit a group by saying its members are lunatics or criminals. That statement itself accepts the existence of a radical division between political and personal action. Rather what is needed to ask is what makes people resort to violent activity in defence of interests that are simultaneously political and personal. And in this way we might analyse the phenomenon of the Red Army Fraction in Germany and its success in developing a protective but non-violent support group during the 1970s.

Rubenstein describes the situation in which a group of middle-class, educated, white men and women came together in what was known in the press as the Baader-Meinhof terrorist group. Certainly the leaders saw themselves as an advanced form of consciousness that would unite with the most exploited in their and other societies. The group have had numerous books written about them, nearly all of which have described them as psychopaths, wild-eyed fanatics and ruthless killers. They have been dismissed as an inexplicable phenomenon in a society noted for its middle-class wealth and opportunities. To designate them as bored, middle-class kids looking for thrills through violence obscures the nearly unbelievable support they received from professional people who were prepared to provide them with safe houses even when they were not themselves prepared to kidnap, bomb and kill government ministers, government lawyers, the police and businessmen. A poll in mid-1971 found that one in ten North Germans would be willing to shelter wanted underground fighters overnight and one in four of all West Germans under 30 professed 'a certain sympathy' with the group. To say that they were simply a bored and spoilt generation of middle-class misfits explains nothing. Rubenstein points to the desperation they expressed which was itself caused by the fact that modern capitalist society had been so successful at solving some of the basic problems of existence. It encouraged idealistic young people to consider the possibility of creating a society that was vastly more just. Rubenstein sees this as a case of rising expectations that are well founded given the technological capacities of modern societies. The Red Army Fraction started their career with the burning down of a department store in Frankfurt. Why? They were not 'back to nature' freaks. They were protesting against the misuse of the technological and financial power of an advanced society to produce trivial goods, consumed by trivial people for trivial purposes. And they definitely saw the creation of this wealth to be at the expense of the poor and deprived of the world.

In general, these middle-class terrorists rekindled that old communist vision of vast abundance and equality of distribution. Rubenstein believes that when European terrorists commit violent acts in pursuance of that vision, they represent traditional values of European culture against the degrading consumerism of modern society. Indeed a book published in 1977 in Sweden which includes key texts of the RAF is not a terrorist cookbook with instructions on the making of bombs. It is a collection of bits of journalism published by important members of the group, letters written to one another and, perhaps most significantly, analyses of German history. It is filled with a terrifying rage, a hatred that is so intense that it sometimes obscures the fact that a coherent message is there to be read. While many, like Astrid Pröll, who was involved with the group for about a year, insist there was little time to discuss political theory, the texts of this RAF Reader draw extensively from the writings of Marx, Mao, Gramsci, Sartre and Lenin. Their insights are then applied to post-war German society.

If we only read these texts, the group's aims are ludicrous in that they had not the slightest chance of achieving them. And it is significant that the catalogue of ills they saw in current German society were not to be corrected by any coherent vision of what Germany might look like should their revolution succeed. This generation of young Germans like Astrid Pröll pointed to a frightening unwillingness and inability on the part of their parents' generation to deal adequately with Germany's past. And a further issue emerges. Anyone who has come to know Germans who survived the Second World War or who were born in its aftermath, will hear a complaint that Germans are permitted no war heroes; that they watch films largely made in America, Britain or France which depict a sinister SS and ruthless Nazis pursuing world domination by thuggish and brutal means. And of course, such forces of evil always lose. What the texts in the RAF Reader indicate is that these forces did not lose at all. They inherited the earth. Not only did their parents' generation refuse to come to terms with what went on in Germany from the 1930s onwards; until very recently no one who studied history in German schools ever studied the rise of the Third Reich. Several years ago a survey was done on what German children knew about Hitler. A huge proportion of youngsters knew nothing about him or indeed where he was born.

No longer is there any doubt that a very large proportion of Germans supported Nazism and not simply out of fear. But the Baader-Meinhof group wanted to tell another story about Germany from the Weimar Republic after the First World War. It was this story that struck a chord with many post-war Germans who may indeed have had parents who were Nazi sympathisers. They were taught to feel a collective shame. Astrid Pröll says that her generation was filled with young Germans who committed suicide out of an inability to cope with what their parents' generation had done in the concentration camps.

But the question concerning to what extent contemporary young Germans had to take on a national shame was deflected by the asking of another question. To what extent is the history of post-war Germany its own autonomous history? The answer that the RAF provided was that post-war German history was nothing more than an aspect of American history, that Germany was a colony of American imperialist interests in America's search to dominate not only Western Europe but also South-east Asia. From Adenauer's time as Chancellor, the Germans had had no self-determining identity. And the politicians of German social democracy were nothing other than a continuation of those politicians who supported the Fascist regime of the Third Reich. Indeed, many politicians and industrialists were the *same men*. America as a foreign occupier had effectively ensured the continuation of Nazi Fascism in Germany. This is why the Baader-Meinhof group continued to call the German Federal Republic 'fascist', a term that seems an outrageous distortion of post-war social democracy to those of us outside. No matter how oversimplified their view of post-war German political history was, it was an oversimplification to which a large number of Germans responded on the political right and left.

Furthermore, the RAF was germinated in that enormously optimistic youth culture of the later 1960s, imported from America and with indigenous outgrowths in France and elsewhere. Drugs, music and a certain sexual liberation made students feel collectively prepared to challenge a status quo that achieved vast wealth through hard work but which kept and proliferated an old legal system that was a continuation of Fascist law. The youth of the Western world seemed united to get America out of the Vietnam War. And the German government that had been formed after the war was seen as doing nothing but playing its allotted role in the world system of American capital.

American fear of communism was so intense that the left-wing opposition to Nazi Fascism was effectively edited out of German history.

We do not hear our own history which is the history of the international proletariat as a people. Instead, what is the natural reaction to German history even on the part of Communists? Shame in that history since 1933. Our history for ourselves and others is therefore reduced to two imperial world wars and twelve years of fascism. What is not relevant is who, in Germany, fought against this. The German Workers' movement which was severely anti-Nazi and which suffered under Nazism has been written out of German history. This is the history we continue through guerrilla warfare. The history of the old left in the Bundesrepublik has been pushed into East Germany. And this is because after 1945 politicians were dominated by an American foreign policy that was so rabidly anti-communist that it virtually annihilated the activities of the old left. The aim of the USA in its three zones was to restore monopoly capitalism, to reconstruct the old ruling élite in the economy and state and, in order to reestablish the middle class, now under the command of American capital, they pursued a remilitarisation and integration of the three western zones into the economic and military system of US imperialism . . . All the key positions in the government and the economy were taken over by the same functionaries who, during the Weimar republic, were FOR capital, for an integration of class warfare into capitalism so that workers' organisations were made illegal.

To the RAF and their supporters all the decisions concerning German policy were taken by Fascists in the state bureaucracy who pursued no line beyond American interests. Even the media were brought within the control of the regime.

This was to be countered by guerrilla warfare, in the form of destructive group action. Ulrike Meinhof, a talented and successful journalist, wrote that the only way people could be set free from the totalising consumer society and its massive bureaucratisation was through its negation in action, in collective battle; group guerrilla warfare with American capital as the enemy.

If the economic miracle of Germany was achieved with the dedicated and single-minded hard work that characterises German attitudes to work, authority and social obligations, so too, Astrid Pröll insists, the guerrilla networks worked with a similar thoroughness. As they saw it, the German state apparatus was proliferated throughout society by ideology in schools, the media and business. Everyone effectively became a civil servant. The institutional strategy of what they called this new Fascism was most prominent in the state justice system. It was nothing more than a counter-insurgency network. Since there was no legitimate opposition, there was no room for radical alternatives of either right or left in Parliament. What there was was a computerisation of information on all citizens. This new, repressive technology of state institutions and mass communication media furthered, they said, the psychological warfare of the State against its own citizens. German society was, they believed, subject by means of propaganda networks to a total manipulation of the facts. Not interested in replacing one bureaucracy with another, the members of the Baader-Meinhof group established policy simply through group terrorist action. This meant fighting until they were either shot themselves or imprisoned.

In 1977 after a long trial, the major figures committed suicide in their cells. There is enough plausibility in their over-schematic account of how German society was reformulated after the war, for us to achieve some understanding of why they did inspire popular support. The media made a meal of them, while behind the headlines, a group of educated, articulate, idealistic and angry people searched for one safe house after another and coped inadequately with the psychological pressure that their own actions and way of life imposed on them. Did 1977 see the calculated martyrdom of the leaders? Were they freedom fighters or terrorists?

It is clear that for professional analysts and ordinary people alike, terrorism is a murky subject. It has frequently been pointed out that the number of people actually killed by terrorists of one sort or another since the Second World War is minuscule in comparison with deaths in road accidents in any given year. But it is precisely because we seem to carry around with us some version of the freedom fighter/terrorist dichotomy that it is of such disproportionate interest to liberal society. It has often been asked why so many apparently morally sensitive people have been thrown into confusion over whether they should support the activities of the ANC, the PLO and the Afghan guerrillas. This is the very dichotomy that terrorists trade on in their attempts to enlist support and indeed to rationalise their own activities to their members and the wider world.

This book has tried to highlight some of the reasons for this dichotomy. Historically we have observed movements which undeniably used what would now be called the tactics of terror to achieve their ends. They seem to have had little option other than to use such means. Their success now seems unimaginable to us without such violence since we see ourselves as the beneficiaries of their actions. Recently, R. W. Johnson has examined the cases of the Patriotic Front in Zimbabwe and the FLN in Algeria (*London Review of Books*, 9 July 1987).

It was surely both historically inevitable and morally just in some fundamental sense that Algeria should be ruled by the Algerians and that Rhodesia should be ruled by its black majority. To imagine, let alone wish, to return to the status quo ante requires a moral as well as a historical Canute-ism. But neither in Rhodesia nor in Algeria was there the slightest sign that the minority white regimes would give way to anything less than overwhelming violence: indeed, all means short of that were tried – and failed.

The FLN and ZANLA could not take on conventional military forces on equal terms. So they attacked strategic 'state' targets – the police. This escalated to placing bombs in supermarkets, massacring outlying farmers, mowing down holiday-makers. And they turned their guns on their own side when 'necessary'. Through terror they intimidated peasant communities to support them. As Johnson says: 'These struggles, of course, have no shortage of sympathisers willing to accept, even to project, a more heroic, romantic and hagiographical picture: but the fact is that what took place both in Algeria and in Zimbabwe were successful terrorist revolutions – or, if one prefers, successful national revolutions carried through by terrorist means.'

While they go on, liberals are repulsed by such violence. But the historical memory is prone to forgetting. Success is ratified. 'And nobody has any qualms about embracing erstwhile terrorist leaders as valuable political partners. The present British government may condemn ANC terrorism now, but if such means bring the ANC to power' (and indeed the organisation is no longer proscribed in South Africa), then 'who can doubt that its leaders will speedily be greeted as honoured guests in Downing Street and Buckingham palace? And would it not be ludicrous to act otherwise?'

For liberals, terrorism is unacceptable when it is contemporary. But retrospectively it is accepted as a legitimate political tactic, especially if it is seen to have been used by men with no real alternative. What is most important is that political history is written on the basis of success. Is this historical justification mere hypocrisy? Johnson rightly points out that our lasting condemnation is reserved for those movements whose terrorism proved futile. 'Nobody loves a loser'. 'Most of us can see why the FLN or Irgun took the road they did – and probably can't find it in ourselves to wish that the French had continued to rule Algeria or the British Palestine. The true puzzle lies with those numerous terrorist groups whose ends are not remotely realisable.'

Was the Baader-Meinhof one such group? It is of some significance that Andreas Baader, Ulrike Meinhof, Gudrun Enslin and many others around them were children whose families had been anti-Nazi during the Second World War and whose fathers had died. They were all active in the anti-Vietnam War movement and the anti-nuclear protest as well as in other Third World 'good causes'. In Berlin in 1967, when a demonstration against the visit of the Shah of Iran took place, the Berlin police, assisted by pro-Shah Iranians organised by Savak, ran amok. They beat up hundreds of demonstrators, shooting one of them dead. This was not seen as a one-off aberration. German police, like their American counterparts, are armed and like their American counterparts were not particularly sympathetic to what they took to be a privileged, lazy and disruptive crowd of middle-class students. When Gudrun Enslin said: 'This fascist state means to kill us all. We must organise resistance. Violence is the only way to answer violence. This is the Auschwitz generation and there's no arguing with them', she voiced what many Germans were thinking. Enslin was the daughter of a Protestant pastor.

And what happened next was what they said would happen, but it was to backfire on the movement itself. The police became increasingly uncomfortable and began to arrest all manner of false suspects. The Criminal Investigation Office developed a vast computerised machine with the almost exclusive aim of hunting the group down. Computer files on 4.7 million people and 3100 organisations were assembled. The implicit police state was made explicit.

After blowing up the department store in Frankfurt, kidnapping industrialists, killing policemen and then a series of bloody raids on American bases in Germany, the group was finally rounded up in 1972. Placed in gaol under maximum security it is extraordinary that sympathisers were able to smuggle in all manner of devices which enabled them to set up an intercom system connecting their cells. Finally they acquired the firearms with which they committed collective suicide in 1977. Others believed they were murdered.

If a coherent definition of terrorism has eluded most analysts, so too students of modern terrorism like Professors Walter Laqueur and Paul Wilkinson are deeply sceptical that there is any comprehensive explanation for it. No scientific sociopolitical theory of terrorism is remotely within reach. This is because there is a wide range of motives, intentions, participants and organisational structure involved. If there is no profile of the typical terrorist and no typical motive beyond unrequited dissent and no single-factor explanation for terrorism, this should not mean that governments must dismiss such movements *en masse* as criminal or lunatic. Professor Townshend has already indicated that a certain self-scrutiny is in order along with a determination to maintain the legal system which in liberal democracies rightly claims mass support. Most analysts also argue that statistics is an ambiguous game. There has not been an inexorable growth in terrorism despite the media coverage such groups are given. It is less clear that in general, terrorism has been singularly ineffective as a technique for seizing power because as Professor Townshend and others have pointed out, when deployed with other means in the spectrum of warfare, some indeed have been successful. And terrorist groups that have been successful have been legitimated by the historical imagination.

But Professor Rubenstein goes further and refuses to dismiss terrorists as psychopaths, fanatics and ruthless killers. Many he says are 'people who are like us, the guy next door'. And he is not averse to depicting mass violence as in some cases a legitimate instrument of social transformation. He too does not differentiate between state violence and terrorist group violence. But his purpose is neither to defend nor to condemn terrorism. Rather he wants to ask whether terrorism as small-group violence for which arguable claims of mass representation can be made is an effective means to the goal of social revolution. And he locates the source of terrorism primarily among the 'disaffected intelligentsia' which is not neces-sarily a class but rather is comprised of 'ambitious idealists without a creative ruling class to follow or a rebellious lower class to lead'. He argues historically that the preconditions for terrorist action are created in periods of rapid and uneven economic development and the weakening of connections between social classes. When there is no militant mass party to win the allegiance of the intelligentsia, the people with ideals, then they turn to violence in a desperate attempt to reconnect with the masses. 'Where the mass organisations are not militant and the militants are not influential, the stage is set for a terrorist response to economic and political crises.' He believes that the Baader-Meinhof group emerged in West Germany after the Social Democrats ceased to offer a clear alternative to the parties of the centre and the right.

But he concludes that terrorism's answer lies in politics rather than in military retaliation or the explanations offered by experts in abnormal psychology or by the proponents of international conspi-racy theories. 'No solution to the problem of terrorism is conceivable that does not reconnect politicized young adults to society by involving them in mass-based movements for change.'

There is no antidote to political violence. Rubenstein is convinced, as Laqueur and Wilkinson are not, that terrorism will *not* remain a fringe activity so long as most people believe that change can be brought about through the political process of the State. While the Green party and the various National Front parties might confine left and right-wing terrorism, there will remain a chorus of disparate voices saying that politics, as we know it, is useless. Which brings us back, in a strange way, to Socrates, urging those who would engage in politics to live the examined life. And if we are to take anything away with us, perhaps it is this, that being Against the State has a long history, an active present and, so far as we can tell, a certain future.

BIBLIOGRAPHY

CHAPTER TWO   SOCRATES

Annas, J., *An Introduction to Plato's Republic*, Oxford, 1981.
Brickhouse, T. C. and Smith, N. D., *Socrates on Trial*, Oxford, 1989.
Camp, J. M., *The Athenian Agora*, Thames and Hudson, 1986.
Guthrie, W. K. C., *A History of Greek Philosophy*, vol. IV, *Plato: the man and his dialogues, earlier period*, Cambridge, 1975.
Klosko, G., *The Development of Plato's Political Theory*, Methuen, 1986.
Kraut, R., *Socrates and the State*, Princeton, 1984.

CHAPTER THREE   MARTYRS

Benko, S., *Pagan Rome and the Early Christians*, Batsford, 1985.
Chester, A., *The Social Context of Early Christianity*, Polity Press, 1988.
Frend, W. H. C., *Martyrdom and Persecution in the Early Church*, Oxford, 1965.
Herrin, J., *The Formation of Christendom*, Blackwell, 1987.
Rowland, C., *Radical Christianity*, Polity Press, 1988.
Sordi, M., *The Christians and the Roman Empire*, Croom Helm, 1983.
Taheri, A., *Holy Terror – the Inside Story of Islamic Terrorism*, Century Hutchinson, 1987.

CHAPTER FOUR   UTOPIANS

Hill, C., *The World Turned Upside Down*, Penguin, 1975 (and later reprints).
Manuel, F. and F., *Utopian Thought in the Western World*, Blackwell, 1979.
Marius, R., *Thomas More*, Dent, 1985.
Passmore, J., *The Perfectibility of Man*, Duckworth, 1970.
Rowland, C.: *see Chapter 3*.

Bibliography

CHAPTER FIVE   OF CROWNED HEADS AND TYRANTS

Ford, F. F., *Political Murder – From Tyrannicide to Terrorism*, Harvard, 1985.

Fraser, A., *Cromwell, Our Chief of Men*, Panther, 1975.

Hampton, C. (ed.), *A Radical Reader*, Penguin, 1984.

Hill, C., *A Turbulent, Seditious and Factious People, John Bunyan and his Church 1628–1688*, Oxford, 1989.

Russell, C., *The Crisis of Parliaments, English History 1509–1660*, Oxford, 1971.

Skinner, Q., *The Foundations of Modern Political Thought*, 2 vols., Cambridge, 1978.

CHAPTER SIX   REVOLUTIONS

Ashcraft, R., *Revolutionary Politics and Locke's 'Two Treatises of Government'*, Princeton, 1986.

Ayling, S., *Edmund Burke – his life and opinions*, John Murray, 1988.

Harris, T., Seaward, P., Goldie, M. (eds.), *The Politics of Religion in Restoration England*, Blackwell, 1990.

Honderich, T., *Violence for Equality – Inquiries in Political Philosophy*, Routledge, 1989.

Miller, J., *Seeds of Liberty: 1688 and the Shaping of Modern Britain*, Souvenir, 1988.

Schama, S., *Citizens – A Chronicle of the French Revolution*, Viking, 1989.

CHAPTER SEVEN   MARX

Carver, T., *Marx's Social Theory*, Oxford, 1982.

Carver, T., *A Marx Dictionary*, Polity Press, 1987.

Cohen, G. A., *History, Labour and Freedom, Themes from Marx*, Oxford, 1988.

Evans, M., *Karl Marx*, Allen and Unwin, 1975.

CHAPTER EIGHT   FREUD

Gay, P., *Freud for Historians*, Oxford, 1985.

Ignatieff, M., *The Needs of Strangers*, Chatto and Windus, 1984.

Roazen, P. (ed.), *Sigmund Freud*, Da Capo, 1973.

Storr, A., *Freud*, Oxford, 1989.

CHAPTER NINE   WOMEN

Elshstain, J. B., *Public Man, Private Woman: Women in Social and Political Thought*, Princeton, 1981.

Pateman, C., *The Sexual Contract*, Polity Press, 1988.

Rowbotham, S., *Women, Resistance and Revolution*, Penguin, 1972.

Scott, J. and Spender, D. (eds.), *Anthology of British Women Writers*, Pandora Press, 1988.

Tomalin, C., *The Life and Death of Mary Wollstonecraft*, Penguin, 1974.

CHAPTER TEN   TERRORISTS

Baumann, B., *Terror or Love?*, John Calder, 1979.

Kupperman, R. and Kamen, J., *Final Warning – Averting Disaster in the New Age of Terrorism*, Doubleday, 1989.

Laqueur, W., *The Age of Terrorism*, Weidenfeld and Nicholson, 1987.

Rubenstein, R. E., *Alchemists of Revolution – Terrorism in the Modern World*, IB Tauris, 1987.

Taheri, A.: *see Chapter 3*.

Townshend, C., *Britain's Civil Wars – Counterinsurgency in the Twentieth Century*, Faber and Faber, 1986.

Tucker, H.H. (ed.), *Combating the Terrorists – Democratic Responses to Political Violence*, Facts on File, 1988.

INDEX

Index

Index